Glass - A world history

GLASS

A world history

The story of 4000 years of fine Glass-Making

by Fritz Kämpfer and Klaus G. Beyer

translated and revised by Dr Edmund Launert

Studio Vista

© 1966 VEB Verlag der Kunst, Dresden
English translation © 1966 Studio Vista Ltd
First published in Great Britain in 1966 by Studio Vista Ltd,
Blue Star House, Highgate Hill, London N 19
Distributed in Canada by
General Publishing Company Limited, 30 Lesmill Road,
Don Mills, Toronto, Ontario
The original edition published by Verlag der Kunst,
Dresden under the title of '4000 Jahre Glas'
Translated from German by Dr Edmund Launert
Printed in Germany by Druckerei Fortschritt Erfurt

Translator's Foreword

The aim of this book is two-fold; to tell the story of glassmaking from its origins down to the present day (see the extended picture captions), and to examine glasses which are typical specimens of each period in an effort to explain to the reader wherein lies their originality and charm (see the explanatory text). The excellent quality of the photographs allows the reader to grasp very easily the point the author is trying to make, and enables him to come to his own conclusions about the aesthetic value of each piece.

A work of this kind cannot, of course, include illustrations and descriptions of every worthwhile piece of glass, and it is to be hoped that readers already familiar with the subject will not be disappointed if they find their favourite piece has been omitted. Indeed it is one of the merits of this book that space has been found for many less well-known, but beautiful, works; and the author must be congratulated in particular on his coverage of some important fields of continental glass all too little known in the U. K. and U. S. A. The result is therefore not only an original and important survey of the whole history of glass, but a work that complements rather than repeats the coverage of other publications.

The translator and publishers would like to thank Mr. R. J. Charleston, Keeper of Ceramics at the Victoria and Albert Museum, London, who so kindly offered suggestions for improvement and correction of the translated text.

E. Launert

Contents

Introduction

A history of glass will naturally concern itself chiefly with the artistic forms into which the material is fashioned, and will disregard the purely functional glass made in the service of science and technology. In an attempt to reveal the factors which determined these artistic forms, a general survey of the technology of glass itself is essential, and only through an understanding of the material can we arrive at a complete appreciation of the individual decorative piece. From the briefest study of the various forms which objects in glass have taken, and of the scientific and technological progress made in glass-making throughout the centuries, it is immediately obvious that these two aspects of our subject are interdependent; the end product is always a direct result of some technological innovation, of the discovery of a way of improving and exploring the qualities of the material.

In some periods of history, glass was worked in imitation of some already familiar material; in other words, objects in glass tended to resemble those being made in metal, porcelain or precious stone. The peculiar qualities and potentialities of glass slowly became apparent, and modern glass, which shows a complete sympathy with the unique nature of the material, serves as an indication of the great advances which have been made.

In the earliest times articles in precious stone served as a model for work done in glass. The Greeks referred to glass as *lithos chyte* which means 'cast stone', and its success depended on how far a jewel-like quality had been obtained.

The most ancient glass objects we know, dating from the third millennium B.C. and discovered in Egypt and Babylon, are tiny, coloured opaque or faintly translucent pieces used for inlay work. The clearest idea of the jewel-like appearance of Egyptian glass may be had by looking at the burial treasure of Tutankhamen, housed in the Cairo Museum. The gold surface of the sarcophagi is inlaid with small pieces of lapis-lazuli blue, turquoise and jasper-red glass. Parts of the throne are of glass. Precious stones and glass were used side by side by the Egyptians, and glass was by no means considered an inferior material. The appearance of precious stone is maintained in the earliest glass vessels known to us. The enchantingly beautiful cup which belonged to Thotmes III, and is the oldest example in existence, is made of turquoise glass ornamented with blue, white and yellow threads.

In later times, Egyptian glass lost its original sacred function, but not its position as a luxury nor its resemblance to precious stone. In the last century B.C., glass vessels in imitation of jasper, agate and onyx were still being made. The Murrhine bowls which were famous in the ancient world, and of which Cleopatra is said to have possessed a costly collection of three thousand, belong to this tradition.

Glass has undergone the same type of treatment from all races in their early attempts to make use of it. The Celts never progressed beyond the first stage, fashioning only rings, beads and bangles from it. The Germanic peoples, who imported glass from the Mediterranean lands, in their turn related it to a precious stone, calling it *glesum*, their word for amber. At this time glass vessels were made in the following manner: a core of sand held by a metal rod was repeatedly dipped into molten glass, rolled and smoothed, so that a thick layer of glass adhered to the core in the manner of a glaze. The core was removed after the glass had cooled.

Just before the first century A.D. the discovery of a new technique in glass-making, which followed on improved furnaces opened the door to new and exciting possibilities. It was discovered that when the glass was red-hot and soft enough it could be blown into a bubble. From that moment, the glass blower's pipe has been the most important instrument involved in the production of glass.

In this period arose the legend of the unbreakable glass. Several Roman authors tell the story of the glass-maker who is said to have proudly offered the Emperor Nero an unbreakable glass. "But Emperor Nero," wrote Johan Mathesius in 1554 in his *Bergpostilla*, "the monster, was not desirous to see the value of gold and silver thus diminished, as would have happened had beautiful glasses lost their fragility; so, it is said, he had the craftsman exiled and his workshop destroyed." The legend is interesting in several respects. It was certainly occasioned by the invention of blown glass, with its unusual, metal-like appearance. The Sidonian glasses of the first century, particularly, which were made by blowing into a mould, and which were exported to Rome in large quantities, give the impression of being made in metal, especially as they have the shape of metal vessels, or a surface treatment resembling that used for metal.

There is also the possibility that the legend, which incidentally attributes the evil deed to various Roman emperors, has some connection with the early glass trade. The market price of Egyptian and Syrian glass was extraordinarily high at the time of the early Roman emperors. Glass objects forming part of the booty of the Persian and Egyptian wars were considered valuable enough to be carried in triumphal processions. Incredible prices were paid for glass at state auctions, and at the lavish banquets of the time glass vessels outdid golden goblets in popularity. There were already glass collectors of note in Rome at this time. Pliny tells us that when Petronius, Nero's master of ceremonies, was languishing on his death-bed he dashed a glass bowl of great beauty to pieces rather than let it fall into his master's hands.

Inevitably glass production was streamlined, and the commodity became cheaper and adapted to daily use. The glass became the normal drinking vessel. Luxury glass was, of course, still made, but along with this household glass was produced, as it still is; in other words, we see the manufacture of ordinary glass, whose basic forms are determined by function, hardly changed up to the present day. Practical shapes easily obtained by the glass-maker have proved their worth to succeeding generations. Among the vessels produced at this early time of glass-making, we note basic, vigorous shapes resulting from the processes involved and not outmoded or improved upon by the modern counterpart of the early glass-maker.

But to return to the luxury glass which represents the highest achievement of craftsmen and artists. This did not undergo all the stages of its manufacture at the hands of the glass-blower, but was enriched by techniques originally adopted for other fields of art; thus glass became the vehicle for the inspiration of the painter and the engraver, was gilded, cut and facetted as other objets d'art had been. Sometimes the application of such forms of decoration has been a case of "gilding the lily" and the actual metal has lost, rather than gained, and is hardly recognisable as glass. This was particularly the case during the latter part of the nineteenth century, and the later rejection of many of the decorative techniques mentioned, and the stress on the nature of the metal and the simplicity of its form were a reaction against the over-lavishness of earlier decorators.

Glass was from the first made in imitation of precious stones, and, logically enough, the art of the gem-cutter was practised on it. The most famous example of this work is the Portland Vase in the British Museum. Just as gem-stones with two or more strata of contrasting colour were cut to reveal this contrast, here the white glass overlay has been cut to reveal the blue glass beneath, but so skilfully that many nuances of blue and white have been achieved. In comparison with the Portland Vase, earlier Cologne *Zirkusschale* attempts at glass-engraving necessarily appear primitive and ill-conceived, although in the latter case the cutter was working on thin blown glass which did not lend itself easily to the technique. The difficulties involved are revealed by the unevenly executed decoration of scratched lines (see plate 39). One and a half thousand years were to pass before a glass of suitable thickness was produced, enabling engraving of a high quality and degree of accuracy to be executed.

On the other hand, decorative techniques which were a natural consequence of the discovery of glass-blowing were soon mastered. By these are implied firstly blowing into a mould, and secondly the application of molten glass to form threads, drops, decorative handles etc. These techniques have persisted, gaining or losing in popularity, throughout the centuries, and are perhaps derived from the craft of the metal-worker.

In the first and second centuries, Syrian glass shows a preference for mould-blown decoration, later for applied ornament. The same development is evident in Rome and in the Rhineland of Roman times. The mould-blown bottles in the form of the human head, grape clusters and so on are already examples of mass-produced objects. It is no more complicated a matter to produce them, once the mould has been prepared, than it is to produce their plain, undecorated sisters.

This cannot, however, be said of the Rhenish snake-trailed glasses, often masterpieces of skill and patience, although vessels with simpler trailed patterns have been produced in great quantities from the time of the main period of Rheno-Roman glass-making, through the Middle Ages, (in the *Waldglashütte* or small forest glass-houses), down to the eighteenth and nineteenth centuries when they again occur in Spanish and Persian work.

The highest achievement of this metal-inspired glass may be seen in the German *Waldglas*. Contemporary artistic taste, along with the technical possibilities and limitations of the craftsmen in these small forest establishments, determined its quality and appearance. It must be remembered that the collapse of the Roman Empire meant an end to Roman trade. The soda which had been imported from Egypt for the use of the Rheno-Roman glass-makers was no longer obtainable. As a result, in the seventh century, potash was adopted as flux by northern glass-makers. This was obtained from beechwood, which was readily available in unlimited quantities, and produced a glass which was sturdier and heavier than the ancient soda-glass. Another ingredient, the local sand, gave it a characteristic green colour, since it had a high iron content. This "impurity" of colour in *Waldglas* is one of its attractions. Its charm also lies in the form of the vessels into which it is made: spiny *Nuppengläser*, prunted *Römers*, ribbed *Maigeleins*, all reflecting the spirit of the late-Gothic period.

A very different kind of glass was made in Venice. Here the ingredients which had been used by the glass-makers of classical times were still available, in particular Egyptian soda, thanks to the city's continued trading connections. These ingredients, the artistic taste of the time and local conditions proved a most fortunate combination of factors. For probably the first time in glass history, our material emerges as something individual, something valuable in its own right. It has been ennobled by the refined simplicity of form given to it by the Venetians. The clean, harmonious lines of Early Renaissance architecture are transferred to the plain thin-walled glasses, produced for a discriminating society which could appreciate and enjoy subtleties of proportion and design. The *cristallo* glass, Venice's most important export commodity, was the main concern of the very highly esteemed Muranese glass-makers, many of whom were adopted into the nobility and were headed by a Burgomaster who had the authority of a doge. The delicate, almost weightless Venetian glasses cannot be compared with any other creation, unless it be that other exquisite product of Venetian skill: lace. The effect of lace was, as we know, reproduced in glassware; the *vetro di trina* of the sixteenth and seventeenth centuries has always been eagerly purchased by connoisseurs and collectors, as the Rosenborg Castle collection near Copenhagen shows.

German *Waldglas* and Venetian soda glass of the classical period nevertheless have one thing in common: both were produced in their finished state by craftsman in the glasshouse, who rejected adventitious decorative additions which were not part and parcel of the actual process of glass-making. The glass-makers of both kinds developed their skill to its utmost heights.

New ideas on the subject of glass were, however, beginning to make themselves felt in Germany during the sixteenth century. While Venice was intent on the transition from Renaissance to Baroque forms, creating increasingly elaborate and ingenious pieces, Germany was turning its attention to the decoration of glass by painting. Enamel painting had reached a very high standard in the East, particularly in Syria and Persia, in the thirteenth and fourteenth centuries. It was richly applied, and enhanced the glass itself, even if it disguised its basic texture. Enamel painting was executed in Venice in the early fifteenth century, and found its way thence to Germany in the sixteenth century, where it developed into a popular and unpretentious art. The word "art" is, in fact, hardly applicable here. The shiny walls of the *Humpen* and *Passgläser* became the canvas of the primitive artist. There was no artistic correlation between the glass-maker and glass-decorator. In Holland, where diamond-point engraving was also used during the same period for the execution of a somewhat primitive art, the same tendency to cover the glass with pictorial decoration is evident.

Meanwhile a new discovery was to revolutionize glass-making yet again. In Prague, the gem-cutter Caspar Lehmann, seeing the possibilities afforded by the improved potash glass, applied the cutting and engraving techniques of rock-crystal to that medium. One of his pupils, Georg Schwanhardt, transferred the imperial privilege for this type of engraving to Nuremberg, which thus became the main centre of glass-engraving in the seventeenth century. *Intaglio* engraving here attained its supreme expression.

The discovery of Bohemian potash-lime glass in the late seventeenth century made it possible to produce a metal of sufficient thickness for engraving in higher relief (*Hochschnitt*). The magnificent covered goblets of this period, cut and facetted to afford the maximum dispersal of light, are an essential manifestation of the spirit of the Baroque. Now it was the turn of Bohemia to become the most important centre of glass manufacture.

The final development in the enhancement of glass by cutting took place in England during the eighteenth century with the production of English lead crystal. Glass-makers were driven on by the desire to extract the maximum effect from the play of light, with the constant comparison of the glitter of the kingly diamond before them. Once more glass was worked in imitation of a precious stone, not this time in the opaque colours of the turquoise, lapis-lazuli or jasper, but colourless like the diamond. Only one other stone has an equal appeal: the ruby, which had driven generations of alchemists, goldsmiths and glass-makers to continual experiment in an effort to produce it artificially, until Johann Kunckel achieved a satisfactory imitation.

The name of Johann Kunckel is bound up with another stage of development. Now the emphasis is placed on the technology of glass-making. His *Ars Vitraria* is a survey of all the known methods of glass-making of his time. Hitherto, all efforts had been directed towards producing a metal of a quality suited to the purposes of the artist-engraver, but now that such a metal had been obtained in English lead-glass, we see a new approach: to create new kinds of glass by experimenting with various techniques held more attraction for the glass-maker than to produce continually the same metal for traditionally engraved vessels. The great names in nineteenth century glass-making are those of men who, like Friedrich Egermann, were first and foremost glass technologists.

We cannot, however, deny that glass in certain ways gained from this attitude. Sometimes it took on an exciting new appearance. New kinds of glass were created, such as Hyalith which resembled black Wedgwood ware, or Lithyalin, closely imitating red or grey marble, and new colours, perhaps in the form of stains or thin flashings. Old colours and techniques were revived, too, in accordance with the prevalent taste for historical rediscovery. At this stage, pressed glass and transfer decorations came into being. The well-proven techniques of preceding centuries were, of course, still employed. At the beginning of the century Samuel and Gottlob Mohn and Anton Kothgasser followed in the steps of the enamel-painter Johann Schaper, and Dominik Bimann continued in the Bohemian tradition of glass-cutting and engraving.

The *Art Nouveau* or *Jugendstil* movement has a remarkable place in the history of glass. One of its sources of inspiration is illustrated by the fact that the French artist Emile Gallé, working in Nancy, and the American, L. C. Tiffany, both took as a model Far Eastern glass which bears a closer resemblance to porcelain than to glass in its usual form. Chinese snuff-bottles, for example, made of opaque white glass with a carved casing of blue or red, are very like the fine semi-translucent porcelain produced by that country. Some of Gallé's opaque glass has the quality of Chinese jade when held against the light, and when light falls on its surface it has the appearance of porcelain. Tiffany's pieces have nothing of the accepted character of glass, but with their metallic surfaces rather remind one of the coppery glazing of modern faïence. This transformation of the natural character of glass marks both Gallé and Tiffany as artists of the nineteenth century, but they nevertheless paved the way for the interpretation given to the material in the twentieth. Certain precepts of theirs are still valid: their vases were not to be mere vehicles for a picture – on Gallé's the decorative element consists of exotic plant forms, on Tiffany's of an overall rainbow-like shimmer. In both cases the ornament has been suggested by the nature of the vessel itself; it is an intrinsic part of the vessel, and not foreign to it. It is, perhaps, a new understanding of this point which has brought about a revision of opinion on the subject of *Art Nouveau* glass.

In the years immediately succeeding this period, it seemed as if a return to cut glass was imminent. In 1925 Emil Pazaurek, the leading glass expert of the day, observed: 'The so-called *Jugendstil* period has quickly flown past, but what I consider to be the supreme expression of glass, namely cut crystal-glass, has experienced a remarkable rise to popularity now that it has cast off the fetters of traditional patterns'. He concluded from this that the twentieth century would be the great century of glass-making.

Pazaurek's prophecy has proved true, but in an entirely different way from what he envisaged. Glass-making developed along other lines. The unforeseen uses to which glass could be put, and the discovery of new and valuable qualities in the material have caused us to consider it afresh. We have discovered that it can be as hard as iron, that it can be elastic and unbreakable, we have learned how to spin it into threads and produce glass fabrics, and we have seen that it can conduct electricity. It has become a valuable part of our lives, and without it scientific experiment and industrial achievement would not be possible.

About the year 1930 came universal appreciation for the new style in glass, which delighted in a thick undecorated metal. In order to give the actual material its best expression, austere, massive forms with a certain tension of line were favoured. Function, a factor which dominates twentieth-century design and which was propounded by the *Bauhaus* group, also determined the forms of glass creations. The most natural forms adopted by glass are those of the sphere and the tear. The glass now relied for its beauty on its own appearance of purity unsullied by distracting decoration, and on the ever-changing intensity of light and colour in its undulating lines. The fifties saw the supreme expression of these principles, but as with all such principles, desire for change or for revision began to appear. The eye has tired of the simple, basic presentation of the material and now seeks pleasure from nuances of colour, contrasts of surface effects, even the demonstration of complicated technique. Cased glass, mosaic techniques, and air-bubble decoration have regained favour in new and adventurous forms. The idea of function and emphasis on the nature of the raw material is gradually being replaced by that of beauty created by technological means.

To sum up, it would seem that with all these means at its disposal, the art of glass-making has returned to its beginnings and is eager to experiment with new meaning in the never ending search to express the beauty of glass.

1 Beaker of Thothmes III

The oldest glass vessels which have come down to us were found in the tombs of the Egyptian Pharaohs. This famous beaker of Thothmes III represents the earliest and most beautiful example.

The glass, which has the shape of a lotus bud, was moulded on a clay core. In Egyptian art the lotus-flower appears time and time again, often stylised, on pottery, metal vessels and in architecture. The petals of the lotus-flower were also often used as a motif for the surface decoration of stone, metal and earthenware. In this beaker the pattern was produced by a technique which is only applicable to glass: threads of glass were superimposed horizontally and rolled into the surface of the hot, and therefore soft, material and at the same time dragged vertically into zig-zag shaped bands by a pointed metal rod. This comb-like ornament is much in evidence on Egyptian glass.

The cartouche gives the names Ra-Men-Kneper of Thothmes and they also appear, in reverse, on the buckle of his statue in the Cairo Museum.

Thothmes III was one of the most important pharaohs of the 18th Dynasty. Under his rule the boundaries of Egypt were at their widest, stretching from the Euphrates to Nubia. After the domination of Egypt by the foreign Hyksos dynasty ceased, cultural activities reached a new peak during the Amarna period, and as a result crafts and a highly sophisticated art of glass-making flourished.

2 Head showing the face of Amenhotep III

The head belongs most probably to a Ushabti-figure modelled after the face of Amenhotep III. He was the father and predecessor of Akhenaten who founded El Amarna. The Ushabti, which means representatives, are images of servants, which were to accompany the deceased in their tombs in order to represent them when their masters were called upon to perform tasks in the after-life.

3 Small amphora

The small amphora, the basic colour of which is lapis-lazuli blue, is one of the most beautiful pieces in the Ägyptische Museum in Berlin. The vessel exhibits the well balanced economical shape that is so characteristic of Greek pottery about half a millennium later. Base, body, and neck are clearly separated. The zone of the largest circumference lies above the middle and is marked by a feathery or fern-like combed ornament. The amphora was made at the time when El Armarna was flourishing (1377–1345 B.C.); this was the place where the pharaoh Akhenaten had built his residence. The town, famous for its cultural activities, was destroyed before her heretic ruler died. Parts of the ruined town, which was never re-inhabited, were excavated by the Deutsche Orientgesellschaft (German Oriental Society) during the years 1911–1914. One of their best known finds is the bust of Queen Nofretete by the sculptor Tutmose.

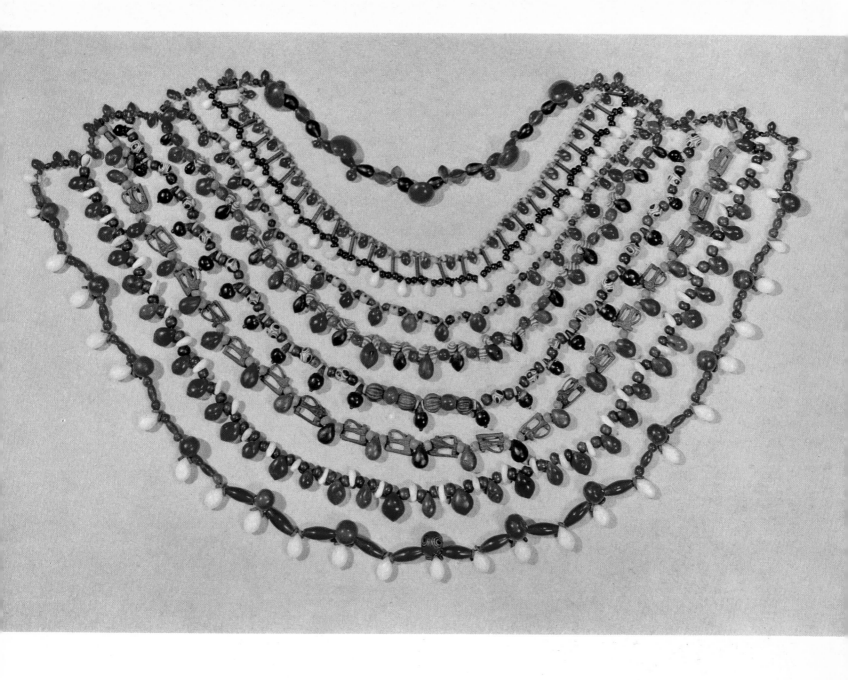

5 Necklace of a Nubian Queen

In his search for antiquities, the Italian Ferlini, who was employed by the Egyptians, started, in 1834, to dismantle one of the small steep-sided pyramids of Meroe, once the capital of the Nubian Kingdom. This venture, which nowadays would be beyond our comprehension, was crowned by success; he found the treasure of a Nubian Queen, unidentified to this day, who reigned in Meroe in the first century B.C. To her treasure belonged the necklace which is illustrated here, though not in its original state. The parts consisting of natural shells, golden links in the form of eye-amulets, cornelian, faience and glass beads, connected simply by traces of string, were reassembled to make two necklaces later. The glass beads appear in a variety of shapes; some are fluted, gilt or layered; others are opaque-white or red and tear-shaped. The Egyptian technique of melting glass threads into glass-surfaces, as employed to make the eye-beads, continued over one and a half millennium.

6 Large amphora

The art of glass-making received no impetus in ancient Greece. There was no demand for household glass because the art of pottery was highly developed. The few glasses which have come down to us were most probably imported from Egypt and Syria. This also applies to the illustrated amphora.

The vessel, about 60 cm. in height, is one of the most exquisite pieces ever produced in glass. It was not blown, but manufactured in two parts which were probably moulded on a clay core and polished. The joined edges are concealed by a gilt metal ribbon.

The shape of the amphora is true to the style of the period and is of the type of panathenaic amphoras. Though it is the only known example of its kind, it demonstrates how the translation of shapes of Greek ceramics into glass forms, even if not wholly appropriate to the material, has resulted in a vessel of outstanding beauty.

Olbia, where the amphora was found, was the most important trading place in the Pontus, a cross-road for the exchange with Kiev and the Baltic countries. The amber trade was also conducted via Olbia.

7 Millefiori bowl

The bowl belongs to a category of glass vessels termed in the ancient tradition *vasa murrhina*. In his 37th book of natural history, Pliny reports that after his victory over the Persian King Mithridates, Pompey brought 2000 Murrhine bowls to Rome which he dedicated to Jupiter. The legendary Murrhine collection of the Egyptian Empress Cleopatra was disposed of by auction in Rome by Augustus. At that time Murrhine vessels were highly valued. Ancient literature reports prices of 70,000 sesterces, which is about £ 1,000 in our currency. The term *vasa murrhina* was a subject of scientific controversy for a long time. Anton Kisa was the first to point out that they were made of glass and not of semi-precious stones.

The production of millefiori glass demanded great skill. A number of coloured glass-canes were placed together to form a certain pattern, such as a flower, and melted together. The resulting rod was cut into slices, and these in turn were placed side by side and melted together. In this way, flat bowls with a continuous pattern were produced which finally had to be ground or polished.

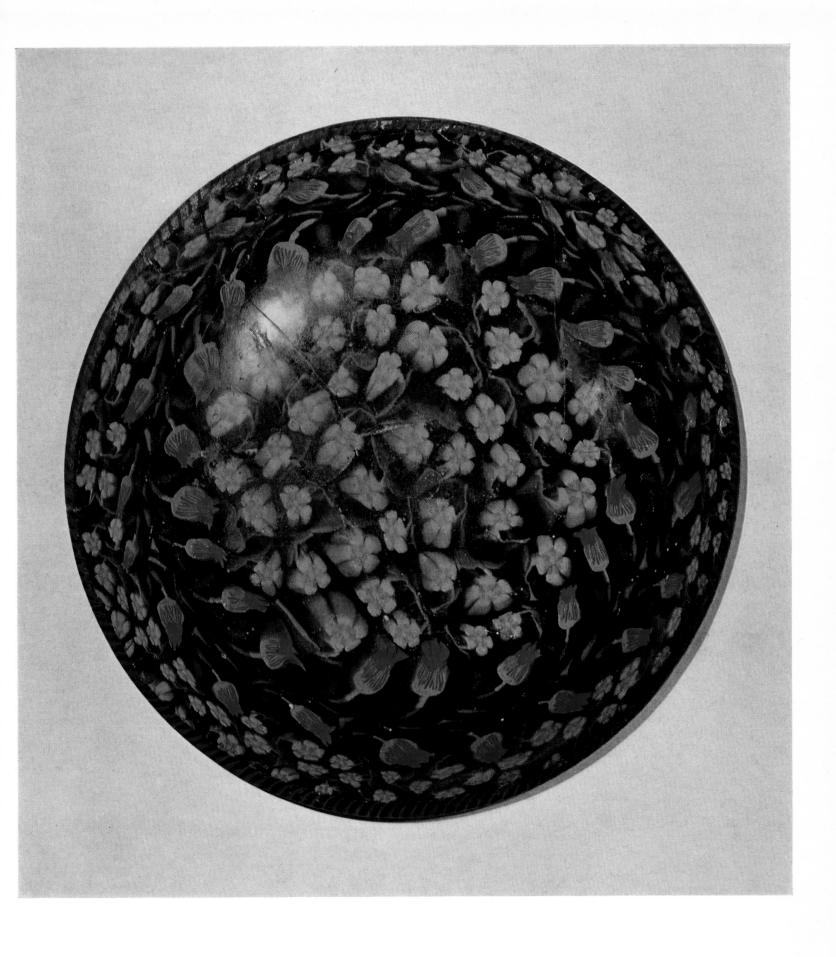

8 Ribbed bowl

9 Tall ribbed bowl

These ribbed bowls were made especially in Rome, Gaul and on the Rhine during the first two centuries. The earliest examples were mould-blown and ground afterwards. Later the method was simplified by applying glass threads to the surface of the blown bowl.

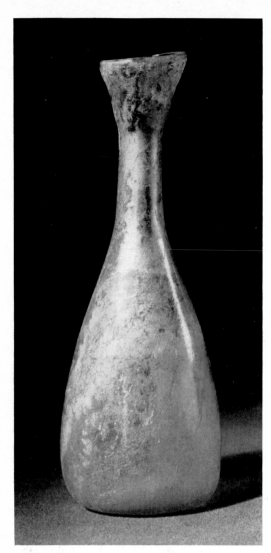 

10/11/12 Syrian domestic glass vessels

With the invention of glass-blowing, the shape of glass vessels changed. The basic shape of all blown glass is a sphere suspended on a hollow iron rod. The hot pliable sphere is transformed, either by its own weight or by a swinging movement, into a club- or tear-shaped body.

In order to make the vessel stand upright, the bottom was flattened or even pressed in (kicked) and later, from about the second century onwards, a ring-shaped foot was fixed underneath the bottle to improve its stability. After cooling, the neck was broken off the blow-pipe. The earliest blown bottles were left as they came off the pipe. In later examples, the mouth, after reheating, was enlarged into a funnel-like shape, pinched into a spout, folded, or, after the first century, a glass-ring was applied just beneath the mouth. At the same time bottles with handles appear which consist of thickish glass-threads melted on to the vessel.

This method of glass-blowing has remained unchanged until to-day. No wonder that the illustrated Syrian bottles appear so surprisingly modern. Though swiftly made for everyday purposes, they have an elegance of shape which shows a true understanding of the material.

13 Bottle with relief decoration

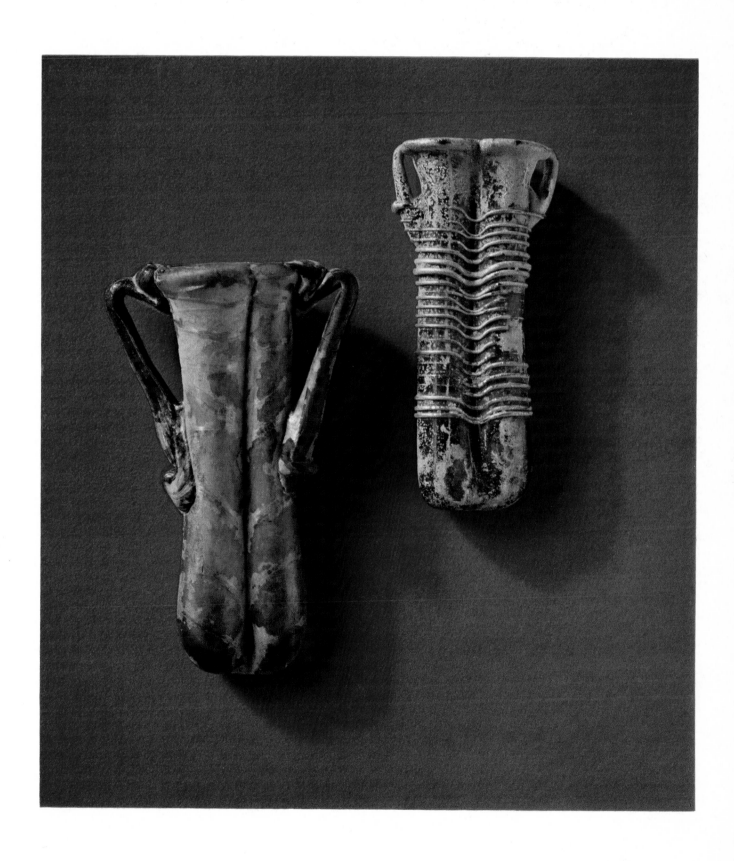

15 Shell-shaped flask

16 Flask in the form of a bunch of grapes

The invention of glass-blowing was soon exploited for artistic purposes. The glass was blown into a mould, which usually consisted of two identical sections. The ornaments were cut in relief into the interior surface of the mould. In some not so carefully executed pieces a vertical line on the glass indicates the joining of the mould.

The earliest mould-blown glasses were made in Sidon (Phoenicia) in the first century. There were several glasshouses, and their products were traded far and wide. The names of the glass-makers appear moulded on their vessels; the best known of these are Ennion, Meges, Artas and Ariston.

Originally the imprinted motifs were confined to parts of the surface, but later they covered the entire vessel. The most common shapes used were shells and grape clusters. In Rome, bottles in the form of a head were much in fashion.

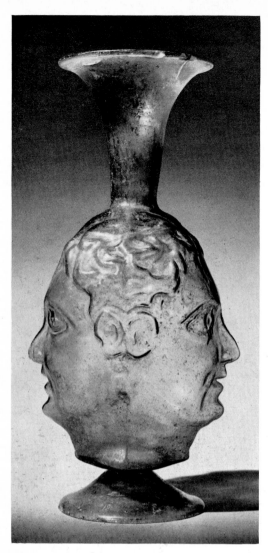 

17 Flask in the form of a Janus head

18 Vessel in the form of a girl's head

19 Negro head bottle

Head-shaped vessels, which played an important part in religious rites in early Greek and Cretan culture, but were adapted for profane use during the Hellenic period, finally lost their serious character in Nero's Rome and turned into a vehicle for caricature. Most of the head-shaped glass vessels realistically depict misshapen faces for sheer amusement. The features of Nero's court fool, a shoemaker, can be found, hence the (German) name *Schustergläser* (shoemaker glasses) which is sometimes attributed to this category of glasses. The Emperor Commodus is said to have made such vessels himself.

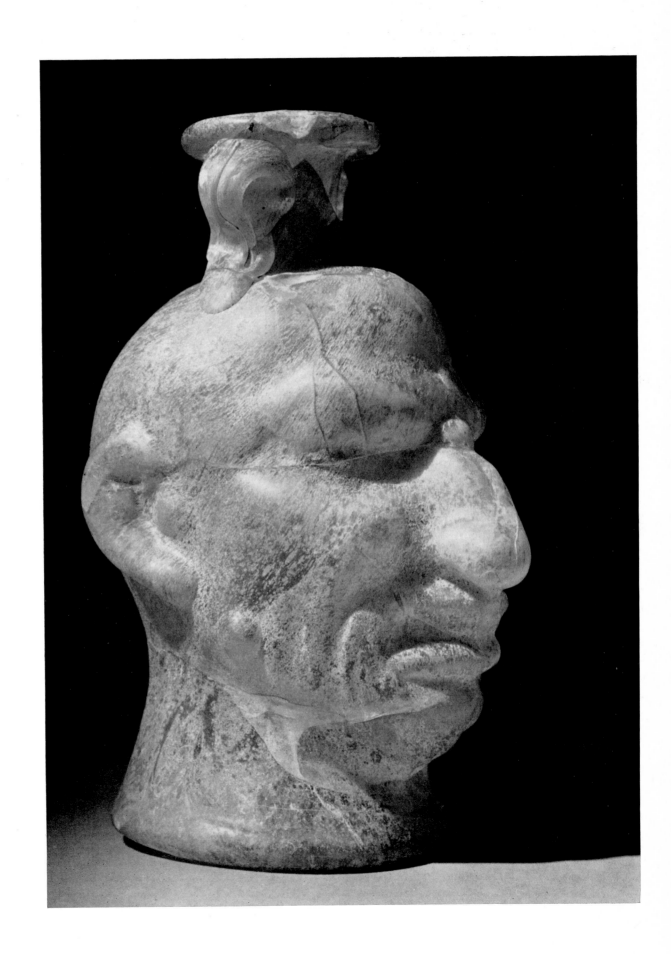

20 Ridged beaker

21 Pear-shaped ewer

At the beginning of the first century the first imports of glass, destined for the Roman upper classes, arrived in Cologne from Egypt, Syria and Italy. Towards the end of the first century the first glass-houses were founded in the Cologne area. Following the Gallo-Roman method of glass-making they produced a simple glass for everyday use in blue-green shades. From about the middle of the second century uncoloured glass was developed, no doubt precipitated by the discovery of a sand which was ideal for the purpose. This furnished the basis for the speedy development of glass-producing around Cologne. In the second half of the third century a light green coloured type of glass was made. The illustrated pear-shaped ewer stems from this period.

The delicate outline of the slender ewer reveals its relationship to metal vessels; nevertheless the use of glass gives a new vigour to a traditional form. The blown sphere was drawn out into a tear-shaped body, and the neck widened into a mouth. Fused to the brim with a knot-shaped twist, the handle displays a delightful elegance. The attractive shimmer of the glass is caused by the fact that the vessel was buried for a considerable time in the earth.

22 Free-blown ewer

23 Cinerary urn

24 Vessel with trailed decoration
25 Small, five-handled amphora

26 Stamnium

27 Pear-shaped ewer

28 Conical ewer, or *Prochus*

Thanks to the late Roman custom of burying with the deceased gifts of food and drink, a large number of works of glass were handed down to posterity. During recent years many well-preserved glass-vessels of Roman origin have come to light during excavation, especially in the Roman burial grounds around Cologne. The immense treasure kept in the Römisch-Germanisches Museum in Cologne nearly all stems from this area. This fact enables us to appreciate the standard and achievement of the Cologne glass industry, and to reconstruct its development in the course of history.

The variety of forms is extraordinary, though there are certain basic types, such as the Prochus, a wide conical ewer, or the Stamnium, a cylindrical bottle with two handles, or the different kinds of the so-called Lekythoi. In each case one gets the impression that the shape achieved cannot be surpassed.

The way in which the glass-threads were applied in the Lekythos with the double-ringed neck is remarkable. First they were laid vertically upon the small, hot sphere, which was then enlarged and twisted at the same time, resulting in the clear spiral relief on the vessel's surface.

30 *Kantharos*

31 Concave beaker

32 Pitcher with trefoil mouth
and trailed snake ornamentation

33 Pear-shaped bottle
with trailed snake decoration

Vessels showing snake-trailing generally indicate Cologne manufacture of the second, third and beginning of the fourth century, although they have occasionally been found within the frontiers of ancient Gaul. The decoration is applied in a somewhat haphazard way, seldom with realistic intentions. These vessels are small masterpieces produced by undoubtedly skilled glass-makers. The jug and bottle reveal their Syrian origin in their simple flowing lines, whereas the classical form of the carchesium shows Graeco-Roman inspiration.

**35 Pilgrim's bottle
with trailed snake decoration,
known as the *Meisterstück***

This is the most outstanding of the Rheno-Roman snake trailed vessels. The flat surface of the bottle is richly ornamented with trailing, with a gold spiral in the centre, leaf motifs with blue midribs and gold edges radiating from it, and garlands in blue, white and gold thread. Thick pinched trailing has been applied to the handles and sides.

Fritz Fremersdorf, the greatest authority on Rheno-Roman glass, gave to this bottle the name of *das Meisterstück* by which it has since been known. The decoration does indeed show masterly skill. Extraordinary virtuosity was obviously called for to manipulate the vessel beneath the hot molten, yet rapidly hardening glass threads and produce such a flowing design.

36 Conical flask with gold painting

37 Cylindrical two-handled bottle

38 Hemispherical bowl
with facetting

The Roman craftsmen were familiar with most of the techniques in glass decoration practised today, including cutting and engraving. Late Roman glass-cutting differs basically from the earlier cameo-like work, of which the most celebrated example is the Portland Vase. In the latter we have the adaptation of gem-cutting to the medium of glass, usually opaque and often two-layered. In real glass-cutting the craftsman was working with an entirely different material: thin transparent glass. As a result the cutting could only consist of shallow, usually matt depressions, or round and oval polished facets. The decorative element is derived from the refraction of light through the concave surfaces.

39 Shallow bowl
with chariot-racing motif

This Rheno-Roman dish, most interesting from both an artistic and historical point of view, was discovered in 1910 in a sarcophagus on the site of a Roman estate in Cologne-Brauns-feld. It lay on the breast of the dead woman, an indication of its superior worth among the burial objects.

The profile of an emperor with crown and whip is surrounded by a view of a chariot-race. Four horses, each with a palm-leaf plume, pull each chariot. The chariot-drivers lean forward, urging on their teams with the whip and grasping the taut reins. Two of them are glancing backwards. The site of the race, the Circus Maximus, may be gathered from the objects depicted between the teams: the two turning points, indicated by two groups of three turreted buildings, which terminate the wall around which seven circuits had to be made, and in addition the obelisk which was situated in the middle of this wall. The seven indicators, showing how many laps remained to be completed, are also visible. In Rome, chariot-racing and gladiatorial combats, two forms of sports introduced from Greece, degenerated, especially in the time of the cruel Emperor Tiberius, into a bloody spectacle which gave the host, usually the Emperor himself, the opportunity to flaunt his wealth, power and favours.

Introduced into the provinces, the games had a particular role to play, participation being granted to subject peoples as a high honour.

40 Goblet with shell decoration

Cologne, capital of the Roman Empire in the West, had developed its own style in glass-making. Even when Eastern fashions arrived, they were adapted by native talent, as this intrinsically beautiful glass illustrates.

The glass shows a combination of technical skill and artistic sensitivity. Its main ornament consists of a cage of vertical trailing standing away from the body, both of twisted and shell-shaped pinched trails. The height of the cage is equal to half that of the vessel itself. Originally colourless, the glass has become opaque white as a result of being buried for a long time.

This mastery of the art of trailing indicates that a Cologne glass-house was the origin of this vessel.

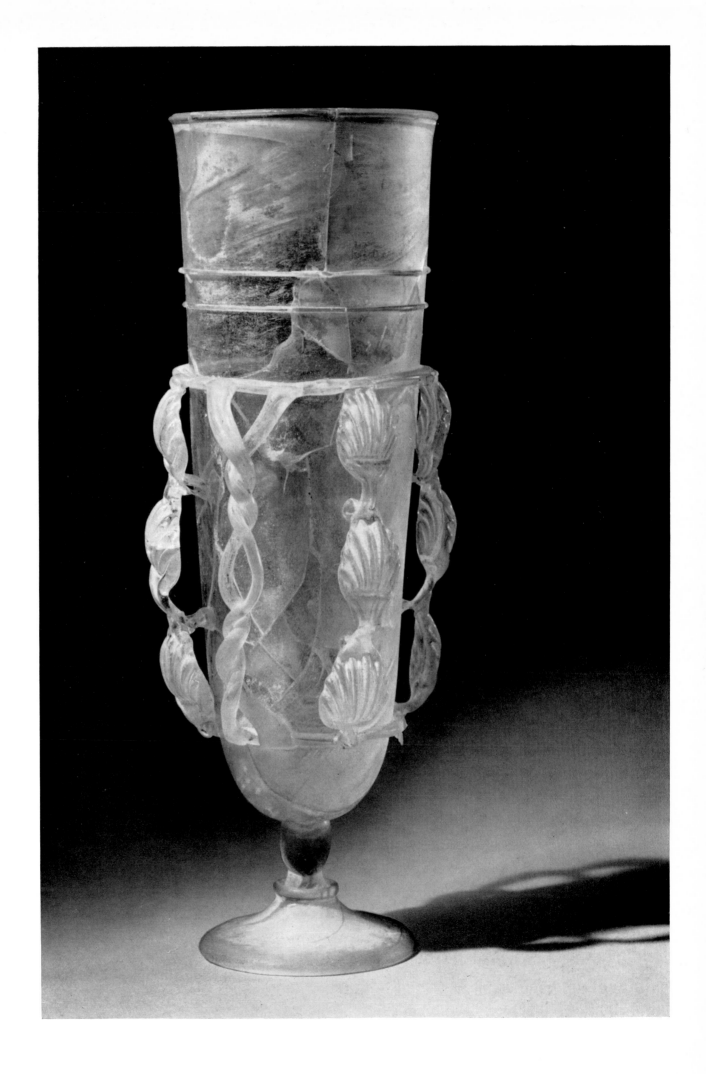

41 Diatreton

The most outstanding products of the Cologne glass-makers are undoubtedly the diatreta glasses. The diatreta have always aroused much speculation among glass historians as to how exactly these intricate objects were made. In 1725, Winckelmann examined the Trivucio cup in Milan, (now housed in the Archaeological Museum in that city), and came to the conclusion that the ornament was "certainly not welded on, but cut out of a solid piece of glass". Objections to this hypothesis have, however, often been made on the grounds of impracticability. In 1880, one Friedrich, a glass-cutter in the Bavarian glassworks of Zwiesel, offered to test this theory. He did in fact succeed in producing a diatreton, by cutting and boring into the metal, although his efforts took him half a year. Unfortunately neither this piece, nor any pictorial record of it, has survived. Later Winckelmann's theory was again attacked, this time by Wilhelm von Eiff, who was convinced that the vessels could not have been obtained by cutting methods in view of the instruments available at that time. He suggested that it was a question of applied decoration. A further critic, Wiedermann, put forward the theory that a complicated prunting technique was involved.

42 Diatreton

Diatreta glasses are among the most precious items a museum collection may possess. Only nineteen such vessels are known, including damaged specimens. The three most beautiful came to light in Cologne.

The first of these, found in 1844, was presented to King Ludwig of Bavaria in recognition of his donation of timber for the roof of Cologne cathedral. It is now in the Museum für Antike Kleinkunst in Munich.

The second specimen, discovered in a sarcophagus not far from the first, went to the Berlin Antiquarium, where it was destroyed by war action in 1945.

It was therefore an exciting occasion when, on 1st April 1960, during the excavation of a building site, a third was unearthed. This was found to be the most beautiful of them all.

This latest discovery was examined by Otto Doppelfeld, who was able to conclude from it that the technique employed in its making was without doubt that of undercutting. The direction of the air-bubbles both in the wall and cage ornament indicates that a single piece of glass was used.

Diatreta glasses have been found in the Rhineland, on the Danube and in Northern Italy. The glasses without inscriptions probably come from Trier, the richer examples from Cologne.

43 Dolphin beaker

The graceful dolphin, friend of the ancient sea-farers, following their ships, did, in fact, symbolise the sea in early art. In Greek mythology it is depicted as the mariner's friend, and is the symbol of Aphrodite, the seaborn goddess. In Early Christian art it came to represent Christ, the letters in the Greek word for fish being taken as an abbreviation for His name and title.

In glass-making, too, which, whether carried out in Rome, in Gaul or in the Rhineland, delighted in shaping natural forms in this plastic material, the dolphin motif occurs. There are few glasses in the shape of a fish, but dolphin decoration is frequent. Dolphin-like handles are a common addition to many Syrian, Roman and Rheno-Roman ewers and bottles.

The dolphin beaker in the illustration, found in a grave near the Severinstrasse in Cologne, is a remarkable piece. The dolphins were hollow-blown, and then perhaps attached to fit over large circular openings in the vessel, a feat which must have demanded considerable mastery of the craft.

The Rhenish glass-makers did not limit themselves to this pattern. Other beakers, ornamented with all kinds of sea creatures and snails, may be seen. Such beakers are known by the general term dolphin beakers. They were apparently produced only in Gaul and the Rhineland.

44 Tall bowl in colourless glass
with trailed coloured
zig-zag ornamentation
and flat button-shaped blobs

45 Beaker with coloured prunts,
known as *Humpen*

At the end of the fourth century the last Roman troops were recalled from the Rhine, and Cologne, the Roman Colonia Claudia Ara Agrippinensis, became a Frankish town. Long before this event, however, as early as 260 A.D., shortly after the collapse of the Limes, strong Germanic influence began to be revealed in Rheno-Roman glass-making. This was partly a consequence of the southernward drive of German tribes on the east of the Rhine. An illustration of a vessel showing Germanic influence is provided by the *Humpen* (nos. 44 and 45), with their blob- decoration and zig-zag frieze. In form they resemble the Germanic *Kummen*, the earliest earthenware serving and drinking bowls. Both the button-shaped blobs and the frieze are of religious origin, being employed to ward off evil spirits. The application of coloured stones to the vessel surface is also typical of Germanic art, and is also a feature of objects worked in gold.

47 *Rüsselbecher*

Recent research has allotted to the *Rüsselbecher*, or Claw-beaker, a more certain place in the history of glass-making, and the trunk- or claw- like appendages are now seen as a development of the earlier dolphin motif. The glasses still, however, pose certain problems. The symbolic meaning of the dolphin was undoubtedly lost by this time, and it is possible that the appendages now represented trunks, or more probably horns, since in Germanic culture, especially in the North, the horn was of religious significance. A curious fact which may be mentioned is that glass drinking horns have been found exclusively in the graves of women.

Rüsselbecher have been discovered in the Rhineland, Western Germany and England. F. Fremersdorf assumes that they were produced in Northern France, where a part of the Cologne glass industry had become established during the migration of tribes.

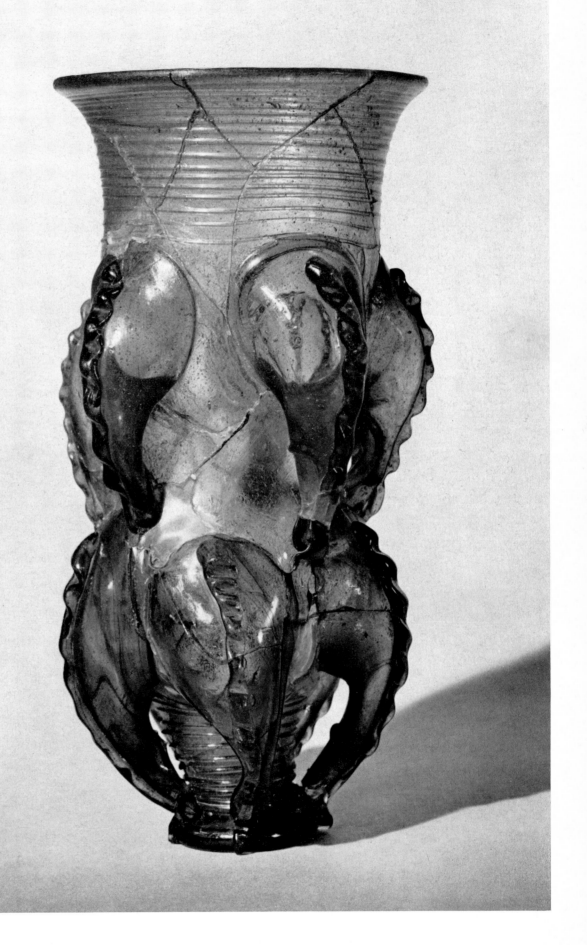

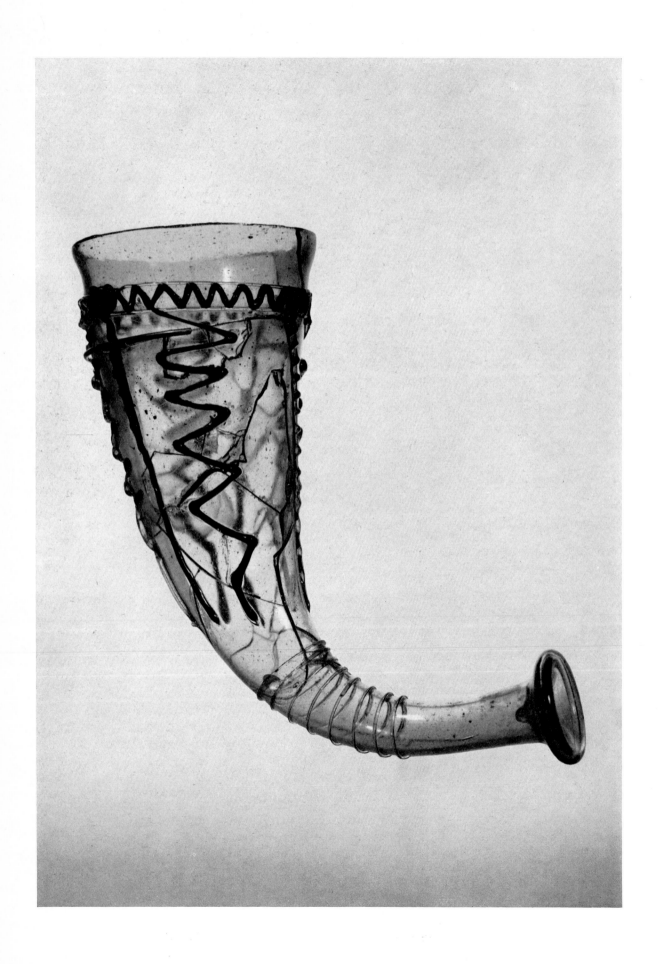

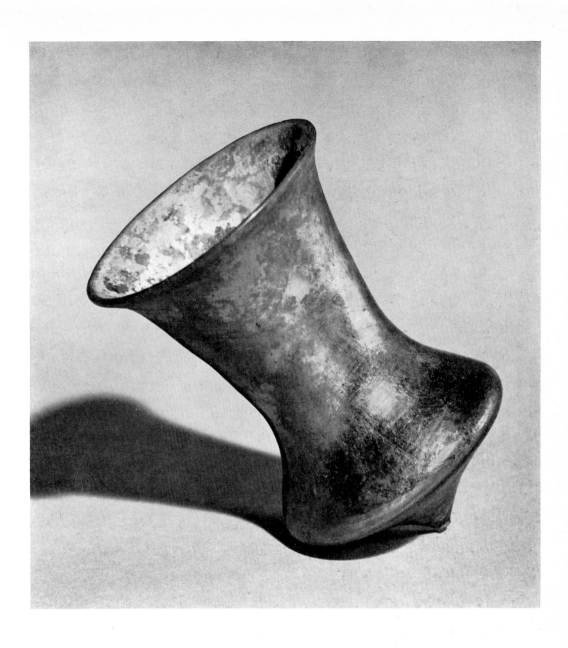

49 Footless beaker

The great period of Rheno-Roman glass-making comes to an end in the fourth and fifth centuries. The centuries of turbulence during the migration of the tribes, as well as a diminution of material assets, lessened the demands and manifestations of civilisation, and glass-making of necessity suffered. In addition the Church forbade the use of glass vessels for the sacrament. The custom of richly furnishing the grave with all kinds of objects died out, also under the influence of the Church. Thus the art, with all its traditions and technical achievements, languished. The glass of the Merovingian and Frankish periods, and of the following centuries of the early Middle Ages, is dull, imperfect and showing impurity of colour. Merovingian glasses show that the art of making a foot for a vessel had been lost, and these footless vessels were the obvious solution to the problem. In Western Europe, with the building of the Romanesque churches and cathedrals, the glass-maker's efforts are henceforth directed towards producing window-glass to be decorated by glass painters, and it is left to the Orient to carry on in the old tradition and raise it to new heights in the Islamic lands.

50 Footed beaker

51 Mould-blown bottle with surface decoration

52 Bowl with winged horse decoration

In the year 224 A.D. the Persian dynasty of the Sassanids succeeded in overthrowing their foreign rulers, the Parthians, who had dominated the land for five hundred years since the destruction of the Ancient Persian Empire by Alexander the Great. The capital of the sultanate was Ktesiphon on the Tigris. The renaissance of the old Persian Empire lasted four centuries, until it was engulfed by the advancing power of Islam. The art of the Sassanian period, an aristocratic art dependent on the ancient Persian religion, Zoroastrianism, is strict in form, ornamental, and rich in symbolism. In comparison with work in precious metal and in bronze, glass is only of minor importance. Nevertheless, although it is hardly formal, this beaker may be regarded, as far as its ornamentation is concerned, as a typical specimen of the period. The haphazardly applied medallions depict winged horses, which have been obtained by pressing a stamp in the soft metal. The glass is said to have been bought from Aleppo dealers and was presented by Wilhelm von Bode to the former Kaiser-Friedrich-Museum in Berlin.

55 Beaker with cut decoration

The beaker comes from Samarra, capital of the rulers of the Abbassid dynasty, who were Caliphs of Baghdad from the sixth to the thirteenth century. Samarra, lying to the north of Baghdad on the Tigris, was founded in the year 836 A.D. by the successor of Caliph Harun-al-Raschid. Its name derives from the Arabic *surra man ra'a*. On the death of the Caliph in 889 A.D., a mere fifty years after its foundation, the city was abandoned and engulfed by the desert sands. Excavations undertaken by German archaeologists at the turn of the century revealed rich treasures of that era of Islamic greatness. The Abbassid style is one of strict geometrical patterns and stylised representation richly used. Upon it all Islamic decorative art is based. The simple facetting of this vessel reflects the architectural ornament of the excavations in Samarra.

Early Islamic glass shows the continuation of late Roman decorative motifs, but is further enriched by the discovery of gold lustre painting. From this point the history of Persian-Islamic glass of the thirteenth and fourteenth centuries may be said to date.

57 *Hedwigsglas*

This glass is one of a famous group of twelve Fatimid *Hochschnitt* or high relief glasses, which take their name from St. Hedwig, the patron saint of Silesia who died in 1243. In such a glass, so legend tells us, the Saint caused a wine miracle to take place. The castle of Coburg houses a *Hedwigsglas* which belonged to St. Elizabeth and subsequently to the house of Wettin, and which was venerated for its alleged powers to give strength to women in labour if they drank from it. The glass was lent on several occasions to courts which were on friendly terms with Wettin. Later, as Mathesius informs us, Martin Luther received the glass as a gift.

Hedwigsgläser belong to the last cut-glass vessels to be produced in the Orient, and are the final masterpieces of Egyptian skill in this genre. It is clear that they are a continuation of the art of rock-crystal cutting. Stylised lions and griffons between palm branches, or sometimes palm branches alone, are the motifs of the deep cutting. Most *Hedwigsgläser* found their way into the treasures of Western churches as the gifts of returning crusaders.

The art of the Fatimite dynasty, which held sway in North Africa from the ninth to the twelfth century with Cairo as its capital, shows an Islamic style with certain original notes. The finer stylisation which derives from the art of the Abbassid realm and finally from Sassanian tradition attains its supreme expression under the influence of Egyptian national tradition.

58 Emerald green bottle with cut ornament

At the end of the first millennium, when this emerald-green bottle was produced in Iran, Persian culture already had a history of six thousand years. The severe lines and geometrical cutting of the bottle are the result of artistic experiment and development dating back to the ceramics of Susa in the third century B.C., and carried on through the period of Greek influence, the Sassanian traditions, and the fusion with Islamic culture before its destruction by the Mongols in the fourteenth century.

The lines of the silhouette have an austerity which appeals to modern taste.

60 Small bottle
with lustre painting

The Caliphs of the Fatimid dynasty ruled from 810 to 1172 over Syria, Egypt and North Africa from their newly-founded capital city of Cairo. This bottle with gold lustre decoration dates back to that period of rule in Egypt. Gold lustre was the discovery of Sumerian potters as a substitute for articles of solid gold, which obedient Moslems were not allowed to possess. The application of this decoration to glass vessels is particularly effective, since here the glitter of the lustre is linked with that of the glass itself.

The vase-shaped glass is decorated at the neck with a calligraphic motif, and the body with a spiral tendril-like motif. Whereas the Cufic-Arabic inscriptions always have an ornamental function, here the ornament has a calligraphic appearance.

61 Beaker with inscribed eulogy

This beaker was discovered in a fourteenth-century Tartar grave in the northwestern Caucasus and was acquired by the Berliner Antiquarium from a private collection in Southern Russia at the beginning of this century. The Tartars of the Caucasus bought such costly enamelled pieces as drinking vessels from Damascus. Many of these highly prized vessels found their way into western Cathedral treasuries as a result of the crusades. The "*Glück von Edenhall*", from an English private collection, now in the Victoria and Albert Museum, and famous because of Ludwig Uhland's ballad of that name, belongs to this group of Islamic enamelled glasses. The *Lutherbecher* in the Quedlinburg Museum must also be included. Further examples may be seen in the Grünes Gewölbe in Dresden and in the Bayrisches Nationalmuseum, Munich.

62 Beaker with horse and rider medallions

63 Bottle with trailed decoration

64 Perfume sprinkler known as an *Omom*

The Omom is a Syrian vessel which was used for sprinkling aromatic essences. The decoration of this piece, somewhat obscured by corrosive action, shows the mingling of Islamic and Chinese motifs. The area between the Caspian Sea and the Persian Gulf was for many centuries the link between the Near and Far East. Chinese influence began to make itself strongly felt, particularly after the Mongol invasion of Mesopotamia and the taking of Baghdad in 1258. Along with the bands of formal foliate pattern we see Chinese flower and animal motifs, the peony, the dragon and the phoenix.

65 Mosque-lamp

Some 230 mosque lamps have survived the centuries. Almost all of them originate from mosques in Cairo, although they were not made in Egypt but in Syria. Their export to Cairo ceased in 1402 – in the year in which Timur, a descendent of Ghengis Khan, whose powerful Mongolian Empire extended from the Great Wall of China as far as Moscow and Egypt, overcame Syria, took Damascus and deported 150,000 people, including of course all the glass-makers, to Samarkand, now the capital of Usbekistan.

The mosque-lamps are masterpieces of the glass-painter's art. Rich gold painting is characteristic of Islamic workmanship, since the use of solid pure gold was forbidden on religious grounds. The text from the Koran inscribed round the neck compares the lamp with a glittering star and with Allah, the light of the heavens. The inscription on the body is in praise of Sultan al-Nasir Muhammed, who ruled from 1293 to 1341. The upper inscription is in blue on gold, the lower in gold on blue. The blue consists of ground lapis-lazuli. The foot is ornamented with coloured friezes showing trefoils and Chinese lotus-flowers. The lamps were suspended from the ceiling on chains. The actual oil-lamp was placed inside them.

Mosque-lamps have long been prized collectors' pieces. At the end of the nineteenth century many reproductions of them were made, and there are no doubt still many fakes in circulation. The glass illustrated here was presented in 1911 to the Kaiser-Friedrich Museum, Berlin, by the German Ambassador at St. Petersburg.

66 Beaker with tracery and spot decoration

The art of making glass, as it had developed in ancient civilisations, was inherited, partly by way of Rome and Byzantium, partly via the Near East, by Venice, which became the centre for the entire European production of new glass. In spite of the extraordinary importance of the Venetian glass industry, we have very little information about its early beginnings. Any attempt to study the derivation of the Venetian style must start with a knowledge of those dates which indicate the city's links with the Orient. The destruction of Constantinople in the year 1204 during the fourth crusade brought rich spoils to Venice, which had placed its fleet at the disposal of the Crusaders. Part of the booty consisted, not only of Byzantine and Islamic glassware, but also of numerous glassworkers.

In the year 1107 Venice established a permanent trading centre in Sidon, the ancient Phoenician trading and glass-making town, and in 1124 another such centre followed in Tyre.

The *Statuti maritimi* of the Doge Remero Zeno dating from 1235 to 1255, and the treaty between Doge Jacopo Contarini and Bohemund VII, ruler of Antioch, brought control over the import from the Orient of cullet, without which the industry could not function. The other necessary ingredients, sand and soda, were also imported from the East.

This close association between Venice and the Near East means that it is often impossible to state with certainty the origin of some fifteenth-century glasses. To this category belongs the glass illustrated. Four such pieces are in existence, in the Corning Museum, New York, the Metropolitan Museum, New York, the Wolf Collection, Buenos Aires, and in the Islamic Section of the former Staatliche Museen, Berlin. All four were found in Syria. The rhombic pattern first occurs in the late Roman period on Mediterranean and Rhenish glasses. The enamel-painted lily-of-the-valley motif, which is seen along with the rhombic pattern on late fifteenth-century glasses of unquestionably Venetian origin, seems to indicate that this vessel was manufactured in Venice for the Syrian market.

67 Ewer

The ewer is partly iridescent as it was buried for a long time, and this effect strengthens the impression that this must be a Syrian piece of c. 500 A.D. The spiral ribbing and the use of blue glass for the spout and handles could confirm this impression. The over-all shape of the vessel is nevertheless Venetian, and the clear distinction between body and foot is a European characteristic of the Renaissance period. None the less, this ewer clearly shows the strong dependence of Venetian glass on its Syrian ancestor. Certain features and techniques have been adopted, but the vessel shows a new inspiration.

The fact that these early unpainted glasses have survived in such small numbers is easily explained by the fact that they were not, like their elaborately ornamented fellows, considered objects of worth and therefore treated with care. A fairly large number of ewers similar to this one have survived, but they too are usually enamel-painted.

68 Bowl with typical
Venetian scale-pattern

69 Marriage goblet

Contact with the Near East was the factor which gave to early Venetian glass its beauty during the early period. The technique of using enamel decoration was highly developed in Islamic glass-making by the thirteenth and fourteenth centuries and was employed by the Venetians, although in a manner reflecting their own contemporary painting, between 1460 and 1530. The Prague Marriage Bowl is an excellent specimen of this period, not so much for the glass as such, although the metal and form are attractive, but for the execution of the enamel painting on it.

The bowl has a wide foot with a raised rib ornament which has a certain Gothic character about it. The bowl is also wide and seems to form the calyx of a flower resting on seven small, leaf-like appendages. The metal is opaque white in colour. The gilt scale decoration is studded with gem-like dots of red and blue enamel, and covers the whole surface of the bowl, except where it is interrupted by two medallions. The ribs and leaves were once gilt. The ornament is formed by the two medallions showing the bridal pair. On the side visible in the illustration we see a portrait of a youth playing a lute. He wears his hair long, and his clothes are of the latest fashion of the day. We are reminded of the self-portrait, executed in a similar delicate manner, of the twenty-nine year old Dürer, who had visited Venice a year earlier, in 1492. Another marriage bowl is to be seen in the Corning Museum, New York, evidently the work of the same artist. The style of the portraits resembles that of the painter Vittore Carpaccio, a pupil of Gentile Bellini.

70 Beaker with grotesque painting Representational painting on glass vessels was no longer the fashion by the beginning of the sixteenth century. Taste inclined more towards clear, plain metal. Glass was appreciated for its own sake, and there was a striving to improve its quality and place the emphasis on beauty of shape.

A transitional phase is represented by those glasses which, although painted, merely have formal patterns, not scenes or portraits. Such glasses are mainly covered with grotesque ornamentation, fantastic, lively patterns built up from arabesque-like flowers and leaves, animal- and human-like forms, such as those which may be seen in the catacombs of Ancient Rome and which were adapted by Raphael in his decoration of the Vatican Loggias. This kind of ornament, greatly used by Italian, French and German engravers, was also employed up to the eighteenth century by cabinet makers, carpet weavers, gold- and silversmiths, and glass and porcelain makers.

The Prague beaker is decorated with winged dragons ridden by putti who hold a gigantic crab. Unattached wavy bands fill in the remaining areas and give unity to the design.

71 Goblet with jewelled enamel border decoration

Oriental influence in Venetian glass was limited to the use of enamel painting. As early as the fifteenth century, Venice had developed its own European style. Inspiration was derived in part from the metalworker's art. The silver goblet in particular was imitated in glass.

The vertical lines of the Gothic style, and the hard silhouette of metal vessels caused by the nature of the material used, determined the shape which glass pieces took. Here we see a stiff, ribbed foot and an austerely shaped cup, which in other examples is also ribbed. Only the slight curving of the bowl indicates the later elegance of silhouette which was to develop. Colour still plays an indispensable role. The foot is of blue glass. The bowl, which has a border in enamel colour, is of clear metal, but is as yet by no means free of impurities, as was the later famous *cristallo*.

73 Wine glass

The wine glass provides an excellent example of the clear elegant lines of the Italian High Renaissance. We note a plain, slightly raised foot, a shapely baluster stem and a simple tall or shallow bowl. Annular knops mark off the foot, stem and bowl, emphasising the proportions of the glass. The metal is still imperfect and bubbled, but its very character, particularly its slight greenish tinge, is an excellent foil for the gold and enamel painting. The border consists of a frieze of gold circles and enamel dots.

74 Ribbed glass

The threat of severe punishment to the families of Venetian glass makers who left the city did not prevent a certain amount of emigration, a problem with which the industry was continually grappling. Working in glasshouses in many foreign countries, the Venetians assured the rapid spread of the techniques and forms familiar to them. The term *façon de Venise* is used to describe this glass produced outside Venice. The glass in the illustration, smoke-coloured and in thickish metal with clean strong ribbing, was probably made in Germany in the sixteenth century.

75 Jug and beaker

76 Flagon with *latticino* decoration

Venetian glass of the classical period of the sixteenth century shows no decoration foreign to the material, no painting, cutting or engraving; its beauty lies in its actual form, in the application of glass ornament at the furnace and, a remarkable innovation, in the patterns within the glass: the *vetro di trina* and *vetro a reticelli*. Both kinds of glass, which demand a high degree of skill on the part of the glassmaker, have been marvelled at right to the present day.

Vetro di trina, or *latticinio a ritorti* as it is sometimes known, is produced by a complicated process. A clay cylinder mould is taken and white glass rods with a colourless casing are arranged with colourless rods in the desired pattern round the inner wall. The remaining space in the mould is filled with molten colourless glass. The glass is then removed from the mould and drawn out and twisted into a long rod. Thus, according to the arrangement of the rods within the mould, a pattern of threads in the new glass rod has been produced. Rods of this kind are then used in their turn in a similar process for the decoration of a vessel: they are placed on the inner wall of a clay mould into which a glass bubble is then blown. The rods adhere and fuse onto the sphere. The ends of the rods are then nipped together with a special instrument. The bubble is then cased with colourless glass and further blowing and manipulation produce the desired shape. The sphere is separated from the pipe, the mouth of the vessel widened, handles and foot (prepared in similar manner) applied, and the vessel is complete. This does, of course, involve extremely quick and skilful manipulation and constant reheating; the glass must always be red-hot during manipulation. The rods, which were round, have become broad and ribbon-like in the course of the blowing.

77 Flute-glass with criss-cross *latticino* work

78 Ewer, *latticino* glass

Venetian lace-glass, or *vetro a reticelli*, represents one of the most subtle and intricate developments in the art of glass-making. Its best period was the end of the sixteenth century when Venice was the leading exponent of another craft: lace-making. Venetian *reticella* lace was much sought after throughout the fashionable world of Europe. The lace pattern book compiled by Cesare Vecellia, who was related to the painter Titian, was printed in sixty editions within the space of thirty-five years.

Delicate tasteful elegance is common at this time to both media, both lace and glass.

The technique of producing *vetro a reticelli* or *reticella* glass was not so complicated as that involved in the making of *latticino* glass with bands and spirals, but it called for a higher degree of skill and accuracy. White glass rods placed side by side were melted on to the glass bubble, the ends of the rods were then pinched together at the top and at the bottom and the bubble turned, so that a spiral band pattern was obtained. By sucking air out of the bubble, the craftsman collapses one half of it into the other, thus producing a double-walled vessel with the rods, or threads, as they now are, lying criss-cross.

Another method of making *reticella* glass was to fuse together two glass bubbles, one inside the other, each with their spirals applied in an opposite direction. *Reticella* glass continued to be produced in Venice during the seventeenth and eighteenth centuries, but glass of this period shows a reduced degree of accuracy.

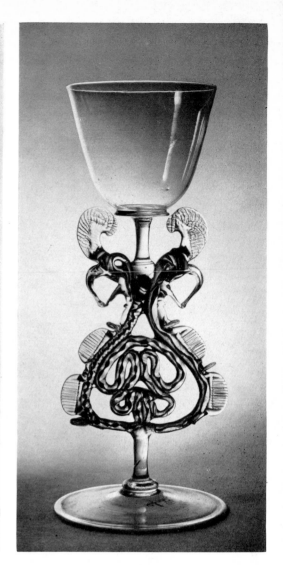

79 Snake-glass in the
façon de Venise

80 Winged glass in the
façon de Venise

81 Winged glass in the
façon de Venise

In the course of the sixteenth century there were considerable variations on the earlier glass shapes. The basic wine-glass form, consisting of foot, stem and bowl, underwent considerable elaboration. After the mid-1500s a form of decoration appeared which is principally responsible for the popular conception of the Venetian glass. This decoration concerns the stem, which is ornamented with handle- or wing-like appendages often resembling the seahorse in shape. These wings are usually in blue glass, upon which a further zig-zag trailing of colourless glass is applied.

In the seventeenth century the wings took over the function of the stem, and evolved into complicated twists of glass, snake-like in appearance –*a serpenti*– or in the double-headed eagle pattern. Such glasses are most frequently of Flemish *façon de Venise* origin.

82 Goblet made to resemble agate

The terminology for a vessel in this type of glass is somewhat confused. Kunckel, the German translator of Antonio Neri's treatise on glass-making uses the word *Calcedonier* for the original Italian term. We gather from Kunckel in his 1744 translation that the glass should be "on the outside sky-blue, sea-green, red, yellow and other streaky colours, and, like an oriental Calcedonio, should have the appearance of jasper and agate, and when held against the light, should glow red, like fire." In view of the usual appearance of its mottling the glass is normally referred to today as agate-glass. Glasses in this metal were produced in Venice from the beginning of the sixteenth century onwards. The colourful streaking and shiny surface of the Munich specimen indicate that this is a nineteenth-century glass.

The production of Calcedonio glass was extensively dealt with in treatises on glass in the Renaissance and Baroque periods. This sort of glass is the triumphant product of alchemical experiments.

A century after Neri, Kunckel criticised the impracticability of the old recipes.

83 Beaker with Neptune motif

The metal of this vessel has the appearance of an opal, glowing bluish-white, yellowish and even violet according to the light. The high relief of the design was produced by mould-blowing. Neptune is shown rising from the waves in a chariot, accompanied by three tritons. Eight pieces of this kind are in existence, all produced from the same mould. The Dresden specimen, in the Grünes Gewölbe Museum, shows eighteenth-century additions, namely a foot and cover in silver-gilt. The glass, from the collection of the Elector Augustus the Strong, is described in the inventory of the ducal treasury as "a large ancient glass beaker, with foot; on the glass are various raised figures such as sea-horses and sirens". All these beaker glasses were originally supplied with ball feet after the manner of Nuremberg beakers of the mid 1600s.

The production of opaque-white opal glass is extensively dealt with in treatises on glass of the Renaissance and of the Baroque period, obviously as a result of the importation of Chinese porcelain. Anton Neri recommends that, if a peach blossom colour is required, Piedmontese manganese should be added to the ingredients of the glass. Johann Kunckel, in his commentary (Ch. 57, Vol. III) on the first volume of Antonio Neri's treatise, gives this recipe for a fine porcelain glass: "60 pounds of sand, 40 pounds of potash and 10 pounds of calcined bone or antler ash. This glass has the peculiarity of emerging from the furnace clear and light, but when heated and worked becomes like opal, or bone-white or milk-white according to how often it is heated, and to how much bone or antler ash has been included".

84 Spouted ewer, *façon de Venise*

A ewer of this type, but with a notched foot-ring and of certain Venetian origin, is shown on Grünewald's "Isenheimer Altar", executed in 1515. This specimen from the Moritzburg-museum in Halle was, as the high conical kick and thickness of the glass indicate, probably produced in Germany. The beauty of its line, which derives from its function, must be attributed to the swift skill of the craftsman, who, with full understanding of the molten metal, has deftly twisted the ewer into shape.

The wide conical neck shows the Syrian influence which played a large part in the early history of Venetian glass.

85 Millefiori tankard

86 Wine glass with ribbed and applied pincered decoration

Towards the end of the classical period of Venetian glass-making, in the latter part of the sixteenth century, pieces of the highest refinement were produced. Now the glass is extremely tall and slender, appearing almost weightless. The properties of the material used have been exploited with great technical skill. The glass seems to have been suspended between the ribs of the bowl. Gothic characteristics are also once more in evidence.

We feel that the craftsman is striving to discover new possibilities for his material, no longer in using simplicity of line, but Baroque exaggeration, and achieving an appearance of unreality by the play of light.

This piece is one of the most interesting variations on an inexhaustible theme: the Venetian wine-glass. The glass has been transformed into a delicate flower, a late-classical development that is far removed from both the severe elegance of the High Renaissance and the lively, naturalistic forms of the seventeenth and eighteenth centuries.

87 Plate with the arms of Duke Ernst of Bavaria

88 Goblet with cover

89 Spouted ewer in the
Venetian style

The glass-house of Hall-in-the-Tyrol was founded in 1534 by Wolfgang Vitl of Augsburg
under the protection of Archduke Ferdinand of the Tyrol, in whose residence, the castle
of Ambras, many pieces originating from this glass-house were kept until they became part
of the well-known Ambras Collection in the Kunsthistorische Museum in Vienna.
Venetian glass-makers worked at Hall-in-the-Tyrol, making vessels in *façon de Venise*, but
heavier in appearance, in line with the German interpretation of the Renaissance. Typical
features are the ornate goblets and tall ewers, the diamond-engraved *Stangengläser* and broad
bowls. The qualities lacking in the imperfect, unclear metal are compensated for by the
delightful decoration. The rich use of diamond-engraved Moresque patterns is combined with
gold, red and blue colours, not fired, but cold-painted, which unfortunately means that they
have not resisted the forces of decay.

90 *Porrón*

91 Drinking vessel

Spanish glass, which from the sixteenth century was subject to Moorish-Islamic influence in the South and to Venetian in the North, can boast of one or two vessels unique to it but which combine both Oriental and European features. First and foremost is the *porrón*, a drinking vessel derived from the wineskin, and from which the flow of wine is directed into the mouth, the vessel itself not coming into contact with it. Secondly there is the *cántaro*, a glass bubble with foot, filler, spout and ring-shaped handle, again descended from skin vessels. Finally we have the *almorratxa*, an extravagantly shaped sprinkler, and the numerous beakers and bowls with their imaginative decoration. The ornament consists mainly of inlaid threads and trailed appendages.

92 *Jarrita*

93 *Cántaro*

94 *Stangenglas*

The *Keulengläser*, which are a club-shaped variant of the *Stangengläser* (q. v.), were originally common vessels belonging to the ordinary glassware of the late Middle Ages. The ring trails have not yet acquired the function of dividing the glass into sections as in the later *Passgläser*, but are merely a simple form of decoration. Their varying sizes show that these glasses were not made for passing round a company of drinkers.

Keulengläser are often depicted in medieval painting and graphic art. A drawing of Albrecht Dürer's showing Aesculapius, the Greek god of medicine, reveals to us that it was considered polite to hold them by the edge of the foot. Perhaps Dürer had observed this custom in Venice, for it was not, as an engraving by Hans Baldung (*Der trunkene Silen*, about 1610) prove, at all general in Germany.

95 Double conical bottle

This curiously shaped vessel was only produced in Germany. The sites of the few specimens found, in western parts of Germany and the Rhineland, would indicate that they were made in the Spessart area. These bottles were current for about a century, from 1430 to 1530. Their shape, so clearly Gothic, must have been very popular, for we see them in many oil paintings, or on copper or wood engravings of the period. A wood engraving executed by an unknown artist c. 1480 shows one in use as a spirit bottle, which is delicately held by the drinker, in accordance with elegant custom, by the rim of the foot. A more usual attitude at the time would be to hold the bottle by the neck.

They were made by reheating a longish glass bubble round the middle, and by pressing one half slightly into the other, thus producing a fold, and a roof-like upper half.

96 Beaker

97 Spouted ewer

98 *Maigelein*

99 *Nuppenbecher*

The origin of the German term *Maigelein* has not been conclusively explained. It is possible that it comes from the word *Magel = Mädchen* (Eng. Maiden), and was a term used jokingly at first. The basic shape of the *Maigelein* is hemispherical and the plain vessel has a high kicked base, but there are variations of this, such as vessels with vertically or spirally ribbed walls.

They were produced by blowing the small soft glass bubble into a ribbed mould. By further blowing and simultaneous twisting of the glass, then blowing into a second mould, still twisting the blowing-iron but in the opposite direction, a diagonal ribbed pattern is obtained. According to the degree of blowing carried out, many variations in strength and direction of ribbing are possible.

100 Honey-comb moulded glass

101 Moulded jug

"As often as he blows down the pipe – and he must blow often – so often does he press it, after quickly removing it from his mouth, against his chin, so that on drawing breath he does not breathe in the flame. He then lifts the pipe high and swings it in a circle round his head to stretch the glass in length, or he shapes it by pressing it into an iron mould, whence, through further heating, blowing, pressing and stretching, it takes on the shape of a beaker, a rounded vessel or any other intended form."

From Georg Agricola's *De re metallica*, Basle 1657.

102 Tall *Stangenglas*

The tall *Stangenglas* in the Prague Municipal Museum is the oldest of its kind in existence. This glass, both ancient and precious, was discovered with a second bricked into a niche in the wall of a house called "Zur Steinernen Jungfrau" in the old quarter of Prague. This is the first of a series of tall glasses decorated with prunts variously known as *Stangengläser*, *Spechter-* and *Passgläser* in Germany where they were popular from the Gothic period down to the Baroque. One of the earliest representations of such glass occurs on a painting dating from 1410, executed by a Lübeck artist, and now kept in the Provinzialmuseum, Hanover. The glass is ornamented with twenty-six rows of small snail-like appliqués. Its slender form reveals its Gothic inspiration, as does its somewhat curious elegance.

The technique of decorating vessels with large drops of molten glass, or prunts, was certainly popularised in Europe by the importation of similarly ornamented vessels from Syria in the fourteenth century, after the tradition in the West had been broken by the decay of the Rheno-Roman glass industry. The earliest glasses showing this kind of decoration have tiny, wart-like drops which developed – some first taking on the form of sharp vertical prickles – into wide, flat prunts drawn upwards to a point. Simultaneously the shape of the glass was changing. The earliest still have the basic Syrian shape, with a sharp division into a cylindrical lower part and a funnel-shaped upper part. In the fifteenth century the "funnel" became the rounded lip of the glass, influenced by contemporary stone-ware drinking vessels, and during the early Renaissance period it is strictly marked off by a circle of glass and is once more funnel-shaped.

The particular development shown throughout the sixteenth and seventeenth centuries by this part of the vessel in Rhenish glass favoured the rounded shape, culminating in the hemispherical bowl, which is typical of the *Römer* and is one of its most important features. This type of glass was not intended for everyday use, as the fact that they have come down to us as relic holders indicates. Throughout the Middle Ages, and for a longer period among the lower classes, the usual drinking vessel was the bottle. In order to drink, one held the bottle in the palm of the hand or grasped it by the foot-ring between finger and thumb.

104 *Stangenglas*

The changes undergone by the *Stangenglas* between the Gothic and Renaissance periods are illustrated by the Hamburg glass. It is wider than the Prague specimen; the drops are larger and obviously applied in rows. After 1500 the drops become larger once more and lie flatter on the surface of the vessel. The bell-shaped rim also disappears.

The much-quoted phrase from the sermon of the Bohemian parson Mathesius, which states that the prunts were applied so that the glasses could be easily grasped by the clumsiest people, is obviously contradicted by this specimen. Here the prunts are a reflection of the late Gothic taste for an exaggeration of form, also evident in the architecture, sculpture and humbler arts of the period.

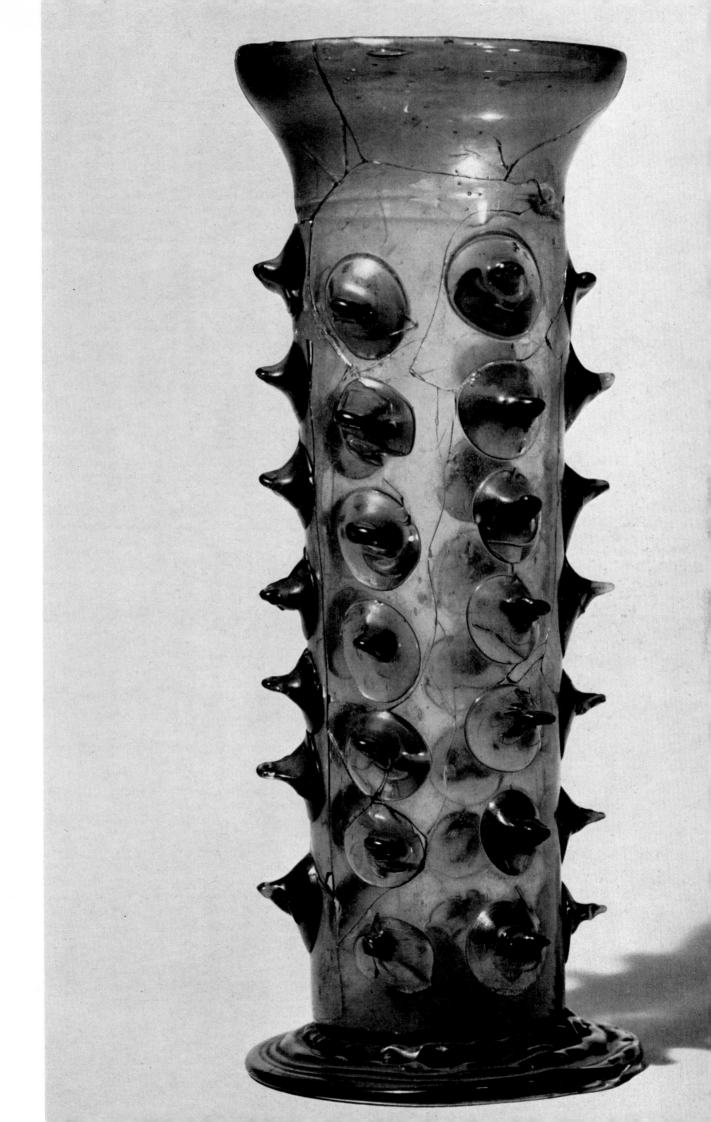

105 *Nuppenbecher* with owner's inscription

The various hues and the manner in which the light is reflected in the German *Nuppengläser* gives them an entirely different appearance from that of the glass of the Venetian makers. The colour green is seen in all its shades, from its palest, most delicate hue to the darkest in the thicker parts of a vessel. Qualities so ardently sought after by the Bohemian glass-cutters are here obtained with the more limited methods of the time. To produce a glass which glows like some precious stone appears to have been the aim of German glass-makers. The irregularity of the prunted surface is typical of the 1500 date. The gold and silver goblets of the time were no doubt the inspiration for creations in glass, although the latter gradually became valuable in their own right, rivalling articles in precious metal.

108 Mallet-shaped (*Bocksbeutelform*) bottle

109 Ribbed spirit-flask

110 Oviform bottle

111 Bottle with spiral trail

"Should you desire to make long-necked bottles, proceed thus: after you have blown the hot glass into a large bubble, stop the opening of the pipe with your thumb, so that the air may not escape; then swing the pipe, with the glass hanging thereupon, over your head, as if you wanted to cast it away. As soon as the neck is stretched, let your hand drop, so that the neck is not bent. Remove the bottle with damp wood, and take it to the annealing chamber."

From: Theophilus Presbyter, *Schedula diversarum artium*.

112 Decanter derived from the *Kuttrolf*

113 Ribbed bottle with pinched neck

The *Kuttrolf* is often mentioned in medieval literature but we are not given a clear indication as to what this vessel looked like. Wolfram von Eschenbach refers in his *Willehalm* to the "Gutterel von Glase"; in the Spessart Ordinances of 1406 we are told that a glass-maker may not make per day "more than 200 Kuttrolf or their equivalent". This cannot, however, be a reference to the complicated vessel, of which there are many variations still to be seen today. One characteristic is to be found in all these vessels; they permit liquid to flow only very slowly, or even merely to drip, from them. Indeed, the name *Kuttrolf*, deriving from the Middle High German *guttern*, to drip, as well as the other name in use, *Angster*, from the Latin *angustus*, meaning narrow, indicate this characteristic. The *Kuttrolf* were used mainly as spirit containers; they were very popular in the Middle Ages and were often depicted in engravings of that period. The complicated form with the triple-tubed, twisted neck is typical of late fifteenth century taste, –in sculpture of the time we note a definite tendency towards twisted forms– but the vessel as a whole is of Syrian and other ancient ancestry. The funnel-shaped mouth is especially indicative of Near-Eastern origin.

114 Four-tubed *Kuttrolf*
115 Four-sided decanter derived from the *Kuttrolf*

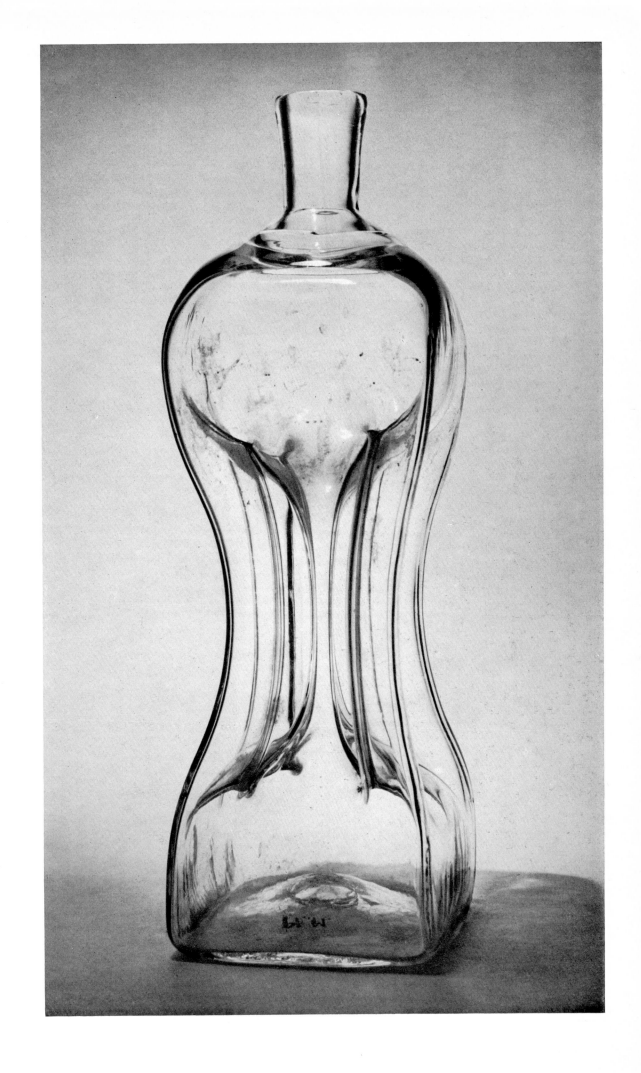

116 Wine jug

"Weil aber das glas von natur weyss und planck ist, wenn zu mahl der sandt und die asche reyn und mit fleyss aussgesotten, und abgefeymet ist, hat man in diesen landen gemeinigklich zum weyn grüne gleser gemacht, darinn ein rebe rechter plancke weyn sehr schön und lieblich steht, und dem weyn ein lüstige farbe gibt."

"Since, however, glass is by nature clear and white, especially when the sand and ash (potash) are carefully sifted and purified, in these countries green wine-glasses have usually been produced, so that the wine appears quite clear, looks appetising and of good colour."

This quotation from the Bohemian parson Mathesius is evidence of the contemporary love for green wine-jugs and glasses. The wine jug is similar to the old German *Doppelscheuer* or *Doppelkopf*, a traditional bridal gift, consisting of two rounded *Kopfen* (heads).

117 *Daumenhumpen*

The fascination for the curious and the unusual, which is so typical of the folk art of the sixteenth century in Germany, brings forth a rich harvest in the medium of glass. The glasshouses which produced the *Waldglas* (q.v.) were far from the centres of refined influence, and glass-making did not often have its patrons as other arts did, with the result that the artist's inventiveness often erred on the side of the grotesque and fantastic. Another factor was pride in technical skill, which led to a continual search for wittier, cleverer creations. The *Daumenhumpen* is an excellent illustration of all these tendencies. The insertion of the finger-holes is a masterly demonstration of the glassmaker's skill.

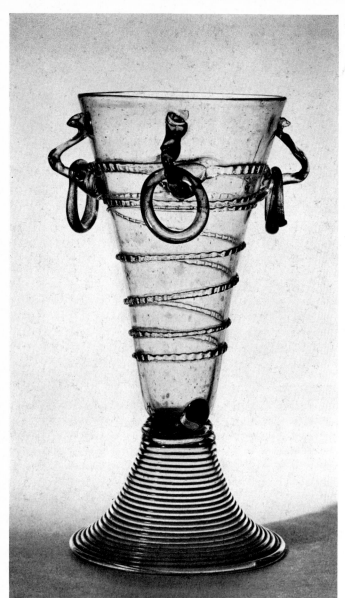 

118 Ring-glass

"Aber es hat sich die Kunst endtlich müssen nach dem lande richten, daher man allerley knöpff, steyn und ringlein an die gleser gesetzet, damit die gleser etwas fester und bestendiger, und von vollen und ungeschickten leuten dest leychter köndten inn feusten behalten werden, daher die starcken, knortzigten, oder knöpffischten gleser in brauch kommen sein."

"But the craft had to adapt itself to the nature of the country, so all kinds of knobs, blobs, stones and rings were set on the glasses so that they were more solid and stable, and could be more easily grasped by clumsy people, and thus the strong, gnarled or knotty glasses came into use."

From: Johann Mathesius, *Bergpostille oder Sarepta*, Nuremberg, 1587.

119 Small ewer
120 *Passglas*

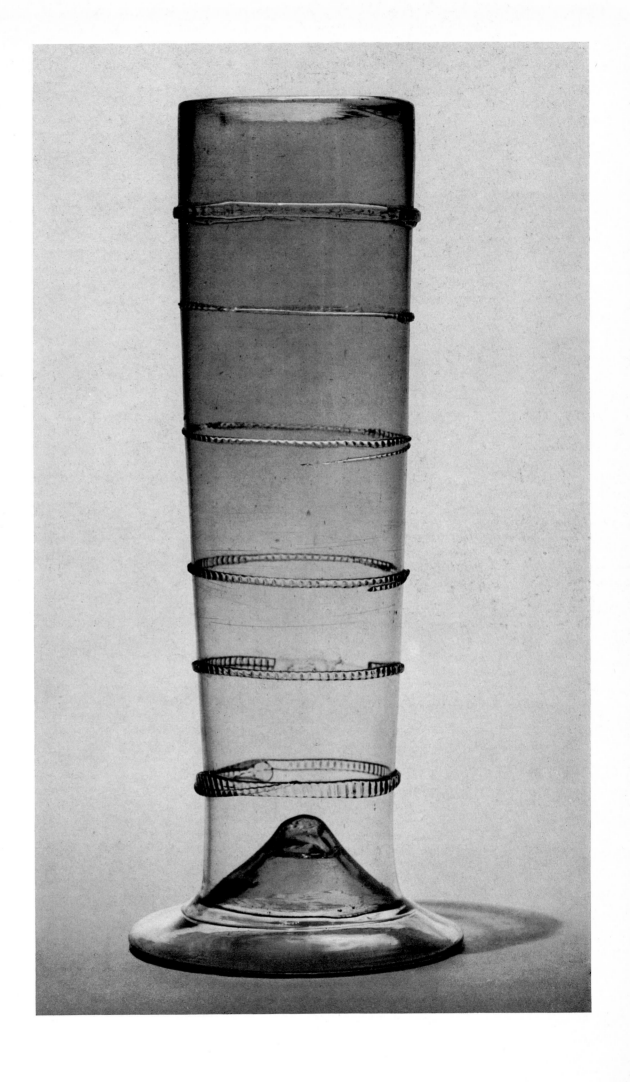

121 Phallus glass

122 Trick glass in the form
of a bear

The pliability of molten glass has always called forth the ingenuity of the glassmaker, tempting him to embark on varied and original creations. There is surely no creature, no part of the human body which has not been reproduced in glass. Virtuosity on the part of the maker was of course required if his works were to sell, for this was a craft lacking permanent patronage. As a result there was a flood of the most fantastic novelty and trick glasses, the most popular being those which rendered drinking difficult for the poor user. Obscenity plays a notable part in this group of glasses. Phallus glasses, which have their origins in some primitive fertility cult, were made in the sixteenth and seventeenth centuries as a form of crude joke.

123/124 The Mainz Dean and Chapter Glass

On the huge bowl we see a finely drawn view of the city of Mainz as it appeared in the year 1617. In the foreground flows the Rhine with ships and small craft, above, the roofs and gables of the citizens' houses, higher still the church spires, and dominating all the Cathedral of St. Martin. On the reverse is the portrait of St. Martin, and the arms of the Archbishop. In two friezes above and below are the arms and initials of the members of the Cathedral Chapter, who may be taken to have been the donors of the glass. Beneath the rim we read the inscription: "Celsitudo atque Nobilitas Florentissimae Metropolitanae Ecclesiae et Civitatis Moguntinae, ut es Anno 1617 constitu."

This excellent piece of work is certainly that of a Dutch engraver. The technique of engraving was practised in Venice, but attained its highest expression in Holland in the seventeenth century. The white lines of the engraving are particularly effective against the green glass of the bowl.

125 Armorial *Humpen*

In the second half of the sixteenth century Germany copied from Venice the fashion of decorating drinking glasses with enamel colours. Up to this time, glasses with armorial bearings had been commissioned from Venetian glass-makers; the German taste for this kind of ornamentation, which advertised the rank of the owner of such vessels, was already well-established. The coats of arms were gradually replaced by pictures, first of a religious nature, then in many other, usually genre, styles. The allegorical representation of Emperor and Empire, the Ages of Man, the Peace of Westphalia, the Apostles, the hunt and views of local interest were most frequent.

The bright colours employed had no doubt an exceptional decorative effect, but the execution of the painting was of no particular quality. Nevertheless, we would have regretted even more bitterly the destruction of so many examples had the glass been a great work of art, for the vessels were made for use during this period when *gross drinken ein Ehr war* (heavy drinking was a point of honor) and many a pretty enamelled glass met its fate during a particularly rowdy session.

The best period of enamel painting was the seventeenth century, and its main exponents Germany and Austria. The rising popularity of cut and engraved glass in the eighteenth century lessened the demand for enamel decorated pieces, and enamel painting was henceforth carried out only in isolated forest glass-houses as a peasant art.

It is difficult to attribute enamel painted glass, with the exception of *Ochsenkopf* and *Hallorenglas*, to any particular source of manufacture, although certain indications are often given by the style of the borders or floral motifs.

126 *Humpen* of the Magdeburg
Cathedral Chapter

127 *Humpen* with equestrian
figure of Gustavus Adolphus

130 *Reichsadlerhumpen*

Although at first sight the *Reichsadlerhumpen* would appear to be little more than an opportunity for an heraldic jig-saw puzzle, they are not without their deeper significance, as becomes obvious when we consider the period from which they originate, the Thirty Years' War with its strife and disruption. "*Das Heilige römische Reich sampt seinen Gliedern*" ("The Holy Roman Empire and its Member States") is inscribed on the reverse of the glass. The main motif is a double-headed eagle with fifty coats of arms arranged in groups of four, according to the so-called Quaternion system. This system, of no contemporary significance, derives from Schedel's *Weltkronik* of 1483.

131 *Ochsenkopfglas*

132 *Hallorenglas*

Another important group of enamel-painted glasses are the *Fichtelgebirgsgläser*. The glass-house in Bischofsgrün was their main centre of manufacture. The popular *Ochsenkopfgläser* depict the Ochsenkopf, the second highest mountain in the range, in a symbolic manner, as a steep tree-covered hill, with forest creatures on it and the four rivers which have their sources there, the Main, the Naab, the Saale and the Eger, emerging from its foot. It is surrounded by a chain fastened with a padlock to secure its riches, which are recounted in a long inscription on the reverse.

The *Hallorengläser* show the procession of the Salters' Guild of Halle-on-the-Saale, with the arms and a view of the town. These glasses were made for a special occasion, the annual Whitsun beer meeting of the Salters.

133/134 Beaker on three feet

The inspiration for the painting on this glass comes from the engraving by Jacques Callot (1592–1635) of a gypsy procession. Callot's illustrations of Italian life were very popular in the seventeenth and eighteenth centuries. They show a sharp characterisation, often indeed a fantastic caricature, of the figures represented. A certain rough humour is present in his works, which are not, however, lacking in grandeur. Some of his characters were the fore-runners of many other figures in European art.

The painting is executed in translucent enamel colours and various strengths of *Schwarzlot*. Johann Schaper, a native of Hamburg but working in Nuremberg from 1640–1670, intro-duced the *Schwarzlot* technique from Northern Germany and was one of the first to employ it; copper oxide, mixed with black enamel pigment, is painted onto the surface of the glass, and the design then scratched out. *Schwarzlot* painting was a Dutch invention, originally used for the decoration of windows. After 1700 it was carried on in Bohemia, mainly for glasses with *Laub- und Bandelwerk* and Chinese motifs.

133/134 Beaker on three feet

135 Wine glass with pear-knopped stem

136 Tall bowl, diamond-point engraved

The bowl is one of the earliest examples of English lead-crystal glass. It probably comes from the London glasshouse of George Ravenscroft, who in 1674 took out a patent on his newly discovered lead-glass. There is remarkable harmony between the vessel's almost modern shape and the heaviness of the metal. The diamond-engraving is, however, still in the tradition of the past. Only with the introduction of cutting was the beauty of this brilliant, thick metal seen at its best. The fact that cut lead-crystal was an eighteenth century development indicates that the decorative techniques of the English Baroque were much more restrained than the Bohemian and German art of the period and lacked its voluptuousness. In the case of this bowl, it is the absence of extravagant cutting which gives it its modern appearance.

137 Glass with diamond point engraving

The second half of the sixteenth century saw the establishment of new glass houses in England. Some were run by Venetian glass-makers and produced glass in the Venetian style. The name of Jacopo Verzelini is one that has come down to us. This maker was granted the privilege of making Venetian glass by Queen Elizabeth I in 1575, and this glass probably comes from his establishment. In clear metal with minute air-bubbles, the glass has a hollow fluted bulb between two knops, a wide flat foot and tall bowl. The diamond-engraving, heraldic in character with parallel arabesques, animal forms and inscription, is a Venetian invention of the same century. The glass may be regarded as a fine example of the Renaissance art of Elizabethan England.

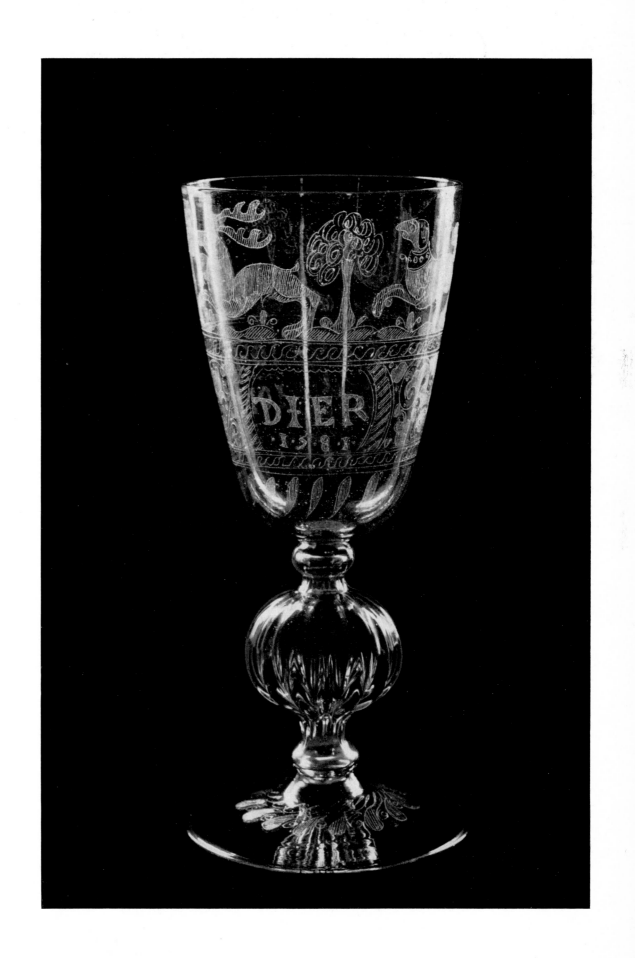

138 Goblet with portrait of a man

139 Goblet showing putti drinking wine

The delicate line of the diamond-point engraving becomes even more indefinite during the eighteenth century, breaking up into a series of dots; in fact the whole design is picked out in minute dots tapped out with the tip of a diamond. One requisite for this technique, which is known as stipple engraving, was good quality glass and this was found in the English lead crystal glass, then known as flint glass, which was exported to Holland, Belgium and France. The most important artists in stipple engraving are Franz Greenwood (1680 to 1762) and David Wolff, who died at the Hague in 1808. In Holland delightful engravings were produced, delicate, showing skilful use of tone, and in their subtle elegance typical of Dutch and French Rococo painting.

Diamond-point engraving had spread from Venice to Germany and Holland during the sixteenth century. In the first half of the seventeenth a large number of diamond-point engravers were active in Holland, and particular mention must be made of the Roemer sisters of Amsterdam and W. J. Heemskerk of Leiden. The delicate effect of seventeenth century Dutch engraved glass forms a marked contrast with the heavy green *Waldglas* and its abundant, deftly executed engravings.

141 Ruby-glass bottle

A problem to which both glassmakers and alchemists of the seventeenth century devoted much of their research was the formula for ruby glass. They were not so much eager to produce a glass of beautiful colour for its own sake, but shared the belief that drinking from such glass would give protection from all manner of ills. In his *Ars Vitraria* of 1679, Johann Kunckel quotes the recipe for ruby glass formulated by Antonio Neri, but adds: "Ich habe hierinnen überaus grosse Mühe angewandt, und kan auch, Gott Lob, neben dem schönsten Rubin, das feinste Roth machen; weil es mir aber gar viel Zeit, Müh und Arbeit gekostet, und es eine sehr rare Sache ist, als wird mich niemand verdencken, dass ichs vor diesmal nicht gemein mache." "I have devoted much time to this subject, and can now, thank Heaven, as well as the finest ruby, produce a most excellent red glass; since it has cost me so much time and trouble, and since it is a very rare product, no-one will object to my keeping it secret this time." Even if he did not succeed in keeping the secret of ruby glass for himself, probably because it had been independently discovered in Southern Germany, he is generally recognised as its inventor. The gold used was soon replaced by copper, which gave a still richer shade. In the nineteenth century many Bohemian glasses were cased with a thin layer of ruby glass. The method of producing the true "gold" ruby glass, which obtains its brilliant colour by being reheated after blowing, was rediscovered in the glass-house at Cologne-Ehrenfelde at the end of the nineteenth century.

142 Ruby-glass beaker
143 Large covered goblet

144 Group of musicians
made at the lamp

145 Lamp-blown centrepiece
of fountain and birds

"This is what I call the minor art of glass-blowing, which is executed at the lamp. Though it is not the most useful of arts, it is nevertheless one of the most delicate in all glass-making and the source of much delight. How these pretty and elegant objects are made I will now relate:

First obtain from a glass-house a number of little rods or tubes of good and pure crystal glass in divers colours; little pieces of broken Venetian glass serve our purpose best. Take a small tube such as I have mentioned above, soften it at one end, and by blowing into it you can form spheres and other shapes; anyone who understands how to manipulate the glass will be able to produce whatever he fancies in this way, such as pictures, figures, crucifixes, small vessels and anything you can imagine. Very often you need for this purpose small pincers and little clamps made of wire, in order to hold a piece when your hands are occupied with various others, and when you have to heat several pieces which are to be welded together in the flame."

Free translation of an extract from J. Kunckel's *Ars Vitraria* (see Kunckel).

146 Glass with allegorical figures

Caspar Lehmann's engraved glass marks a new phase in the history of glass decoration. As in Roman times, the technique employed in gem cutting has been applied to glass. This deeper cutting, and the high relief produced by the *Hochschnitt* techniques, was principally used for the ornamentation of rock crystal, a material favoured by the Renaissance and Baroque but not by the Romans, who preferred the various coloured precious stones. The artists most sought after for this work were Italians. One of the centres of rock crystal cutting was the court of King Rudolf II in Prague. This monarch was described by Sandrart as "einen rechten Vater und Pflegevater der Künste und Künstler"; (a true father and patron of the arts and of artists). Caspar Lehmann, one of the gem cutters employed there since 1588, is accredited by Sandrart as having "rediscovered and brought to light the art of glass-engraving". As a result he received the Imperial privilege for the exploitation of his discovery throughout the entire Empire.

The unpolished engraving is of the same overall shallowness in view of the thinness of the glass, and the graphic engraving is two dimensional. Polished engraving, which enhances the relief, is not yet in evidence. The appearance of the engraving reflects that executed on rock crystal, which is equally flatly cut and obtains its decorative effect from the contrast of the white surfaces and lines with the dark background of the transparent crystal.

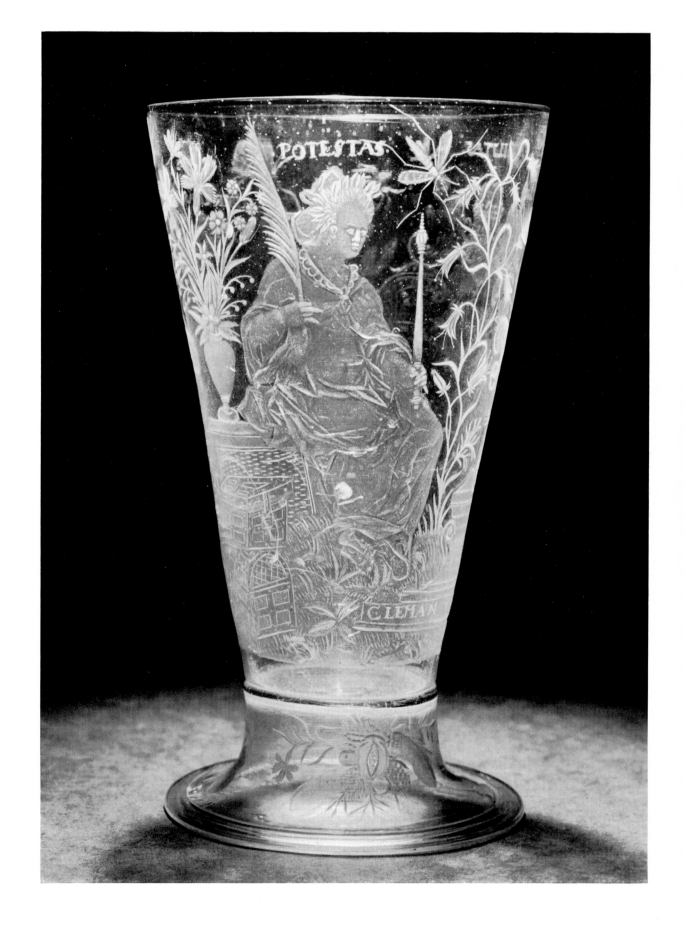

147 Covered goblet with hollow stem

Caspar Lehmann bequeathed his privilege for glass engraving to his pupil Georg Schwanhardt the Elder, who was born in Nuremberg and who worked with him at the Prague Court. In 1622 Schwanhardt returned to his native town where the new technique, so important for the future of glass-making, soon became known and spread rapidly.

The Nuremberg marriage goblet is made of thin glass which is somewhat impure in colour. The stem and finial consist of a series of hollow ball knops and one baluster knop interspersed with discs. Bowl and cover form a harmonious whole. The decoration –landscape, hunting, and genre scenes– is executed in shallow intaglio and covers the entire bowl and cover.

A style of representing certain features typical of Nuremberg, such as trees or the human face, developed and distinguished this school of engraving from others, but rendered the task of identifying the individual Nuremberg artists very difficult. The quality of Nuremberg engraving lies in the nuances obtained by the discreet use of polished and unpolished surfaces, and the resulting impression of high relief on a thin-walled glass. Towards the end of the 7th century it lost ground to its Bohemian –Silesian rival, executed on thick-walled potash-lime glass.

The engraving on the goblet illustrated, previously held to be the work of Georg Schwanhardt the Elder, is now attributed to the Thuringian engraver IH.

148 Covered goblet with floral decoration

During the first important period of engraving of potash-lime glass, from the end of the 16th century until about 1725, Bohemia was the main exponent of the art. Here we see a goblet with plain foot, a baluster-stem and a facetted bowl, crowned by a heavy cover which is also facetted, as is the finial.

Around 1700 plant motifs were most favoured, these gradually becoming finer in execution and more formal in design. By 1720 scroll-work is the usual form of decoration. The inspiration for the newly-introduced grotesque shapes lies in the copper-engraved pattern books of the period, of which the *Neue Grotesgen Werk* by Paul Decker, Nuremberg, 1710, was the most frequently used.

In the same decade the Bohemian glass trade was enjoying its hey-day. Trading companies for Bohemian glass were to be found the world over, and salesmen travelled the length and breadth of Europe. One of these, Franz Kreibich from Steinschönau, went as far as Russia, Sweden and Constantinople. Bohemia had at last triumphed over Venice, her great rival.

149 Goblet with arms of Count Schaffgotsch

Potash-lime glass was first made in Bohemia in 1680. Kunckel gives its formula as "15 pounds of sand, 100 pounds of potash, 20 pounds of pure chalk and 10 lot (old German weight) of pyrolusite (manganese dioxide)." The metal this produced was so clear that even thick-walled vessels still exhibited an uncommon brilliance. This discovery opened the way to the vigorous high relief engraving of the Baroque period.

Baroque taste is most evident in the *Hochschnitt*, or cameo-relief technique, carried out mainly in Silesia.

The model upon which engraved glass vessels were based was again work done in rock-crystal, but in this case no longer the flatly engraved Renaissance pieces but the bizarre facetted ones of the second half of the seventeenth century.

The motifs of the earlier period of this engraving were acanthus leaves and branches, completely covering the surface of the vessel. The massive shafts and covers of the goblets are cut geometrically or after motifs from nature. The facet-cutting of the wall of the bowl broke up the surface, allowing for a greater exploitation of the metal's light-reflecting quality.

150 Covered goblet with view of Leipzig

In the second quarter of the eighteenth century Silesia emerges as the leading exponent in the art of glass engraving. Wide decorative borders are typical of Silesian work, usually recognisable from the combination of minute strokes and large curly leaf shapes. The style of ornament extended into other artistic fields at the time. On Silesian glasses it usually encloses small scenes, generally the view of some town. The shape of the vessel is generally somewhat waisted.

In the mid-eighteenth century Rococo motifs predominated, e.g. rocaille ornament and decorative panels. A large group of Silesian goblets show a combination of cameo relief and the more usual *intaglio* work. Two palmettes, which were executed in *Hochschnitt*, divide the glass into two areas which enclose scenes or views of towns. In some vessels the palm-decoration was gilt.

151 Covered goblet
with Venus and Adonis motif

152 Two engraved glasses

154 Covered goblet with Neptune

In contrast to Silesian and Bohemian glass, this shows mainly scenic decoration or figure compositions usually of mythological inspiration. The area of illustration comprises the entire wall of the glass. Very little of the surface area has been left untouched by the wheel; the foot is heavily cut in a scale pattern, the stem is decorated by shallow relief diamonds, the base of the bowl shows short, shallow fluting, whereas the rim is embellished with cut beading. Elias Rossbach was from 1735 to 1736 Master of the Potsdam glass guild. Some of his work is signed and his signature has thus become well-known.

155 Wine glass with Silesian stem

156 Wine glass with gilt decoration

Whereas German glass-makers of the eighteenth century expended their finest efforts on special pieces, such as commemorative goblets or showpieces for the ducal table, or collectors' cabinets, their English counterparts were already exploring the possibility of producing glass on a commercial scale and of perfecting a selection of fine shapes. The existence of a discriminating middle class in England provided a market for table-ware which combined function and good taste. Consequently, however, glass engraving never attained the heights reached in Germany and Bohemia.

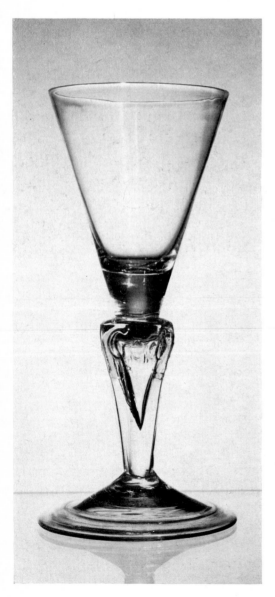

157 Glasses with engraved decoration

Although some glasshouses had been founded in North America in the seventeenth century, usually by Dutchmen, the eighteenth century sees the setting-up of the first important ones, mainly by Germans and Englishmen. To these belong Johann Friedrich Amelung's glassworks, established at New Bremen in Maryland. The three dated glasses show that American ware of the period was still European or Anglo-German in style. The glasses have a sturdy form, the metal is pure and clear, and the decoration consists of restrained engraving with foliage and rocaille motifs and finely drawn inscriptions.

158 Mug with painted decoration

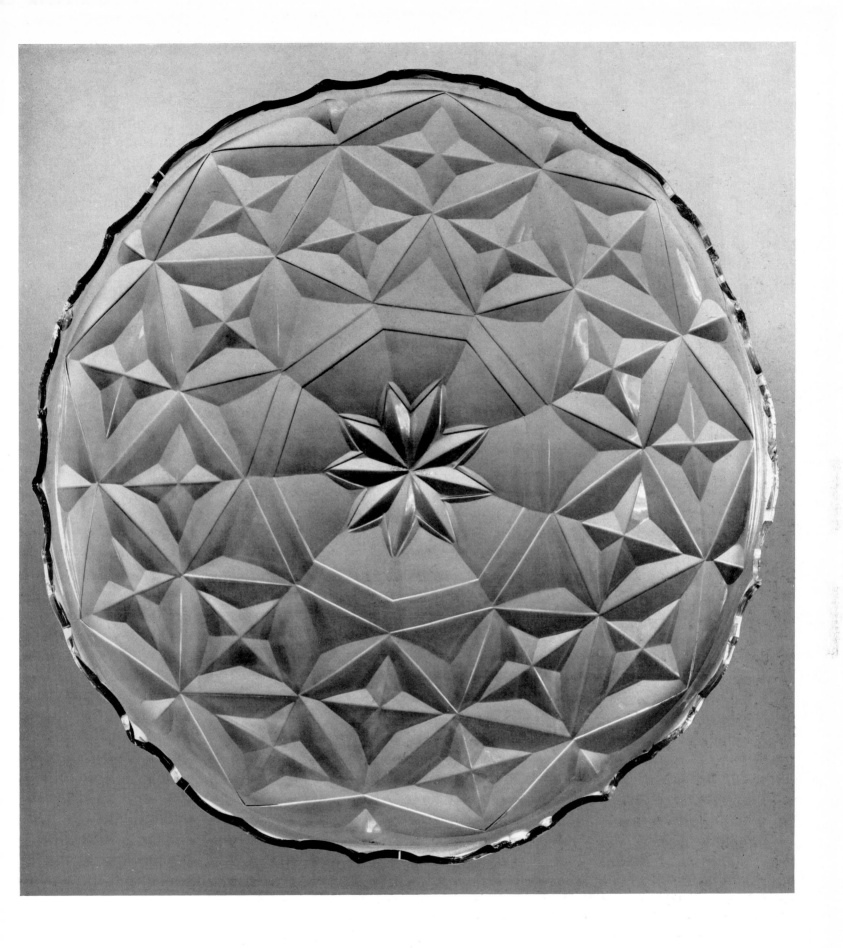

159 Cut-glass dish

160 *Zwischengoldglas* with painted decoration in several colours

161 *Zwischengoldglas* with hunting scene

Zwischengoldgläser are a Bohemian phenomenon of the period 1730 to 1740. They are composed of two beakers one fitting exactly into the other and with a layer of gold leaf between them. The slit where the edges meet is either at the rim or slightly below it on the outside of the glass. Sometimes the gold leaf effect is enhanced by the use of silver foil and coloured lacquer painting.

162 Glass with gilt monogram

Johann Joseph Mildner (1764 to 1808) worked at the glasshouse of Gutenbrunn (Lower Austria). Signed works of his dating from 1787 to 1808 are in existence. A typical feature of his glass is a medallion in *Zwischengold* technique. A cut is made in the surface of the glass and into it is inserted a piece of etched gold leaf on a red background, then a glass disc is placed on top, sealing off the ornament. The usual motifs are portraits, monograms or arms, or more rarely allegories and representations of saints. Sometimes a poem is scratched onto the reverse side of the medallion. The base of the glass also usually contains a scratched picture. Mildner's glasses are among the most charming specimens of the glass decorator's art. Technical precision, good artistic taste and graphic skill ensure the success of these very personal and poetic creations.

163 Glass with view of Dresden

There still exist today many glasses by the Saxon porcelain painter Samuel Mohn, who was born near Merseburg in 1762, and died in Dresden in 1815, and his son Gottlob Samuel Mohn, born in Weissenfels, 1789, died in Vienna, 1825. They are decorated with views of famous places in translucent enamel pigment. They cannot equal the work of J. J. Mildner in elegance –the Mohns worked on a large scale, producing their panoramic glasses with the help of apprentices and making use of transfer prints to produce outlines for their paintings– but with their delicate colours these paintings of well-known views may be considered as interesting specimens from the history of the souvenir trade.

**164 Glass showing
St Stephen's Cathedral, Vienna**

Kothgasser's glasses are among the finest examples of the Viennese Biedermeier style. Anton Kothgasser (1769 to 1851), a Viennese porcelain painter, was introduced to the medium of glass by Gottlob Samuel Mohn, but produced work that is unquestionably personal in style. In shape, his glasses –usually waisted with a heavy cut base– exhibit a greater degree of taste, and surpass Mohn's in the painting and more refined decoration.

An ornamental frame, painted in gold on silver-stain, surrounds the generally darker area of the painted scene and gives a greater feeling of neatness and unity. The relationship to Viennese porcelain painting is obvious in the lavish use of gold. As for his themes, Kothgasser shows a wider range than the two Mohns. Although views of towns predominate, portraits, genre scenes, and flowers, sometimes copied from the work of other artists, are found.

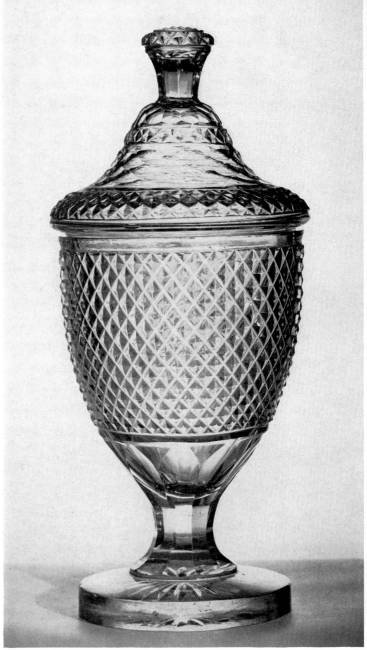

165 Glass showing the ages of man

166 Sweetmeat bowl and cover

167 Pear-shaped ewer showing Cupid and Psyche

168 Glass with engraving of Venus

France has made only a limited contribution to the history of European glass-making. In the Middle Ages she had many flourishing makers of *Waldglas* but from the sixteenth century onwards preferred to import Venetian ware. Nevertheless one glasshouse is worthy of mention, that of Nevers, founded in 1581, and it must be added that France was renowned for the manufacture of excellent mirror and window glass.

In the eighteenth century English lead-crystal was imported, and this was sometimes decorated by French engravers. The glass illustrated, engraved by the Parisian artist Charpentier, shows excellent workmanship which reproduces in perfect detail the tiniest flowers and the delicate curls of the goddess, who is drawn in her chariot by a pair of swans.

169 Goblet

In 1777 the tax on glass was doubled in England, but this did not apply to Ireland, which indeed benefited from it. Up to this time Ireland had produced glass for the home market alone, but now she was able to conduct a successful international trade. The introduction of the higher tax therefore marks the beginning of the rise of the Irish industry, which produced work of excellent quality for three quarters of a century. The entry of English glass-makers and engravers brought about the establishment of more glassworks, of which the most important were the Waterford (1783–1851), Belfast (founded 1776) and Waterloo glass-works in Cork (1783–1811). Anglo-Irish flint glass was at that time as celebrated as Venetian glass had been two centuries earlier.

In Ireland, as in England, more interest was shown in producing high quality table-ware than in single show pieces. Typical of Irish manufacture are the decanters with three neck-rings and mushroom stoppers –the countless pieces which have come down to us often show only the slightest variation in design, a factor which makes it difficult to attribute them with certainty to any one glasshouse– wine, beer and punch glasses, sweetmeat bowls and pickle urns. Characteristic designs in the cutting are stars and bands, diamonds and lines in various combinations. The bodies of the decanter are almost invariably mould-blown.

170 Mould-blown vessels

171 Sugar bowl and jug

The beginning of the nineteenth century saw the development of a unique and peculiar style in North America. The vessels are blown into a mould, decorated with applied trails, and coloured green or brown, rather in the manner of medieval *Waldglas*. Typical examples of this style are the moulded ribbed bottles, or vessels with a moulded portrait or other decoration, possibly merely the name of a firm. Medieval German, seventeenth century English and eighteenth century Scandinavian glass no doubt influenced this style, but of greater importance was the part played by current ideas which were also reflected in the romantic literature of the time. The glasses are not without character and originality, and are in no way comparable to the late romantic products of the Cologne-Ehrenfeld glassworks at the end of the nineteenth century. These American mould-blown relief glasses led directly to the invention of pressed glass.

172 *Rosenwasserflasche*

There was a renewal of Persian glass-making in the eighteenth and nineteenth centuries, which had as its centre the town of Shiraz. The demand for these exotic, typically oriental vessels was so great that it could not be met by Eastern manufacture and the market turned to the Bohemian, Thuringian and Spessart glasshouses to make up the quantity. The use of pincered trailing and rich threaded decoration was also typical of German workmanship. Evidently the Persian article had its influence on German style, and in Dexel's *Deutsches Handwerksgerät* we see an illustration of a Spessart bottle showing all the signs of Persian influence. As a rule the German products show a metal of higher quality than their Persian counterparts. It is interesting to note that Persian glass of this period re-introduces a form already two thousand years old: the single tubed *Kuttrolf* with the bent neck, which had been so popular in late Gothic Germany.

173 Ewer

174　Vase in Persian style

177 Snuff bottle

178 Snuff bottle

179 Tall vase

Just as Ancient Greece knew almost exclusively pottery vessels, China, too, concentrated on stone and porcelain ware. Glass could not rival the masterly products in these other materials. Although from the third century onwards glass-making was carried out here and there —we know, for example, that a glasshouse was founded near the palace in Peking in 1680— the results were not finely blown, clear glass of the Venetian kind, nor glittering cut-crystal glass, but a metal that had little that is characteristic of glass, coming nearer to porcelain or other materials in appearance. The Chinese glass-makers were particularly fond of imitating jade, with its milky-white colouring and waxy sheen. Another type of glass produced was the so-called "Rice-glass", with its cloudy speckled effect. Chinese glass is mainly moulded and opaque white or coloured. Its resemblance to semi-precious stone called for the decorative technique of that medium, cutting. The snuff and perfume bottles which are painted on the inside are uniquely Chinese; they are small masterpieces of the craftsman's skill.

The snuff-bottles of the seventeenth to the nineteenth century are of opaque white or light-grey glass, cased with a second contrasting glass layer. They are then wheel-cut, releasing a motif in relief on the light background. They do not, however, exhibit fine modelling or delicate use of tones, as does for example the Portland Vase.

180 Vase of cut overlay glass

Emile Gallé (1864 to 1904) derived, like many other artists and craftsmen of the late nineteenth century, much of his inspiration from oriental art. Chinese snuff-bottles were the prototypes of his cut cased glasses. In early examples of his work the elegant motifs have been produced by cutting away the unwanted areas of overlay with the wheel. Later the artist used acid in the first stages for this purpose, finishing the vessel at the wheel. The most complicated processes of ornamentation entailed the fusing on of isolated glass motifs and the inlaying of metal and mother-of-pearl decoration, which were then enhanced by the cutting away of surrounding areas.

At first strongly oriental in appearance, the ornamentation gradually became typical of the Art Nouveau movement, consisting of sinuous plant motifs designed to harmonise with the general shape of the vessel, which in its turn is influenced by plant forms, so that entirely new lines in the history of the glass vessel are produced. The unity of shape and ornamentation, an Art Nouveau principle still valid for modern artists, is further assisted by the use of colour, mainly subtle dusky shades reminiscent of musk mallow flowers. Most of Gallé's work is signed.

A factory producing pieces very similar to those of Gallé was that of the brothers Daum in Nancy, although as well as plant motifs landscapes and figures appear on their work.

181 Vase with clematis-flowers
182 Vase of cut overlay glass

183 Vase with inlaid and trailed thread decoration

184 Onion-shaped vase

Louis Comfort Tiffany succeeded in producing glass with a metallic lustre, obtained by the use of metallic compounds and resinous substances. Unlike Gallé's work, his pieces are the product of the glass-maker as opposed to the artist decorator. They are masterpieces of glass-blowing, not of glass-cutting. Glass threads are laid in the Ancient Egyptian manner on the vessel, then combed with a pencil-like tool. The pattern of the threads undergoes some changes through repeated heating and reforming, until the blue-green and silver-violet surface, shimmering like peacocks' feathers or butterflies' wings, is produced. The iridescent glow of Tiffany's glass reflects perfectly the *fin-de-siècle* atmosphere and taste of the Art Nouveau movement. Tiffany pieces had their immediate imitators. The most important of these was the factory of Joh. Lötz Witwe in Klostermühle in Bohemia.

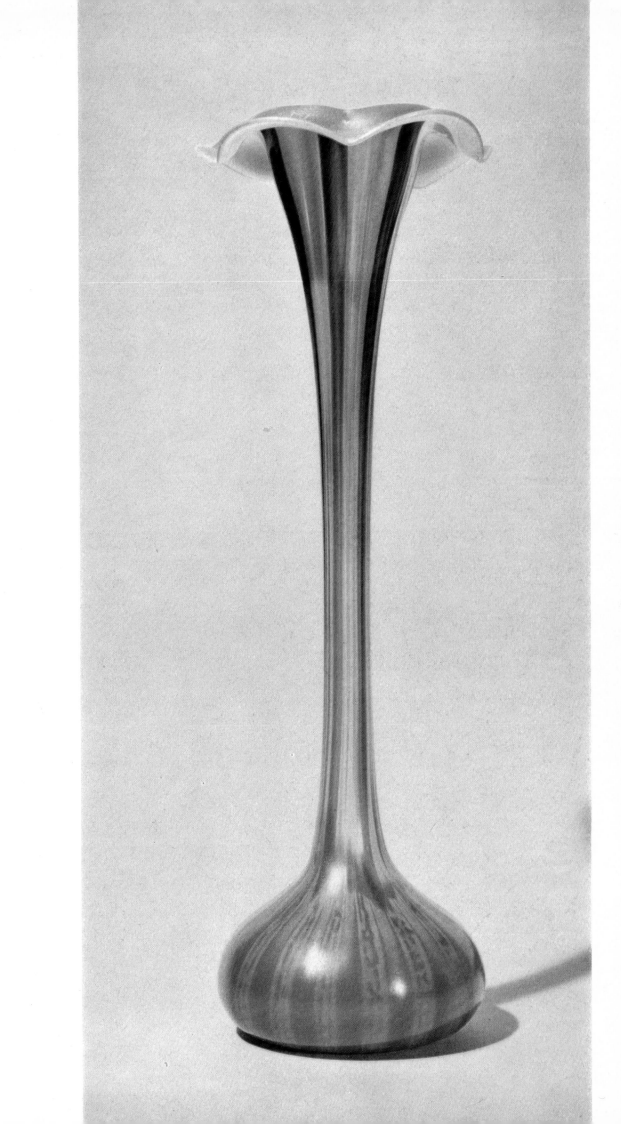

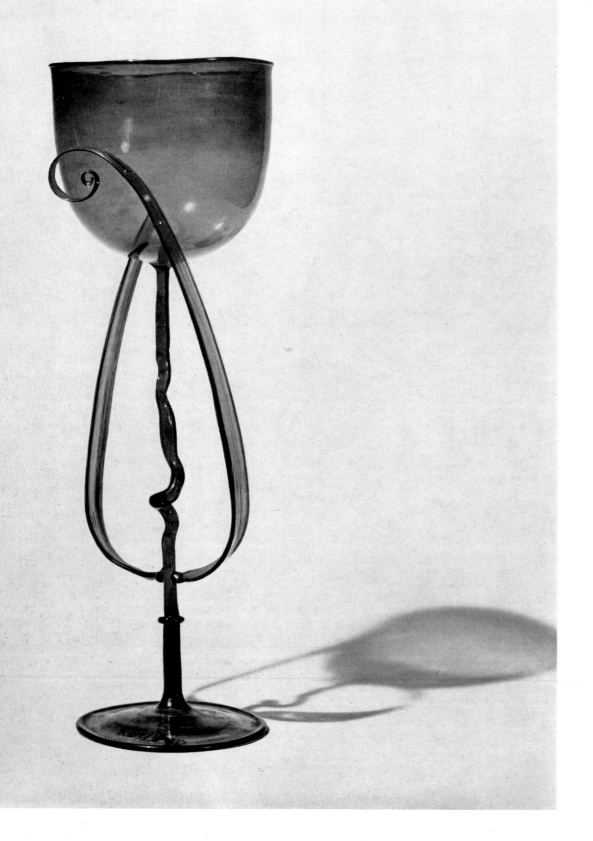

185 Tulip-shaped glass

This glass by the Berlin artist Karl Köpping may be said to epitomise the *Jugendstil*, the German version of the Art Nouveau movement. The stem of the glass has become the true stem of a flower, rising gracefully upwards with slender leaves growing from it. The glass has been accused of being completely unfunctional, and not without cause; but considered as a decorative piece, as the embodiment of an artistic ideal, it can refute any criticism. Köpping also designed functional glasses which, with their tall thin stems and small bowls, have their place in the history of glass forms.

186 Bowl with inward curving rim

187 Beaker with *Broncit* decoration

In 1911, Josef Hoffmann, founder of the Wiener Werkstätte (Vienna Crafts Centre) in 1903, built the Palais Stoclet in Brussels. Of this building Peter Behrens said that everything inside it, décor, furniture and ornaments were part of a single architectural theme. Le Corbusier has praised Hoffmann's works as being the expression of the refined, the witty, the agreable and the noble. This harmony with architecture is demonstrated by Hoffmann's *broncit décor* glasses.

Just as his interiors are based on the contrast of dark constructional parts with light areas of wall, so here the blackish-brown parts contrast with the transparent or matt areas of glass. The strong stylisation of the plants and figures and the geometrical design in which the motifs are placed give the glass a certain cool elegance.

189 Tumbler

190 Glass sculpture – hyaloplastic

Baccarat, lying in the French department of Meurthe et Moselle to the south east of Lune-ville, has gained fame for its crystal-glass industry. The first glasshouse, the St. Anne House, was founded in 1765. In 1816 it was purchased by d'Artiques and began to specialise in English-style crystal glass. In 1822 it became known as the Compagnie des Cristalleries de Baccarat, Paris, which name it still bears today. The first great period of this manufacture came in the fourth and fifth decades of the nineteenth century, although Baccarat pieces have at all times borne their own stamp: the brilliance of an exquisite metal set off by the elegance of classical form.

191 Tall bowl

193 Beaker-shaped vase

194 Wine glass

195 Tall bowl with dancing maidens

The Orrefors factory in Småland, Sweden, was founded in 1898. No other glass-works has had such an influence over glass-production throughout the world, or done so much to determine an international style. The history of Orrefors glass, particularly that by Simon Gate and Edvard Hald, is representative of that of all glass of recent times. In the first three decades of this century, attention was mainly centred on the ornamentation of glass by engraving, which was carried out with acute awareness of the relationship it must bear to the general character of the glass. After 1930 experiments were made with heavy thick glass, worked free hand.

Since the reorganisation of the Steuben Glassworks in Corning (New York) in 1933, three factors have governed the work of this establishment: high quality metal, artistic merit and good craftsmanship, and Steuben glass has taken its place among the best in the world. The table glass with its good design is in the best lead-crystal metal and usually undecorated, although glass-engraving is carried out. One of the most famous pieces of Steuben manufacture engraved decoration is the Merry-go-Round Bowl offered to Queen Elizabeth II, then Princess Elizabeth, by President Truman on the occasion of her marriage in 1947.

201 Flower bowl

202 Urn-shaped vase

Wilhelm Wagenfeld, born in 1900, is one of the pioneers of modern ideas in factory-produced glass. He has been graphic artist, sculptor, and silversmith, and took part in the celebrated *Bauhaus* venture, which was at that time centred on Weimar. Later he taught metal-work at the Weimar College of Architecture, as well as designing for the glass, metal, jewellery and porcelain industries. He then became a professor at the Academy of Fine Art in Berlin and finally took over the artistic direction of the then *Vereinigte Lausitzer Glaswerke*, with the result that their entire production was of the highest quality. His personal ideas on the subject of glass-making and this timely opportunity to put them into practice influenced the products of a whole industry, so that not only the art pieces, but also the mass-produced articles for everyday use exhibit aesthetic as well as technical quality. The enrichment obtained by decorative techniques is not, however, neglected, if it is considered to add to, and not detract from, these basic qualities.

203 Ewer

204 Bottle with matt surface

Paolo Venini, who died in 1959, was one of the most important artists in glass of recent times. The Venini factory, founded in 1921, employed at the time of Venini's death more than a hundred glass-blowers who were experienced in the ancient and complicated techniques involved. It was Venini's aim to marry the Venetian tradition in glass-making to modern Italian taste. The early pieces still show a strong resemblance to classical Renaissance forms.

In his modern *latticino* and mosaic glass, there is always an exciting silhouette, a brilliant colour scheme and an interesting surface structure. Paolo Venini has succeded in restoring to Murano glass the aristocratic charm and witty elegance it had in its classical period.

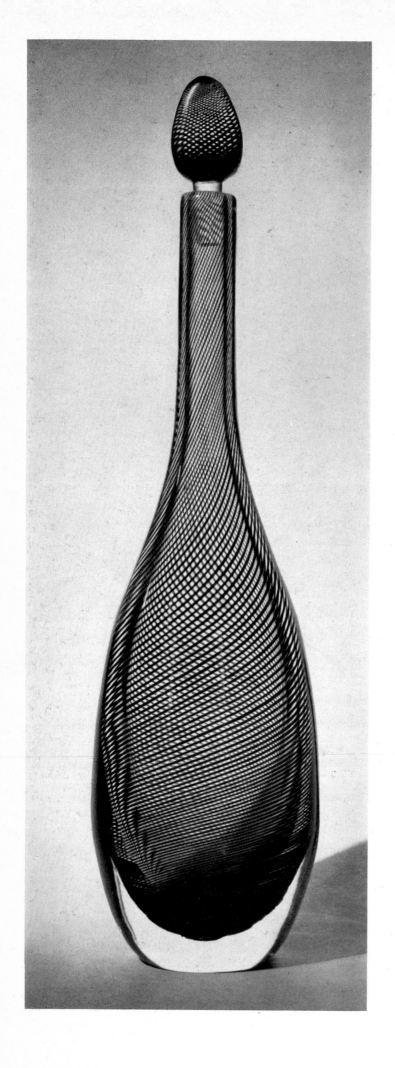

205 Flask in the *filigrana* technique

206 *Fazzoletto* bowl in the *sanfirico* technique

207 Multi-coloured vase
208 Shouldered bottle with matt surface

209 Large bowl

210 Four-coloured vase

Since 1934 the chief designer for the Seguso factory in Murano has been Flavio Poli. His glasses are simple and clear – a direct result of the technique of blowing – and yet full of careful harmony and balance. In the cased glasses the lines of the vessel bear an important relationship to the brilliantly contrasting colours, producing a tense, exciting effect. Here, glass is not treated like a semi-precious stone, but is exploited for its own powers of expression, and with its unique and very modern colouring is certainly a worthy rival to any material.

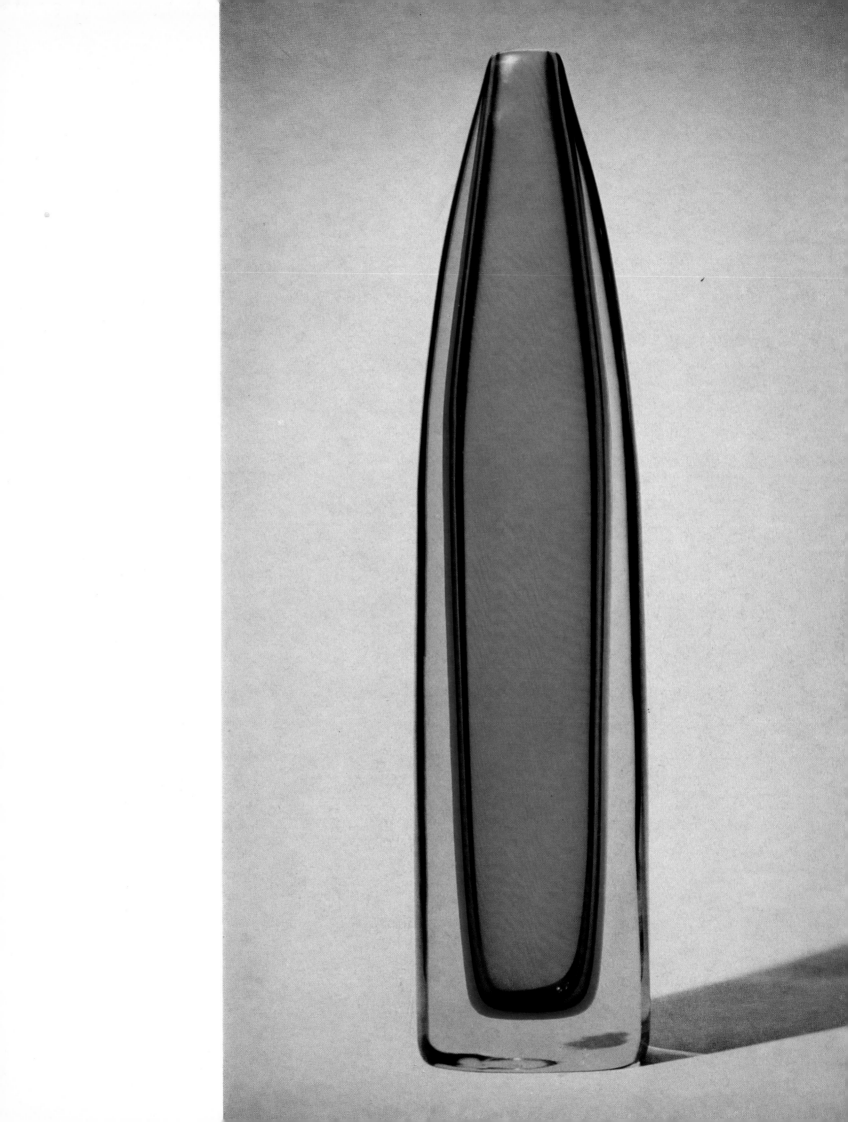

211 Squat bottle of speckled glass

212 Bowl in mosaic-glass

Flavio Poli's credo, "simplicity of form, but variety of colour and material" applies not only to the Muranese artist, nor to the medium of glass alone, but to all contemporary art work, and also to the field of architecture.

Many of the modern pieces illustrated here demonstrate this fact. However clear and simple the overall shape, the actual metal is used in many different ways to produce very varied effects, often one of great richness. One method of rendering the material interesting is to give the vessel a new dimension through colour or texture. The spirit in which millefiori or mosaic techniques, air-bubbles in Ariel glass or flashing and casing are used, corresponds to that on which decorative methods in present-day ceramics, textiles and metal-work are applied.

213 Vase with air-bubble decoration

The most important achievements of Orrefors glass are Ariel-glass, Gral-glass and Ravenna-glass. The unique character of Ariel-glass is obtained by manipulating air-bubbles within the mass of glass. Air-bubbles may be introduced into the soft glass by sticking a pointed tool into it, then sealing them in by smoothing over the surface. On reheating the air-bubble becomes round, but may be guided into many shapes, even into figurative representations. The foremost exponent of these techniques is Edvin Öhrström.

214 Flower vase
with overlay reticulated pattern

215 Bottle with
two superimposed layers

Modern glass of all countries favours the use of thick heavy glass. Glass should, according to many artists, have the appearance of frozen liquid. The thick crystal-clear bases give the impression that the vessels contain water. Thick clear-glass casings often enclose a coloured inner wall. The austere tense lines emphasise the character and qualities of the material, its immaculate purity and glowing transparency. The beauty of the glass and the form it has been given should not, it is thought, be spoiled by additional ornamentation. Glass is not a frame or canvas but the medium itself, and a fascinating one at that. Free-hand glass completed at the furnace is therefore the main interest of the modern glass artist.

218 Bottle

219 Two cylindrical vases

Finnish glass has also played its part in influencing international style. The most important Finnish designers are Tapio Virkkara, Kaj Franck, Timo Sarpaneva and Saara Hopea. The Finnish glass industry aims at producing not individual art pieces, but everyday ware of artistic value. In its simple lines and appealing decor, Finnish glass shows a close resemblance to other Scandinavian work, particularly Swedish. In its considerable use of round shapes it is closer to the Danish in spirit. The most important manufacturers are Iittala and Notsjö.

220 Vase

221 Brandy bottle
in the style of a *Kuttrolf*

Although Danish glass is strongly influenced by Swedish, it does have characteristics of its own. Fuller, round shapes predominate and give it, whilst depriving it of none of its modernity, a jollier, warmer appearance. The decanter, based on the medieval *Kuttrolf*, is typical of its homelier elegance. The most important factories are Holmegaards Glasværk at Holmegaard and Copenhagen, and Kastrup Glasværk in Copenhagen.

224 Dish

The main glass manufacture in Holland is the Koninklije Nederlandsche Glasfabriek at Leerdam, founded in 1765 and reorganised in 1915. The artistic director is Adrian Dirk Copier, who, together with the designers Floris Meydan and Willem Heesen, has given Dutch glass, after a century of little significance, a new lease of life and a unique Dutch style about it. Its forms are heavier and sturdier than those of Scandinavian or Italian glass.

226 Parts of a drinking service

The name Lobmeyr has been associated with the production of quality glass in the Austrian industry for more than a hundred years. The more conservative approach to the material shown by Ludwig Lobmeyr (1829 to 1917) resulted in his adherence to an elegant decoration, carried out in the Northern Bohemian centres of Haida and Steinschönau. After 1902, when Stephan Rath joined the company, there came a re-orientation towards the contemporary Viennese style of the early twentieth century, to the development of which Josef Hoffmann and his Viennese Studio (founded 1903) greatly contributed. Grace of form and a feeling for proportion have characterised Lobmeyr pieces up to the present day, and are to be seen in the illustrated wine-service, reminiscent of classical Venetian glass.

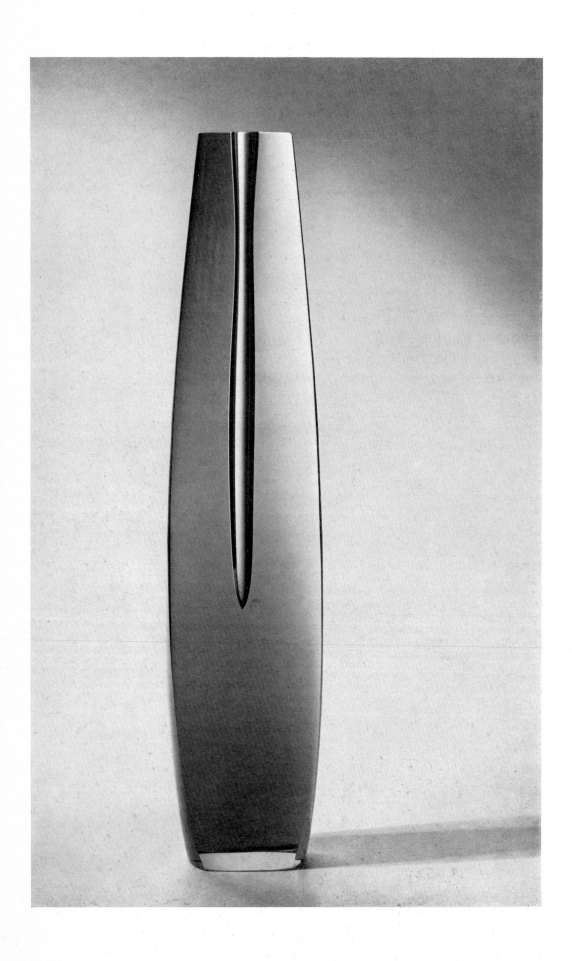

228 Two-layer vase

**229/230 Plate
with sand-blast engraving**

The technique of sand blasting enables Ladislaus Oliva to give thick lead crystal glass a new and exciting appearance. His decorative themes, tending towards the monumental, which have evolved from an earlier, somewhat rigid tectonic to increasingly free and irregular rhythmic forms, always appear to result from the natural lights of the heavy glass mass.

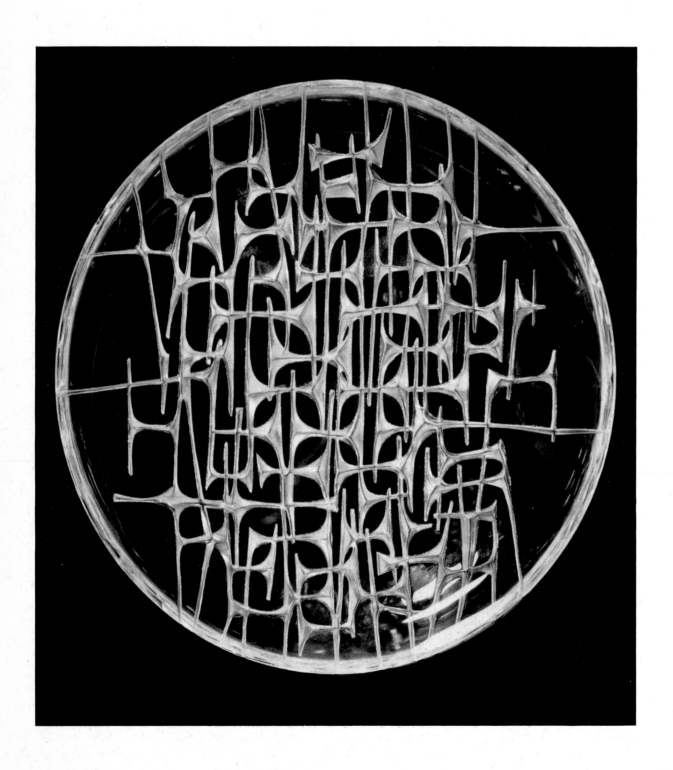

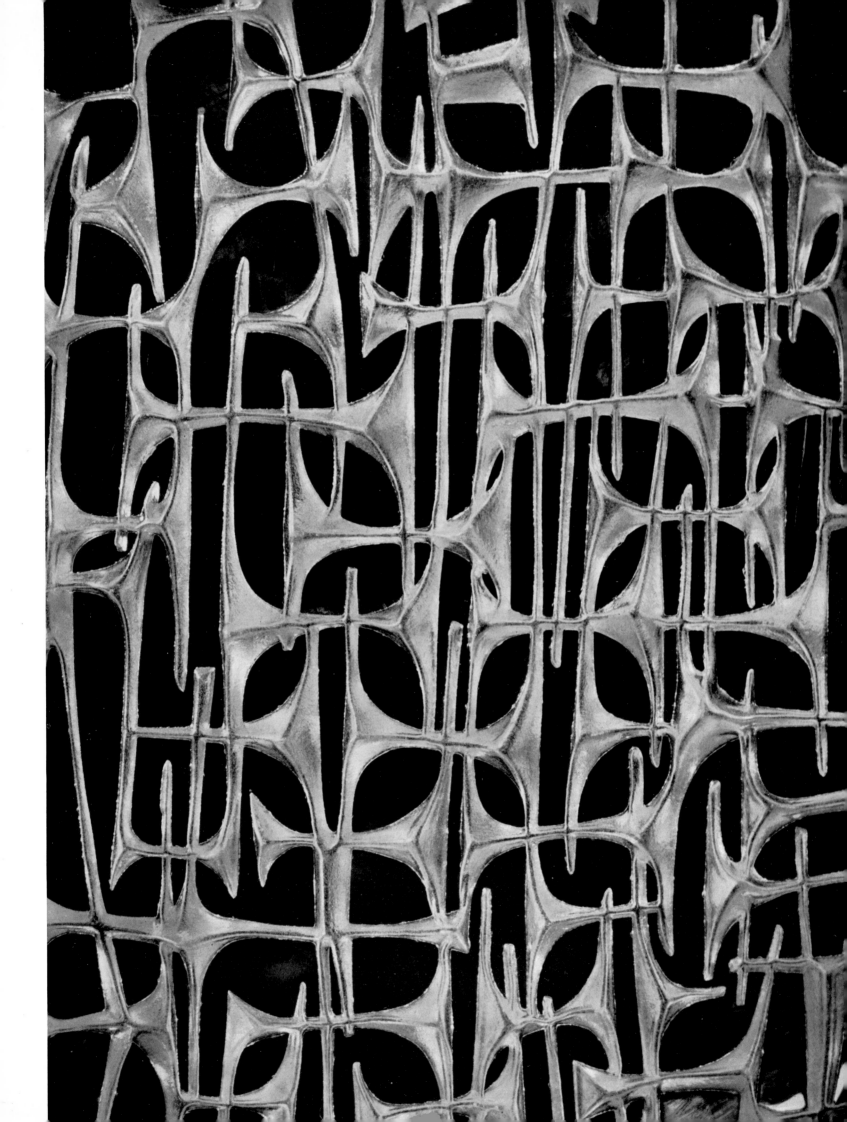

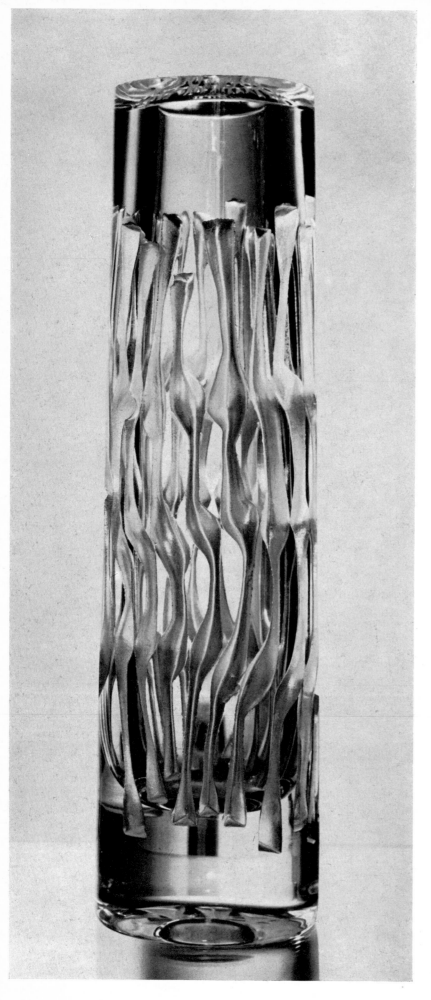

231 Vase decorated
with sand-blast engraving

Rene Roubiček directs his efforts towards creating free-hand worked pieces, with brilliant effects. We see in his work a continuation of the medieval glass-making tradition heightened into an even more cultured art form. His hollow-blown pieces take on the appearance of modern sculpture, and are imbued with that poetry which results when the craftsman's creations rise above the utilitarian and are conceived with quiet humour or happy fantasy.

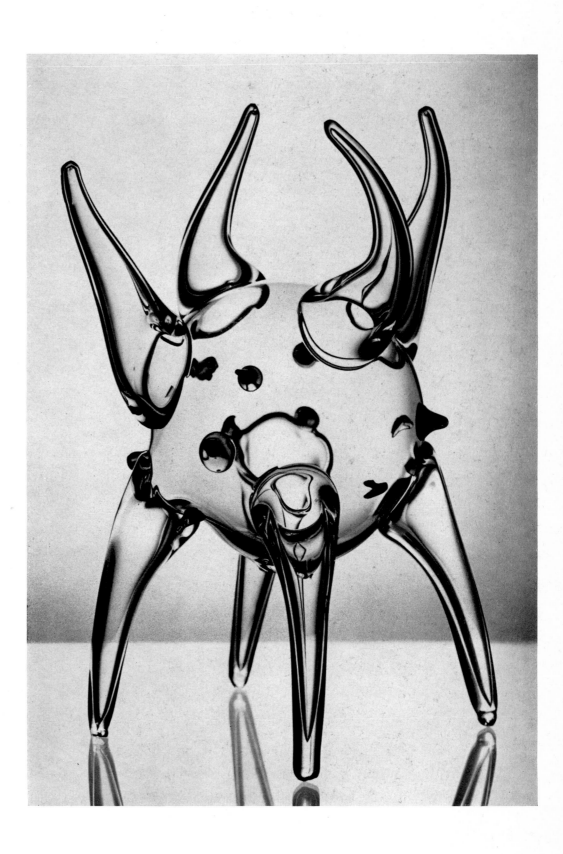

233 Lustre-decorated vase

234 Vase with engraved line pattern

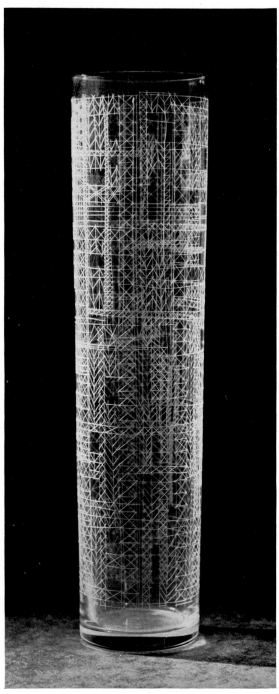

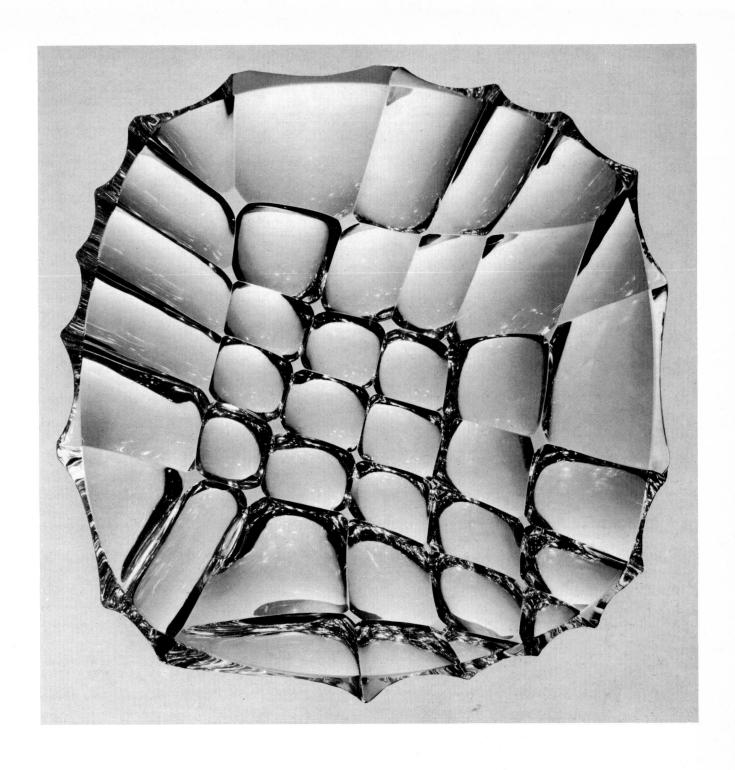

235 Hollow bowl
with deep facetting

Czechoslovakian glass is known for its great tradition in lead-crystal cutting. This is not only continued at the present time, but is constantly finding new expression. It is still worthwhile to enhance the brilliance of this high quality glass by clever cutting. The style of cutting has nevertheless changed considerably. Instead of the usual diamond or star motifs, free, irregular patterns have now come to the fore.

236 Jug
237 Tall jug

In both jugs we see the blending of the traditions of German *Waldglas* of the seventeenth century with the principles of the German Werkbund, which sought harmony of form and function in every object produced. Functions such as fitting, storing, carrying and pouring determined the shape of the vessel. Here the lively outline derives from the basic form of blown glass, the sphere. Here also is a material which, owing to the very nature of its manipulation, requiring swiftness, readily meets modern mass-production's demand for speed. And yet all parts, all the lines in the piece are so delicately balanced one against the other that the overall effect is one of simplicity and economy resulting in elegance of form: an excellent model for all industrial design.

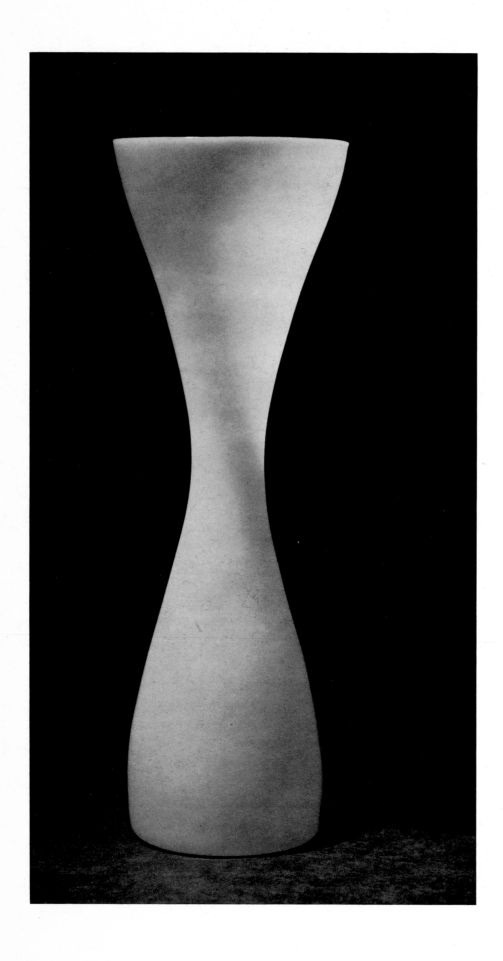

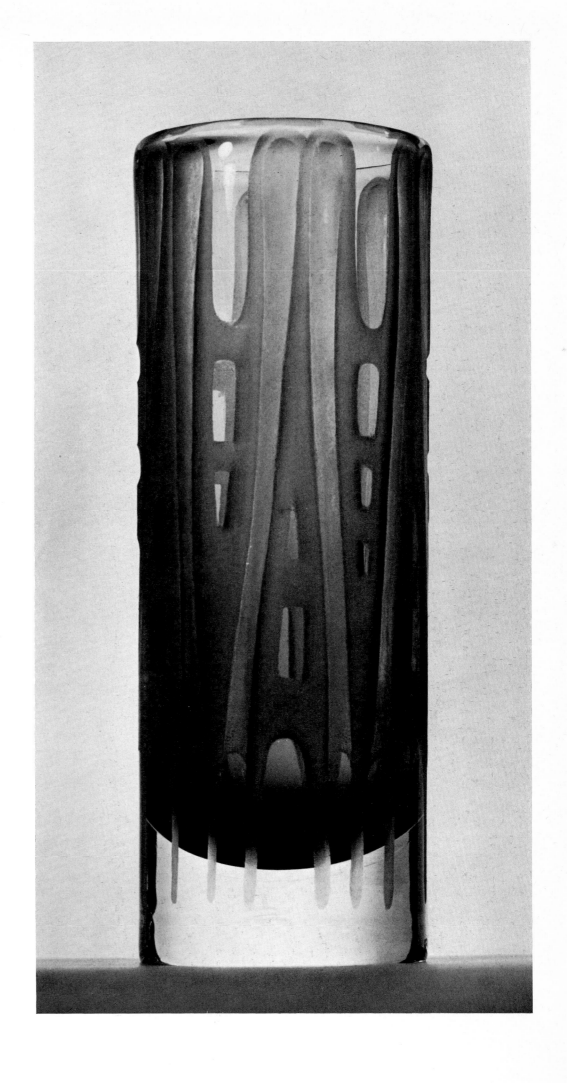

239 Vase with cut decoration

240 Table glasses
241 Blue glass vase with colourless insertions

242 Table glasses
243 Drug jars

Catalogue

1. Beaker of Thothmes III

Turquoise coloured, opaque glass with blue and yellow thread decoration
Height 8.4 cm.
Munich, Ägyptische Staatssammlung

The glass, moulded over a clay core, has the shape of a lotus bud. It has a small foot and a short, squat stem bearing the slightly conical cup. On it are garland-like glass threads fused into the surface, and the cartouche of Pharaoh Thothmes III.

Egypt, 18th Dynasty, about 1450 B.C.

References: Frederic Neuburg, *Antikes Glas*, Darmstadt 1962, Colour plate Ia; Ludwig F. Fuchs, *Die Glaskunst im Wandel der Jahrtausende*, Darmstadt 1956, fig. 1

2. Head showing the face of Amenhotep III

A mixture of dark blue and yellowish glass
Height 3.8 cm.
Munich, Ägyptische Staatssammlung

This head, made from glass of two colours, moulded, then cut, wears the Royal head-dress with the symbol of the snake's head on the forehead.

Egypt, c. 1375 B.C.

Reference: *Journal of Glass Studies*, The Corning Museum of Glass, Corning, New York, Vol. II 1960, p. 138, fig. 1

3. Small amphora

Opaque blue glass with coloured combed decoration
Height 12.5 cm.
Berlin, Staatliche Museen, Ägyptisches Museum

This egg-shaped vessel stands on a wide conical foot. It has light blue, white and yellow combed decoration, which on the lower part and on the neck is garland-like, and in the middle forms a palm-leaf pattern. The neck is cylindrical, curving slightly at the top, and provided with small dolphin handles.

Egypt, c. 1350 B.C.

Reference: compare a similar piece in "Glass from The Corning Museum of Glass, a Guide to the Collections", Corning, New York 1958, fig. 2.

4. Two containers for balm or cosmetics.
(On the right an alabastron, on the left an unguentarium)

a) Opaque blue glass with yellow and white combed decoration
Height 7 cm.
Berlin-Charlottenburg, formerly Staatliche Museen, Department of Antiquities

Squat bottle with flattened base, with a wide rim over a narrow neck. Two small loops for a carrying string are seen on the side of the bottle. Decorated with palm-leaf pattern in yellow and white.

Egypt, 3rd Century B.C.

b) Opaque white glass with brown combed decoration
Height 13 cm.
Berlin-Charlottenburg, formerly Staatliche Museen, Department of Antiquities

Raindrop-shaped bottle with four carrying loops, short neck and wide rim. Spiral thread decoration in brown, drawn horizontally, is seen on the upper part of the bottle, turning into a zig-zag pattern in the lower part.

Egypt, 6th Century B.C.

Reference: similar vessels are to be seen in Frederic Neuburg's *Antikes Glas*, Darmstadt 1962, Colour plate IIb and fig. 11.

5. Necklace of a Nubian Queen

Glass beads, faience, shells and gold chain links
Berlin, Staatliche Museen, Ägyptisches Museum

The necklace consists of eight rows, the inner two joined by small tubular beads. The fourth row contains many shells, threaded in pairs, of a brown and white spiral pattern. In the middle of the fifth row are ridged glass beads, gilt and covered with a layer of glass, and to the right and left of them are many "eye"-beads and red glass beads in the form of round berries. In the sixth row there are nineteen components with eye insets (amulets) forming links in the necklace. The arrangement of the beads as seen today is not original. The components that have come down to us were probably those of a larger collar ornament, and after purchase by the Berlin Ägyptische Museum were arranged to form two necklaces.

Nubia, first half of the 1st Century B.C.

Reference: Heinrich Schäfer, *Ägyptische Goldschmiedearbeiten*, Mitteilungen aus der Ägyptischen Sammlung, Königliche Museen zu Berlin, Berlin 1910, plate 33.

6. Large amphora

Colourless glass with gilt bronze mount
Height 59.6 cm.
Berlin-Dahlem, formerly Staatliche Museen, Department of Antiquities

The vessel has a bell-shaped foot, an egg-shaped body, flattened above the shoulder, a tall, slender neck, an outward-curving rim, and a conical lid. It is made in two parts.

Alexandria, c. 200 B.C.

Reference: Adolf Greifenhagen, *Antike Kunstwerke*, Berlin 1960, fig. 85.

7. Millefiori bowl

Glass in four colours
Diameter 11.5 cm.
Berlin-Charlottenburg, formerly Staatliche Museen, Department of Antiquities

Shallow bowl with a wide, raised edge. Background colour violet with a yellow flower pattern, green stalks and a wreath of yellow-red tulips.

Alexandria, 1st Century B.C.

Reference: Robert Zahn, *Die Sammlung Friedrich Ludwig von Gans im Antiquarium*, in the *Amtliche Berichte aus den Königlichen Kunstsammlungen 35*, fig. 50 (1913).

8. Ribbed bowl

Azure blue glass, moulded, then cut
Diameter 18 cm.
Cologne, Römisch-Germanisches Museum

Shallow, footless bowl with vertical, slightly twisted rib ornament, producing a very bold effect, but cut away at the rim.

Roman, second half of the 1st Century A.D.

Reference: Fritz Fremersdorf, *Römisches geformtes Glas in Köln, Die Denkmäler des römischen Köln, Vol. VI*, Cologne 1961, fig. 55.

9. Tall ribbed bowl

Azure blue with a pronounced iridescence, either mould-blown or with applied trailed decoration
Diameter 9 cm.
Berlin-Charlottenburg, formerly Staatliche Museen, Department of Antiquities

Rounded bowl with distinct inward curve at the neck and slightly widening rim. Vertical ribs are the sole decoration, and give the impression of having been trailed onto the vessel.

Roman, middle of the 1st Century A.D.

References: *Amtliche Berichte aus den Königlichen Kunstsammlungen*, Berlin 1907, p. 59, fig. 41; for similar bowls see also Fritz Fremersdorf, *Römisches geformtes Glas in Köln, Die Denkmäler des römischen Köln, Vol. VI*, Cologne 1961, plate 62.

10. Syrian domestic glass vessel

Impure glass in light green
Height 14.5 cm.
Weimar, Museum für Ur- und Frühgeschichte Thüringens
Club-shaped standing bottle.

Syria, found at Garizim 1–2 Century A.D.

11. Syrian domestic glass vessel

Height 12 cm.
Weimar, Museum für Ur- und Frühgeschichte Thüringens
Jug with trefoil mouth in light green transparent metal, top of the handle forming a snake's head.

Syria, found at Garizim, 1–2 Century A.D.

12. Syrian domestic glass vessel

Height 8 cm.
Weimar, Museum für Ur- und Frühgeschichte Thüringens
Globular vessel with short neck and folded rim, whitish, slightly transparent glass.

Syria, found at Garizim, 1–2 Century A.D.

13. Bottle with relief decoration

Blue glass, mould-blown
Height 9 cm.
Leipzig, private collection

Hexagonal, vase-shaped vessel standing on a small base. Tall neck terminating in a thickish rim. On the walls, relief decoration with Jewish motifs (vases between pillars).

Sidon c. 200 A.D.

Reference: Compare a similar bottle in Frederic Neuburg's *Antikes Glas*, Darmstadt 1962, fig. 41.

14. Two twin Alabastra

a) Bluish-green glass with white trailing, with triangular-shaped handles, showing a silvery iridescence
Height 11 cm.
b) Green glass. A hollow tube was bent and white threads were trailed round the two parts of it. Tiny handles; silvery iridescence
Height 9 cm.
Eisenach, Thüringer Museum

Syria, 2nd to 3rd Century A.D.

15. Shell-shaped flask

Green glass, mould-blown, with trailed decoration
Height 19 cm.

Cologne, Römisch-Germanisches Museum

The body of the vessel takes the form of a pilgrim's shell with distinct grooves. This is supported by a short, thickish stem on a sturdy, rounded foot. Spiral trailing decoration is seen on the neck, and two slender handles curve from the shoulders of the vessel to the widening rim, where they form two small loops.

Rhenish, c. 300 A.D.

Reference: Fritz Fremersdorf, *Römisches geformtes Glas in Köln, Die Denkmäler des römischen Köln, Vol. VI*, Cologne 1961, fig. 165.

16. Flask in the form of a bunch of grapes

Blue glass with yellow handles and yellow trailed decoration
Height 17 cm.
Cologne, Römisch-Germanisches Museum

Mould blown consisting of two identical halves with the result that the seam is clearly seen; the vessel stands on a broad flattened foot. The body of the vessel is in the form of a grape cluster. The neck is long and slender with a funnel-shaped opening, and delicate, ingeniously twisted handles. A yellow thread of glass in a spiral round the neck is an additional decoration.

Cologne, 3rd Century A.D.

Reference: Fritz Fremersdorf, *Römisches Buntglas in Köln, Die Denkmäler des römischen Köln, Vol. III*, Cologne 1958, fig. 81.

17. Flask in the form of a Janus head

Pale greenish metal
Height 25.3 cm.
Cologne, Römisch-Germanisches Museum

The vessel has a conical foot and a funnel-shaped neck with wide opening. The body of the vessel, blown into a mould, consists of two almost identical halves, each in the form of a man's face.

Rhenish, 3rd to 4th Century A.D.

Reference: Fritz Fremersdorf, *Römisches geformtes Glas in Köln*, *Die Denkmäler des römischen Köln*, *Vol. VI*, Cologne 1961, fig. 172.

18. Vessel in the form of a girl's head

Blue glass
Height 20 cm.
Berlin-Charlottenburg, formerly Staatliche Museen, Department of Antiquities

The foot is of modest proportions, the neck funnel-shaped and wide, with a sharply bent handle joining the neck horizontally, and attached at the lower end to the main body of the vessel. The latter takes the form of the head of a girl with long, wavy hair. Another piece from the same mould is to be seen in the Corning Museum, New York.

Gaul, 2nd Century A.D.

References: Adolf Greifenhagen, *Antike Kunstwerke*, Berlin 1960, Plate 86; *Glass from the Ancient World*, *The R. W. Smith Collection*, *Exhibition Catalogue*, Corning Museum, New York, 1957, p. 141; Frederic Neuburg, *Antikes Glas*, Darmstadt 1962, fig. 101.

19. Negro head bottle

Whitish-green glass
Height 15.5 cm.
Cologne, Römisch-Germanisches Museum

This bottle takes the shape of a negro head. The features are somewhat caricatured: the mouth with its thick lips is half open, the nose flattened, the forehead has bulging brows, and there is a wart on the right cheek. The neck of the bottle is short with a wide rim and two dolphin handles attached to it. The bottle was blown into a two-part mould.

Roman, 2nd–3rd Century A.D.

References: Anton Kisa, *Das Glas im Altertum*, Leipzig 1908, p. 757, fig. 305; Fritz Fremersdorf, *Römisches geformtes Glas in Köln*, *Die Denkmäler des römischen Köln*, Vol. VI, Cologne 1961, fig. 169.

20. Ridged beaker

Bluish-green, the glass containing numerous small bubbles
Height 20.7 cm.
Cologne, Römisch-Germanisches Museum

This beaker-like vessel, gradually widening out towards the rim, has five folds or ridges on the body and a primitive trailed spiral decoration around the neck. It was found on the Alteburg near Cologne on the site of the home port of the Roman Rhine fleet.

Rhenish, c. 200 A.D.

References: Fritz Fremersdorf, *Zur Geschichte des fränkischen Rüsselbechers*, *Wallraf-Richartz-Jahrbuch*, N. F., Cologne 1933/34, p. 16, Plate 11; Ignaz Schlosser, *Das alte Glas*, Brunswick 1956, plate 12.

21. Pear-shaped ewer

Light green to dark green metal streaked with white
Height 31 cm.
Cologne, Römisch-Germanisches Museum

The slender, pear-shaped ewer has a steep, conical foot with a folded rim. The neck widens at the top into a funnel shape and has an inwardly folded rim. The handle, which is round in cross-section, forms a knot where it meets the rim. Found at Cologne.

Cologne, end of the 3rd Century A.D.

22. Free-blown ewer

Light green metal with blown spiral decoration
Height 27 cm.
Berlin, Staatliche Museen, Department of Antiquities

Above the widish foot, the kicked base of the ewer protrudes into the main part of the vessel and is visible through the thin wall. The ewer is pear-shaped, widening rapidly above the foot, and narrowing even more abruptly above the shoulders into a slender neck with a decoration of a double ring. The opening is funnel-shaped, and the ribbon-like handle is looped beneath the rim.

Romano-Rhenish, 3rd–4th Century A.D.

Reference: Department of Antiquities, Katalog der Staatlichen Museen Berlin, Berlin 1957, fig. 59.

23. Cinerary urn

Green glass with blue handles
Height 31 cm.
Nuremberg, Germanisches Nationalmuseum

A globular vessel with a somewhat narrow neck, which opens out considerably, however, so that the rim almost touches the M-shaped handles. A tall conical lid crowns the whole.

Rhenish, beginning of the 2nd Century A.D.

24. Vessel with trailed decoration

Height 8 cm.
Berlin-Charlottenburg, formerly Staatliche Museen, Department of Antiquities

A small globular body, with a neck curving sharply inwards and a wide funnel-shaped mouth. A zig-zag decoration stretches between the rim and the shoulders of the vessel, masking the slender neck.

Syrian or Roman, 3rd–4th Century A.D.

25. Small, five-handled amphora

Light, bluish-green with blue handles and blue trailed decoration
Height 11 cm.
Berlin-Charlottenburg, formerly Staatliche Museen, Department of Antiquities

The round body of the jug stands on a fairly wide foot-ring. The neck is long, widening into a funnel shape and decorated with spiral trailing below the mouth and below the point where the five handles meet the neck. The handles, rising at points on the shoulders of the vessel, have the appearance of celery stalks.

Syria, 3rd Century A.D.

References: Compare W. B. Honey, *Glass, Victoria and Albert Museum*, London 1946, plate 11, fig. b, and *Glas, Katalog des Kunstgewerbemuseums der Stadt Köln*, edited by Brigitte Klesse, Cologne 1963, no. 19.

26. Stamnium

Greenish glass
Height 32 cm.
Berlin, Staatliche Museen, Antikensammlung

Cylindrical body with kicked base and long neck; funnel-shaped throat is double ringed; wide, flat handles attached to throat run vertically down to shoulders.

Roman or Rhenish, 3rd to 4th Century A.D.

27. Pear-shaped ewer

Yellowish-green metal with spiral decoration
Height 22.3 cm.
Cologne, Römisch-Germanisches Museum

The foot is wide, the body of the vessel slender at its base, widening sharply towards the middle, then narrowing again into a slender neck, and the mouth is wide with a flat rim. Two rings, pincered flat, ornament the neck, and a handle stretches vertically from the widest part of the body to the rim, where it forms a knot. The surface of the vessel is decorated with a spiral of four threads trailed close together.

Cologne, end of the 3rd, beginning of the 4th Century A.D.

Reference: *Deutsches Glas, 2000 Jahre Glasveredelung, Hessisches Landesmuseum Darmstadt, Exhibition Catalogue*, edited by H. Merten, Darmstadt 1935, plate 239.

28. Conical ewer, or Prochus

Green glass with white marbling
Height 23 cm.
Cologne, Römisch-Germanisches Museum

This conical vessel, widest at the base, stands on a thick foot. The rim is decorated with a frilly ribbon of glass. The handle is flat, and strongly ribbed. There is a vigourous marbling pattern in the glass from which the ewer is made.

Cologne, end of 3rd – beginning of 4th Century A.D.

Reference: See vessels with similar marbling in Fritz Fremersdorf's *Römisches Buntglas in Köln, Die Denkmäler des römischen Köln*, Vol. III, Cologne 1958, plate 106.

29. Small amphora with applied decoration

Originally clear, now clouded glass with applied decoration and white inlaid threads
Height 17 cm.
Berlin-Charlottenburg, formerly Staatliche Museen, Department of Antiquities

Small, flat foot, and compressed knop, both in glass with spiral thread ornament. Broad, pear-shaped body with inlaid pattern of wavy lines on the lower part. Two bands of three threads run round the shoulder. Slender, funnel-like neck. The general shape reveals Greek influence. The authenticity of the foot is questionable.

Syria or Greece, 3rd to 4th Century A.D.

30. Kantharos

Chestnut-brown glass
Height 10.5 cm.
Cologne, Römisch-Germanisches Museum

Wide cup-shaped vessel with small foot, stem consisting merely of a compressed knop, deep rim, large flat handles. The elegant shape is inspired by that of certain metal vessels.

Italy, 1st Century A.D.

Reference: Fritz Fremersdorf, *Römisches Buntglas in Köln, Die Denkmäler des römischen Köln*, Vol. III, Cologne 1958, plate 35.

31. Concave beaker

Dark olive green glass
Height 10.5 cm.
Cologne, Römisch-Germanisches Museum

The green beaker with concave sides stands on a small base. Found in Cologne.

Northern Italy, 1st Century A.D.

Reference: Fritz Fremersdorf, *Römisches Buntglas in Köln, Die Denkmäler des römischen Köln*, Vol. III, Cologne 1958, Plate 51.

32. Pitcher with trefoil mouth and trailed snake ornamentation

Light green clouded metal with white and blue trailing
Height 12 cm.
Nuremberg, Germanisches Nationalmuseum

The round jug, with foot-ring, trefoil mouth and elegantly curving handle has a snake-like, blue and white trailed decoration.

Rhenish, 2nd Century A.D.

33. Pear-shaped bottle with trailed snake decoration

Colourless glass with blue and white trailing and metallic iridescence

Height 13.9 cm.

Cologne, Römisch-Germanisches Museum

This bottle, with its elegant line, has a thick foot-ring and a tall, funnel-shaped neck. The blue and white trailed snake decoration can be seen on the body of the vessel. A ring of blue glass around the neck is an additional decoration. The bottle was found in the Aachener Strasse in Cologne.

Rhenish, 3rd Century A.D.

Reference: Fritz Fremersdorf, *Römische Gläser mit Fadenauflage in Köln, Die Denkmäler des römischen Köln, Vol. V*, Cologne 1959, plates 28 and 29.

34. Bell-shaped beaker with stem (Carchesium)

Sea-green glass with white and gold trailing
Height 12 cm.

Cologne, Römisch-Germanisches Museum

The foot is broad, and at the point where it joins the stem there is a white ring decoration. The knopped stem is rather short. The trailed ornament is in the region between the widening mouth and the bulging base of the cup. It consists of gold scrolls forming a cross, and white haphazard squiggles. There is a thick line of trailed glass along the rim. The beaker was found in the Weiherstrasse in Cologne.

Rhenish, 3rd Century A.D.

References: Anton Kisa, *Das Glas im Altertum*, Leipzig 1908, Part 2, Plate V, 1 facing p. 452, p. 239, fig. 119; Fritz Fremersdorf, *Römische Gläser aus Köln*, Cologne 1939, colour plate no. 1; Fritz Fremersdorf, *Römische Gläser mit Fadenauflage in Köln, Die Denkmäler des römischen Köln, Vol. V*, Cologne 1959, plate 67; "Deutsches Glas, 2000 Jahre Glasveredelung, Hessisches Landesmuseum Darmstadt," Exhibition Catalogue, H. Merten, Darmstadt 1935, plate 25 no. 256.

35. Pilgrim's bottle with trailed snake decoration, known as the *Meisterstück* (Masterpiece)

Colourless glass with rich, blue, white and gold trailing
Height 27 cm.

Cologne, Römisch-Germanisches Museum

A short stem connects the foot and the body of the vessel which is circular and flat. Trailed decoration appears on both sides of the vessel. This consists of a central gold spiral, from which four blue lines lead out, forming the midribs of four leaves, the silhouettes of which are trailed in gold. In the angles formed by the leaves, we see four garlands, which consist of a ruffle pattern in gilt, red and blue trailing. The neck of the vessel is tall, and has a funnel-shaped mouth. The sides of the body and the handles are ornamented with pincered ridges. The bottle was found in the Luxemburger Strasse in Cologne in 1893. The given date was confirmed by the presence of the fragments of a similar bottle in a hoard containing coins of the period.

Cologne 3rd Century A.D.

References: Fritz Fremersdorf, *Römische Gläser aus Köln*, Cologne 1939; coloured plate II; Fritz Fremersdorf, *Römische Gläser mit Fadenauflage in Köln, Die Denkmäler des römischen Köln, Vol. V*, Cologne 1959, plates 70, 71.

36. Conical flask with gold painting

Extremely thin colourless glass
Height 10 cm.

Leipzig, Museum des Kunsthandwerks

This conical vessel has a slightly rounded base and a small funnel-shaped neck. The decoration is confined to a panel running round the sides of the bottle, marked off by two fine engraved lines. The painting represents three trees and figures of praying, working, and playing youths.

Rome, 1st–2nd Century A.D.

37. Cylindrical two-handled bottle (Stamnium)

Greenish glass with shallow cutting
Height 33.6 cm.

Cologne, Römisch-Germanisches Museum

The surface of the vessel is marked off into four areas by double engraved lines running horizontally. The three lower areas are decorated by shallow cutting into simple geometrical designs (hobnail patterns, circles, straight lines) and oval facets. A plain stamnium is illustrated in plate 26 (q. v.).

Cologne, 4th Century A.D.

Reference: compare similar vessels in Fritz Fremersdorf's *Römische Gläser aus Köln*, Cologne 1939, plate 41.

38. Hemispherical bowl with facetting

Clear, colourless glass with cut decoration
Diameter 13 cm.

Cologne, Römisch-Germanisches Museum

This hemispherical bowl has three ridges cut into it below the rim, and below them a row of eyelet-shaped shallow facetting, and below that four rows of disc-shaped cuts.

Cologne, 2nd half of the 3rd Century A.D.

Reference: Fritz Fremersdorf, *Römische Gläser aus Köln*, Cologne 1939, plate 36.

39. Shallow bowl with chariot-racing motif

Colourless glass with line and (wheel?) engraving
Diameter 27 cm.

Cologne, Römisch-Germanisches Museum

In a small round area in the centre of the bowl we see a representation of a Roman emperor, and surrounding this four chariot-racing teams taking part in a race. The dish was found on the site of a Roman estate in Cologne-Braunsfeld in the year 1910. Coins of the time of the Emperor Constantine found with the dish made it possible to date it accurately.

Rhenish, c. 320 A.D.

References: Fritz Fremersdorf, *Der Römische Gutshof in der Stolberger Straße zu Köln-Braunsfeld, Bonner Jahrbücher*, 1930, no. 135, p. 131; Fritz Fremersdorf, *Kurzer Führer durch die Römische Abteilung des Wallraf-Richartz-Museums zu Köln*, Cologne 1927, plate 2; Fritz Fremersdorf, *Römische Gläser aus Köln*, Cologne 1939, plate 46.

40. Goblet with shell decoration

Once colourless, now opaque whitish glass
Height 21.5 cm.
Cologne, Römisch-Germanisches Museum

The goblet has a short knopped stem, and a slightly domed foot. The cup is tall, slender and slightly conical, and, forming a kind of cage round it, there is a decoration of trailed glass moulded into shell shapes, which is, however, raised away from it.
Cologne, beginning of the 4th Century A.D.

Reference: Otto Doppelfeld, *Der Muschelpokal von Köln*, Bonner Jahrbücher *1959*, no. *159*, p. *153* ff.

41. Diatreton

A single piece of almost colourless glass
Height 10.5 cm.
Munich, Museum of Antiquities (Antikensammlung)

The very fine rim of this glass was ground on the wheel. Below it we see the raised inscription: "Bibe multis annis"; and beneath this a network which also extends underneath and supports the vessel. The glass was found in 1844 in the Benenisstrasse, Cologne, on the site of the western gate of the Roman Colony. It was presented to King Ludwig I of Bavaria in acknowledgment of his donation of timber for the roof of the Cologne Cathedral. Another diatreton was found at the same time in a sarcophagus nearby, and was sent to Berlin, where it was destroyed by war action in 1945.

Rhineland (most probably Cologne), beginning of the 4th Century A.D.

Reference: Otto Doppelfeld, *Das Kölner Diatretglas und die anderen Netzdiatrete*, Gymnasium, Heidelberg, Vol. 68, 1961, p. 410–424, fig. 3, 1.

42. Diatreton

Inner wall in colourless glass, inscription purplish-red, collar honey-yellow, surrounding network green
Height 12.1 cm.
Cologne, Römisch-Germanisches Museum.

The beaker has an outward curving rim, and beneath this a Greek inscription, consisting of seventeen raised letters, and expressing an exhortation to drink: *ΠΙΕ ΖΗΣΑΙΣ ΚΑΛΩΣ ΑΕΙ*. Collar decoration in the form of loops. Network consisting of three rows of circles, twelve in each row, and one row of six oval shapes, surrounding the vessel and extending underneath it, where one large circle acts as a base. The inner wall of the vessel is 1.5 mm. thick, the network c. 2 mm. thick, and the space between network and inner wall c. 5 mm. It would appear from the shape and position of air bubbles in the cup and connecting shanks that the vessel was produced from a single, solidly blown body. The coloured layers are overlaid. The rim, the lower edge of the undercut collar, and the furrow between collar and network were cut on a kind of turning-lathe. Signs of grinding on the shanks and on the network would indicate the use of a wheel. The glass was found as part of the burial hoard of a sandstone sarcophagus on the site of a Roman cemetery in Cologne-Braunsfeld, on 1st April 1960. The position of the sites where such diatreta glasses have been found, and the nature of the vessels, lead us to conclude that they were manufactured in Cologne.

Cologne or Rhineland, beginning of the 4th Century A.D.

References: Otto Doppelfeld, *Das neue Kölner Diatretglas*, Germania, Berlin, Vol. 38 1960, p. 403–417; Otto Doppelfeld, *Das Kölner Diatretglas und die anderen Netzdiatrete*, Gymnasium, Heidelberg, Vol. 68, No. 5, 1961, p. 410–424; Otto Doppelfeld, *Das Diatretglas aus dem Gräberbezirk des römischen Gutshofs in Köln-Braunsfeld*, Kölner Jahrbuch für Vor- und Frühgeschichte, Berlin, Vol. 5 1960/61, p. 7 ff.

43. Dolphin beaker

Greenish glass with blue decoration
Height 13 cm.
Cologne, Römisch-Germanisches Museum

There are two rows of hollow prunts drawn downwards so as to resemble elephants' trunks. The lower row reaches the foot-ring and the upper row terminates in a fish-like tail, so that the ornaments of this row resemble dolphins. This resemblance is enhanced by applications of blue glass representing the dolphins' mouths and fins. Part of a burial hoard found in the Severinstrasse in Cologne.

Cologne, 4th Century A.D.

Reference: Fritz Fremersdorf, *Zur Geschichte des fränkischen Rüsselbechers*, Wallraf-Richartz-Jahrbuch, N. F., Cologne 1933/34, p. 7 ff.

44. Tall bowl in colourless glass with trailed coloured zig-zag ornamentation and flat button-shaped blobs

Diameter 12 cm.
Cologne, Römisch-Germanisches Museum

The rim is curved slightly outward with the trailed decoration (so-called dog tooth pattern) beneath. The blobs have raised edges and a somewhat protruding centre.

Cologne, beginning of the 4th Century A.D.

Reference: compare similar pieces in Fritz Fremersdorf, *Römische Gläser mit Fadenauflage in Köln*, Die Denkmäler des römischen Köln, *Vol. V*, Cologne 1959, plates 131, 132, 133.

45. Beaker with coloured prunts, known as *Humpen*

Colourless glass with blue and green decoration fused on to it
Height 14.5 cm.
Cologne, Römisch-Germanisches Museum

A footless beaker with rounded base and conical in shape. There is a thin engraved line below the rim. The decorative elements are in two layers and consist of coloured ovals and small prunts.

Rhenish, 4th Century A.D.

Reference: Fritz Fremersdorf, *Die römischen Gläser mit aufgelegten Nuppen in Köln*, Die Denkmäler des römischen Köln, *Vol. VII*, Cologne 1962, plate 9

46. Two Frankish beakers

Light, moss-green glass with blue spots
Height 10 cm.
Berlin-Charlottenburg, formerly Staatliche Museen, Department of Antiquities
Rhenish, 6th Century A.D.

47. Rüsselbecher (Rüssel = proboscis) also termed trunk- or claw beaker

Dark green glass with large, hollow prunts
Height 19 cm.
Cologne, Römisch-Germanisches Museum

The basic shape of this vessel is conical. It has a small foot-ring, and the part immediately above it is slender and decorated with horizontally trailed glass-threads. Another area ornamented in this way lies below the rim, much wider than the foot. Between these two areas is the claw decoration; there are two rows of five claws, each claw is hollow and has a line of pincered glass trailed on the length of its outer surface.

Rhenish, 5th Century.

Reference: Fritz Fremersdorf, *Zur Geschichte des fränkischen Rüsselbechers, Wallraf-Richartz-Jahrbuch*, N.F., Cologne 1933/34, p. 7ff.; Ludwig F. Fuchs, *Die Glaskunst im Wandel der Jahrtausende*, Darmstadt 1956, fig. 12.

48. Drinking horn

Greenish glass with dark brown and green trailing
Length 24.5 cm.
Cologne, Römisch-Germanisches Museum

The foot end is tilted upwards and strengthened with a ring of glass. The lower part of the horn is decorated with fine spiral trailing. On the body of the horn the trailing is lengthwise, in zig-zag pattern or straight lines. A more compressed zig-zag pattern runs horizontally below the rim between two thin threads.

Rhenish, 4th Century A.D.

Reference: Fritz Fremersdorf, *Römisches geformtes Glas in Köln, Die Denkmäler des römischen Köln*, Vol. VI, Cologne 1961, fig. 44.

49. Footless beaker

Light blue glass
Height 10 cm.
Leipzig, Museum des Kunsthandwerks

Footless glass resembling a whipping-top in shape, with waisted body and pointed base.

Frankish, 6th to 7th Century A.D.

50. Footed beaker

Brownish, rather incrustated iridescent glass
Height 8 cm.
Berlin, Staatliche Museen, Vorderasiatisches Museum

The foot is flattened, the stem which supports the broadly conical beaker rather short.

Syria, 5th Century A.D.

Reference: compare similar glass in *Glas, Katalog des Kunstgewerbemuseums der Stadt Köln*, edited by Brigitte Klesse, Cologne 1963, no. 28.

51. Mould-blown bottle with surface decoration

Height 15 cm.
Berlin-Dahlem, formerly Staatliche Museen Islamic Department

Bell-shaped bottle with tall, funnel-shaped neck. The decoration is in the form of arcading and almond-shaped motifs, obtained by blowing into a mould. This bottle was acquired in Teheran.

Egypt, 10th–12th Century.

References: see similar work in Carl Johan Lamm, *Mittelalterliche Gläser und Steinschnittarbeiten aus dem Nahen Osten*, Berlin 1929, plates 12 and 13; *Journal of Glass Studies*, The Corning Museum of Glass, Corning Glass Centre, Corning, New York, Vol. III, 1961, p. 138, fig. 15, which shows the same motifs, although cut, not mould-blown, on a bottle in the City Art Museum, Missouri, U.S.A.; *Ergänzung zu dem Katalog "Islamische Kunst aus den Berliner Museen, formerly Staatliche Museen Berlin, Museum Dahlem"*, edited by Ernst Kühnel, Berlin 1954, p. 10, No. 463.

52. Bowl with winged horse decoration

Opaque, light brown glass
Diameter 10 cm.
Berlin, Staatliche Museen, Islamisches Museum

The sides of the vessel are decorated with seven moulded medallions representing winged horses. A glass thread runs horizontally round the bowl some distance below the rim.

Syria, c. 700 A.D.

References: Carl Johan Lamm, *Mittelalterliche Gläser und Steinschnittarbeiten aus dem Nahen Osten*, Berlin 1929, plates 10 and 15; Robert Schmidt, *Das Glas*, Berlin 1912, fig. 20.

53. Hexagonal flask

Light-brownish glass with geometrical relief decoration
Height 16.5 cm.
Berlin, Staatliche Museen, Early Christian-Byzantine Department

The six-sided bottle was blown into a mould. It is shouldered, and the neck narrows upwards to a point slightly above half its length, then widens out into a funnel-shape. A thickish ring decorates the neck below the rim.

Syria, 5th Century A.D.

References: see similar vessels in Frederic Neuburg's *Antikes Glas*, Darmstadt 1962, fig. 40; *Journal of Glass Studies*, The Corning Museum of Glass, Corning Glass Centre, Corning, New York, Vol. III 1961, p. 137, fig. 9.

54. Small ewer with disc decoration

Greenish glass, greatly corroded and iridescent
Height 12.8 cm.
Berlin, Staatliche Museen, Vorderasiatisches Museum

A round body with inverted conical neck, bulbous throat and rim extended to form a lip. An upright handle curves over to join the rim. The button-like blobs, which decorate the body of the vessel in three rows, were obtained by the technique of mould-blowing.

Syria, 9th Century A.D.

Reference: see similar glass in *Glas, Katalog des Kunstgewerbemuseums der Stadt Köln*, edited by *Brigitte Klesse*, Cologne 1963, No. 34.

55. Beaker with cut decoration

Greenish glass
Diameter 9.5 cm.
Berlin, Staatliche Museen, Islamic Museum

The decoration consists of cuts in straight and curved lines forming a geometrical pattern. The beaker was excavated on the terrace of the Caliph's Palace in Samarra in 1911.

Mesopotamia, 9th Century A.D.

Reference: Carl Johan Lamm, *Das Glas von Samarra*, Berlin 1928, plate V.

56. Jug with thread decoration

Greenish, iridescent glass with green and blue trailing
Height 22.5 cm.
Berlin-Dahlem, formerly Staatliche Museen, Islamic Department

Jug in the shape of a mosque lamp: conical foot, wide, rounded body, tall funnel-shaped neck. Small handle meets the neck and shoulders, where they are ornamented with three and two circuits of blue threads respectively. Below the two threads, zig-zag trailing, and three groups of three applied rosettes. A further trailed line round the lower part of the body.

Syria, c. 1200.

Reference: Carl Johan Lamm, *Mittelalterliche Gläser und Steinschnittarbeiten aus dem Nahen Osten*, Berlin 1929, plates 27 and 13.

57. Hedwigsglas

Light brown glass with cutting in high relief. The gilt copper foot is a later addition
Total height 29 cm.

Nuremberg, Germanisches Nationalmuseum
The cup is slightly conical. Stylised representations of lions and griffons in high relief, with contrasting plain and ribbed surfaces, form the decoration. Between the animal representations are patterns arranged in bands.

Egypt, 11th Century.

Reference: Carl Johan Lamm, *Mittelalterliche Gläser und Steinschnittarbeiten aus dem Nahen Osten*, Berlin 1929, plate 63 and 64.

58. Emerald green bottle with cut ornament

Height 29 cm.
Berlin-Dahlem, formerly Staatliche Museen, Islamic Department

Plant-pot shaped body, wide shoulders, slender conical neck, wide, flat rim. On the shoulders there is a frieze with facet cutting, and on the neck a geometrical pattern. There is diamond-shaped cutting and circular facetting on the body of the vessel. Similar vessels may be seen in the Corning Museum, New York, and in the Museum für Kunst und Gewerbe, Hamburg

Persia, 9th to 10th Century A.D.

References: *Glass from the Corning Museum of Glass, Guide to the collections*, Corning, New York 1958, fig. 21; Lise Lotte Möller, *Flasche von smaragdgrünem Glas*, in: *Stiftung zur Förderung der Hamburgischen Kunstsammlungen, Erwerbungen 1962*, Hamburg 1962, p. 50–52 with colour plates; *Ergänzung zu dem Katalog Islamische Kunst aus den Berliner Museen, Staatliche Museen Berlin, Museum Dahlem*, edited by Ernst Kühnel, Berlin 1954, p. 12, no. 489.

59. Beaker with gold and enamel painting

Pale purple coloured glass with blue and white enamel colours and gold painting
Height 7.2 cm.
Berlin, Staatliche Museen, Islamisches Museum

The beaker is funnel-shaped, has a two-tiered foot and painted decoration in the "combed" pattern.

Egypt, 12th Century.

Reference: Ernst Kühnel, *Neuerwerbungen an islamischen Gerät, Berliner Museen, Berichte aus den preussischen Kunstsammlungen*, LXIII.–LXIV. 1942/43, p. 31, fig. 10.

60. Small bottle with lustre painting

Greenish glass with brownish-gold lustre painting
Height 9.5 cm.
Berlin-Dahlem, formerly Staatliche Museen, Islamic Section

A pear-shaped bottle with tyre-shaped foot and funnel-shaped neck, complete with a bulge forming a ring, extending to a widish opening. The bottle is lustre painted, the pattern consisting of a row of spirals between two thick horizontal lines. The neck-decoration, calligraphy-like, does not mean anything.

Egypt, 11th Century.

Reference: Carl Johan Lamm, *Mittelalterliche Gläser und Steinschnittarbeiten aus dem Nahen Osten*, Berlin 1929–1930, *Vol. I*, colour plate B/2, Vol. II, plate 34, 3; compare a similar glass in the Victoria and Albert Museum, London: W. B. Honey, *Glass*, London 1946, plate 16a.

61. Beaker with inscribed eulogy

Pale, slightly yellow glass, with red, blue, white and light green enamel painting
Height 19.5 cm.

Berlin-Dahlem, formerly Staatliche Museen, Islamic Section
Cylindrical body widening towards the mouth, with fused foot-ring. There is a decorative border in lustre and enamel painting below the rim, and, some distance below this, a swimming fish motif. Then comes a frieze with trefoil pattern and arabesque foliage in gold and enamel. Around the

middle of the vessel is a calligraphic border consisting of a eulogy, the words painted in gold surrounded by red. This is interrupted by three medallions with coloured leaves and arabesque foliage.

Syria, c. 13th Century.

References: Robert Schmidt, *Das Glas*, Berlin 1912, plate 26; *Islamische Kunst aus den Berliner Museen, Staatliche Museen Berlin, Museum Dahlem*, Catalogue, edited by Ernst Kühnel, Berlin 1954, p. 31, no. 293.

62. Beaker with horse and rider medallions

Yellowish, shallowly fluted glass with lustre and enamel painting
Height 31 cm.
Munich, Bayerisches Nationalmuseum

Straight-sided body, widening towards the mouth, flat, spreading foot. Trefoil frieze in lustre painting below the rim, below this a border of painted spirals. There is a wide border at the point where the vessel narrows, showing seated women and wine drinkers in gold and enamel painting executed on a fine background of gold scroll-work. The lowest frieze has three medallions each depicting a horse and rider.

Syria, c. 1290.

Reference: Carl Johan Lamm, *Mittelalterliche Gläser und Steinschnittarbeiten aus dem Nahen Osten*, Berlin 1929, plate 159, 1.

63. Bottle with trailed decoration

Blue corroded glass
Height 21 cm.
Berlin-Dahlem, formerly Staatliche Museen, Islamic Section

Squat, rounded body, on a thick foot-ring; a tall slender neck terminating in a flattened rim. At the base of the neck a thick ring of glass, twisted so as to form a series of scrolls (running dog), has been applied. The original gold decoration, three griffons and an inscription, can hardly be distinguished to-day.

Syria, end of the 12th Century.

Reference: Carl Johan Lamm, *Mittelalterliche Gläser und Steinschnittarbeiten aus dem Nahen Osten*, Berlin 1929, plate 89.

64. Perfume sprinkler, known as an Omom

Heavily corroded glass with rich gold enamel painting
Height 20 cm.
Berlin-Dahlem, formerly Staatliche Museen, Islamic Section

The body of the vessel is spherical, and a slender, chimney-like neck emerges from it. The decoration is hardly visible, owing to corrosion. On the shoulder, however, we can distinguish a frieze with a zig-zag pattern and gilt festooning on a blue background, punctured by medallions showing birds of prey and ducks. Between the medallions are yellow and green parrots. C. J. Lamm considers this bottle to belong to the group of vessels of acknowledged Chinese influence.

274

Persian, c. 1350.

References: Carl Johan Lamm, *Mittelalterliche Gläser und Steinschnittarbeiten aus dem Nahen Osten*, Berlin 1929, plate 176, 5; *Islamische Kunst aus den Berliner Museen, Staatliche Museen Berlin, Museum Dahlem*, Catalogue, edited by Ernst Kühnel, Berlin 1954, p. 31, no. 292.

65. Mosque-lamp

Light green glass with rich gold and enamel painting
Height 33.5 cm.
Berlin-Dahlem, formerly Staatliche Museen, Islamic Section

The lamp has a high, domed foot with a frieze of floral medallions and trefoils. The lower surface of the large body shows Chinese lotus flowers, and on the sides there is an inscription in praise of the Sultan al-Nasir Muhammed, in gold on a blue ground. There are six loops for suspending the vessel. Round the throat we see a gold painted frieze of leaves and flowers. A text from the Koran ornaments the neck, (Sure 24, 38) in blue on a gold background.

Syria, first half of the 14th Century.

References: Carl Johan Lamm, *Mittelalterliche Gläser und Steinschnittarbeiten aus dem Nahen Osten*, Berlin 1929, plate 190, 10; *Islamische Kunst aus den Berliner Museen, Staatliche Museen Berlin, Museum Dahlem*, Catalogue, edited by Ernst Kühnel, Berlin 1954, plate p. 13.

66. Beaker with tracery and spot decoration

Light glass with trailing and enamel spots
Height 8 cm.
Berlin-Dahlem, formerly Staatliche Museen, Islamic Section

The foot-ring is pincered, and the beaker is decorated in a pattern of tracery, produced by trailing, and in the spaces enamel spots in white, yellow, red and green, the "Lily-of-the-Valley" decoration, have been applied. The beaker was found in Syria, and was in the collection of F. v. Gans until 1913, when it was bequeathed to the Berliner Antiquarium.

Venice, 15th Century.

References: Robert Zahn, *Die Sammlung Friedrich Ludwig von Gans im Antiquarium*, in: *Amtliche Berichte aus den Königlichen Kunstsammlungen*, Berlin, XXXV, 1913, fig. 56; *Three Great Centuries of Venetian Glass*, The Corning Museum of Glass, Exhibition Catalogue, Corning, New York 1958, p. 29 and 31, fig. 3, 4 and 5; *Glass from the Corning Museum of Glass, Guide to the collections*, Corning, New York 1958, p. 35, fig. 30; *Glas aus vier Jahrtausenden*, Helmhaus Zürich, Exhibition Catalogue, Zürich 1956, fig. 23; Giovanni Mariacher, *Edle Gläser von der Antike bis Murano*, Munich 1962, plate 34.

67. Ewer

Dull yellow glass with blue spout and handle
Height 17 cm.
Berlin-Dahlem, formerly Staatliche Museen, Islamic Section

Spreading, ribbed foot, rounded body with spiral ribs, tighter round the tall, slender neck.

Venice (?) end of the 15th Century.

Reference: *Islamische Kunst aus den Berliner Museen, Staatliche Museen Berlin, Museum Dahlem*, Catalogue, edited by Ernst Kühnel, Berlin 1954, p. 31, no. 276. The ewer is here identified as Syrian, 10th–11th Century.

68. Bowl with typical Venetian scale-pattern

Dark green glass
Height 6 cm.
Munich, Bayerisches Nationalmuseum

The squat, rounded vessel stands on a relatively large foot-ring. A wide band round the body of the bowl shows light gilding, and white enamel spots, round which thin lines have been drawn, producing a scale-like pattern. A row of blue enamel spots is seen on the shoulders.

Venice, c. 1500.

69. Marriage goblet

Opaque white glass with enamel painting
Height 12.7 cm.
Prague, Národní Museum

Foot with raised ribs, bowl resting on seven leaf-like projections. Gilt scale decoration with red and blue enamel dots, and two medallions, each showing one of a marriage pair.

Venice, end of the 15th Century.

References: Karel Hettes, *Venezianisches Glas*, Prague 1960, fig. 1; For the style of painting see: *Three Great Centuries of Venetian Glass*, *The Corning Museum of Glass*, *Exhibition Catalogue*, Corning, New York 1958, fig. 11.

70. Beaker with grotesque painting

Colourless glass with enamel painting in various colours
Height 11.5 cm.
Prague, Národní Galerie

Hollow spreading foot with folded edge. Beaker, conical with blue and white gemmed border and grotesque painting showing putti mounted on dragons and crabs. Red and blue enamel streaks on the foot.

Venice, beginning of the 16th Century.

Reference: Karel Hettes, *Venezianisches Glas*, Prague 1960, fig. 10.

71. Goblet with jewelled enamel border decoration

Cup, clear glass with enamel painting; foot, blue glass
Height 17 cm.
Nuremberg, Germanisches Nationalmuseum

The foot is tall, conical and with a ribbed decoration. The base of the bowl is ornamented with a pincered ring, the cup itself bell-shaped with a border of enamel spots below the rim (gemmed or jewelled border).

Venice, late 15th – early 16th Century.

72. Four wine glasses

Colourless glass
Prague, Národní Galerie

The foot of each glass is flat and disc-like; one goblet has a thin stem gradually widening upwards, the remaining three have baluster stems; all stems are hollow. The bowls are conical, two waisted, and of various proportions.

Venice, first half of the 16th Century.

Reference: Compare Karel Hettes, *Venezianisches Glas*, Prague 1960, fig. 15.

73. Wine glass

Green, clouded glass, scale-gilt and jewelled
Height 14.5 cm.
Halle, Staatliche Galerie Moritzburg

Flat foot, hollow baluster stem and wide conical cup with gilt border and enamel spot (gemmed or jewelled) decoration beneath the rim.

Venice, c. 1500.

74. Ribbed glass

Light smoke-coloured glass
Height 20.5 cm.
Munich, Bayerisches Nationalmuseum

Hollow pedestal stem with folded rim, ribbed knop between two rings, and a trumpet bowl, ornamented with vertical ribbing on the lower two-thirds of its surface.

Hall-in-the-Tyrol, c. 1550.

References: Walther Bernt, *Altes Glas*, Munich 1950, fig. 6; Erich Egg, *Die Glashütten zu Hall und Innsbruck im 16. Jahrhundert, Tiroler Wirtschaftsstudien, 15.*, Innsbruck 1962, fig. 16.

75. Jug and beaker

Light coloured glass with gold and enamel painting
Height of jug 28 cm.; height of beaker 13 cm.
Leipzig, Museum des Kunsthandwerks

The jug shows a hollow pedestal foot with hollow shaft-ring, pear-shaped body, funnel-shaped neck and curving handle. Three lustre-painted friezes bordered with enamel dots ornament the neck. Four diamond-shaped medallions, also lustre-painted, may be seen on the body of the vessel. The base of the slightly conical beaker is kicked; there is a border of enamel dots below the rim.

Venice, first half of the 16th Century.

76. Flagon with *latticino* decoration

Colourless glass with opaque *latticino* decoration
Height 12 cm.
Halle, Staatliche Galerie Moritzburg

Pear-shaped vessel with plain foot-ring and bell-shaped cover. Two decorative handles in the form of sea-horses, in white glass with pincered additions linked by a ring of zig-zag trailing. *Latticino* decoration in vertical stripes with two alternating interlaced patterns.

Venice, c. 1600.

Reference: Otto Heinz Werner, *Schönes Glas in der Moritzburg zu Halle, Katalog der Staatlichen Galerie Moritzburg*, Halle 1957, fig. 13.

77. Flute-glass with criss-cross *latticino* work (*reticella* glass)

Clear glass with *latticino* decoration and silver-mount
Height 35 cm.
Nuremberg, Germanisches Nationalmuseum

Flat, disc-shaped foot, hollow baluster stem with silver knop, very tall, slender body. All the glass part exhibits the *latticino* technique.

Venice, early 17th Century.

78. Ewer, *latticino (reticella)* glass

Colourless glass with opaque white threads
Height 24 cm.
Dresden, Grünes Gewölbe

Foot in *latticino* glass with folded edge, and blue shaft-ring. Egg-shaped body with trefoil opening and high, curving handle.

Venice, c. 1600.

79. Snake-glass in the *façon de Venise*

Colourless glass, showing air bubbles, with blue, red and white glass in the wings
Height 17.5 cm.
Leipzig, Museum des Kunsthandwerks

Flat, spreading foot, short shaft linked to the trumpet-shaped bowl by an elaborate twist of red and white glass with blue pincered wings.

Cassel (in Germany), 17th Century.

80. Winged glass in the *façon de Venise*

Colourless glass with blue ornament
Height 20.5 cm.
Hamburg, Museum für Kunst und Gewerbe

Flat disc-like foot, stem consisting of six hollow knops alternately large and small, conical bowl. Attached to the stem, wings of blue threads with colourless pincered ornament, giving the appearance of sea-horses.

Probably Holland or Belgium, 17th Century.

References: A similar piece is illustrated in *Journal of Glass Studies, The Corning Museum of Glass, Corning Glass Centre, Corning, New York, Vol. III*, 1961, p. 139, fig. 20; It belongs to the collection of F. Smith jr., and is identified as "perhaps" Liège, 17th Century; Trenton, New Jersey.

81. Winged glass in the *façon de Venise*

Colourless glass with white and blue thread ornament
Height 18 cm.
Nuremberg, Germanisches Nationalmuseum

Flat, disc-like foot, plain shaft evident above and below the snake-like twist, this ornament having four pincered tabs and terminating upwards in two eagle-head-shaped wings. Slightly rounded bowl on a slender upper stem.

Probably Belgium, beginning of the 17th Century.

Reference: compare glass, shape and colour in *Die alten Gläser und Glasgemälde der Sammlung Bremen in Krefeld, Rheinisches Landesmuseum in Bonn, Exhibition catalogue*, 1964, No. 209, fig. 45, with similar decoration.

82. Goblet made to resemble agate (German: *Schmelzglas*)

Glass streaked with blue, green and yellow tones
Height 17 cm.
Munich, Bayerisches Nationalmuseum

Slightly domed foot, mould-blown stem with impressions of lions' heads, bell-shaped bowl.

Venice, most probably 19th Century. There are much earlier examples of *Schmelzglas* (compare B. Honey, *Glass*, London, Victoria and Albert Museum 1946, p. 8).

83. Beaker with Neptune motif

Opaque white glass
Height 15.5 cm.
Leipzig, Museum des Kunsthandwerks

The straight-sided, mould-blown beaker shows a lively image of Neptune with sea-chariots and tritons in high relief. The colour of the vessel changes according to how the light falls from white, through yellow, to purple tones.

Venice, 17th Century.

Reference: Walter Holzhausen, *Sächsische Gläser des Barock*, in: *Zeitschrift für Kunstwissenschaft*, Berlin, Vol. VIII, 1954, p. 107; *Three Great Centuries of Venetian Glass, The Corning Museum of Glass, Exhibition catalogue*, Corning. New York 1958, fig. 120; *Glass from The Corning Museum of Glass, Führer zu den Sammlungen*, Corning, New York 1958, fig. 39.

84. Spouted ewer, *façon de Venise*

Colourless glass
Height 11.5 cm.
Halle, Staatliche Galerie Moritzburg

Conical body with projecting kick in base, funnel throat, and curving spout. The tightly curving handle is knotted to a frilled ring, greenish-blue in colour, encircling the neck, and terminates in a spreading leaf-like extension.

Probably German, 16th Century.

85. Millefiori tankard

A mixture of colourless, yellow, white, reddish-brown and purple glass
Height 15 cm.
Halle, Staatliche Galerie Moritzburg

The slightly bulging tankard has a thick handle of clear glass and a silver lid with foliage ornament.

Venetian, c. 1600.

Reference: Otto Heinz Werner, *Schönes Glas in der Moritzburg zu Halle, Katalog der Staatlichen Galerie Moritzburg*, Halle 1957, fig. 14.

86. Wine glass with ribbed and applied pincered decoration

Very thin, colourless glass
Height 19 cm.
Hamburg, Museum für Kunst und Gewerbe

Flat, disc-like foot, tall, hollow blown stem, nipped towards the top, flowerlike bowl with eight ribs, and pincered trailing on the lower half.

Venice, late 16th–early 17th Century.

Reference: *Three Great Centuries of Venetian Glass, The Corning Museum of Glass, Exhibition catalogue*, Corning, New York 1958, fig. 114.

87. Plate with the arms of Duke Ernst of Bavaria

Colourless glass with gilding and unfired painting
Diameter 42.5 cm.
Munich, Bayerisches Nationalmuseum

In the centre of the plate, the arms of Bavaria with the date 1536, surrounded by bands of wreathed foliage. On the rim, more foliage decoration and four medallions showing heads of ancients. The plate belongs to the ewer shown in illustration No. 89.

Hall-in-the-Tyrol, 1536.

Reference: Erich Egg, *Die Glashütten zu Hall und Innsbruck im 16. Jahrhundert, Tiroler Wirtschaftsstudien, 15.*, Innsbruck 1962, fig. 6.

88. Goblet with cover

Colourless glass with diamond engraving, gilding and unfired painting
Height 34 cm.
Munich, Bayerisches Nationalmuseum.

Smallish foot, flattened ball knop, large egg-shaped body curving in at the shoulders, concave neck and double-domed cover ornamented with raspberry prunts. Four mask medallions are set on the shoulders. The painted decoration on the body shows Tyrolean eagles and wreaths of fruit framed by diamond engraved arcading. Moorish patterns embellish the remaining areas.

Innsbruck, Hofglashütte, 1570–1580.

References: Heinrich Kohlhaussen, *Geschichte des deutschen Kunsthandwerks*, Munich 1955, fig. 348; Erich Egg, *Die Glashütten zu Hall und Innsbruck im 16. Jahrhundert, Tiroler Wirtschaftsstudien, 15.*, Innsbruck 1962, fig. 31.

89. Spouted ewer in the Venetian style

Colourless glass with gilding and unfired painting
Height 33.5 cm.
Munich, Bayerisches Nationalmuseum

The foot of this vessel is hollow and conical. The lower part of the pear-shaped body shows carefully executed ribbing. A horizontal rib marks the beginning of the shoulder, which narrows towards the double ring encircling the neck at the point where it is joined by an S-shaped handle. Above this point the neck widens into a funnel shape and another double ring may be seen below the rim. The spout is tall and curved. The motifs of the painted decoration are as follows: on the foot, straight and wavy lines; on the lower part of the body, floral swags; above the horizontal rib, the arms of Bavaria (on either side of the ewer) surrounded by foliage; on the neck, foliage and line ornament. At the base of the spout, a medallion showing human figures has been applied.

Hall-in-the-Tyrol, 1536.

Reference: Erich Egg, *Die Glashütten zu Hall und Innsbruck im 16. Jahrbundert, Tiroler Wirtschaftsstudien, 15.*, Innsbruck 1962, fig. 7.

90. Porrón

Colourless glass with *latticino* decoration
Height 21 cm.
Berlin, Staatliche Museen, Kunstgewerbemuseum

Conical vessel with slender neck and wide, funnel-shaped rim, and straight conical spout jutting out at an angle from the body near the base. *Latticino* stripes and rosettes form the only decoration.

Spain, 17th Century.

91. Drinking vessel

Light, yellowish-brown, imperfect glass with blue additions
Height 19 cm.
Munich, Bayerisches Nationalmuseum

The base exhibits a conical kick, and foot-ring. Urn-shaped body, narrowing into a truncheon-shaped neck with no opening, but terminating in a double knop in blue. The handle, curving like a question-mark, joins a wavy line of glass which surrounds the neck. The spout is straight, almost vertical, and has a lip of blue glass. The Venetian influence is marked in this vessel.

Spain, possibly Barcelona, 16–17th Century.

92. Jarrita

Pale green glass with thread decoration
Height 15 cm.
Berlin, Staatliche Museen, Kunstgewerbemuseum

Solid, ribbed foot-ring; squat, rounded body extending into a large funnel-shaped neck, spiral trailing on neck and body, and wavy trailing near base. Four handles with pincered trails, and applied drops. A *Waldglas* with Moorish influence.

Southern Spain, 17th Century.

93. Cántaro

Colourless glass with white spirals
Height 28 cm.
Berlin, Staatliche Museen, Kunstgewerbemuseum

Hollow conical base with high kick, oval-shaped body with filler and sharp spout. Large circular loop as handle. Striped glass, with the exception of the handle.

Spain, Catalonia, 17th Century.

94. Stangenglas (in this shape also termed Keulenglas from German: *Keule* = club)

Pale yellow-green glass with impurities
Height 15 cm.
Eisenach, Thüringer Museum

Wide foot, high projecting kick, slightly conical body with three notched trailed spirals.

German, c. 1500.

Reference: Franz Rademacher, *Die deutschen Gläser des Mittlalters*, Berlin 1963, Plate 33.

95. Double conical bottle

Height 16 cm.
Nuremberg, Germanisches Nationalmuseum

Sturdy foot-ring, body in the form of two cones meeting at the base, formed by folding one bubble of glass. Upper part, roof-like, broader than the lower. Short, chimney-like neck.

German, c. 1500.

References: Bottles of this type are illustrated by Robert Schmidt, *Das Glas*, Berlin 1912, fig. 75, und Franz Rademacher, *Die deutschen Gläser des Mittelalters*, Berlin 1963, plate 16.

96. Beaker

Pale green glass with impurities
Height 10.2 cm.
Leipzig, Museum des Kunsthandwerks

Flared beaker with flattened foot-ring and high kick.

German, 15th Century.

Reference: Similar beakers in Franz Rademacher, *Die deutschen Gläser des Mittelalters*, Berlin 1963, plates 28a und b.

97. Spouted ewer

Pale green glass, ribbed
Height 10.8 cm.
Hamburg, Museum für Kunst und Gewerbe

Pear-shaped body with high kick, no foot-ring; S-shaped spout and handle pinched to form a tight loop. Ten slightly swirled ribs.

German, 15th Century.

Reference: Franz Rademacher, *Die deutschen Gläser des Mittelalters*, Berlin 1963, plate 17a.

98. Maigelein

Bluish-green glass
Diameter 10 cm.
Nuremberg, Germanisches Nationalmuseum

Footless, boat-shaped beaker with vertical ribbing.

German, 15th Century.

99. Nuppenbecher

Green glass
Diameter 9 cm.
Nuremberg, Germanisches Nationalmuseum

Crinkled foot-ring; squat, rounded body with seven applied drops drawn upwards to a point; heightened drinking rim.

German, 16th Century.

100. Honey-comb moulded glass

Green glass
Height 7 cm.
Cologne, Römisch-Germanisches Museum

Beaker-shaped with honey-comb ribbing, produced by blowing twice into a mould.

German, 15th Century.

101. Moulded jug

Dark green glass
Height 10.5 cm.
Eisenach, Thüringer Museum

Round foot-ring, pear-shaped body flaring towards the mouth, and diagonal ribbing. Applied handle pinched into shape.

Thuringia, 16th Century.

102. Tall Stangenglass

Brownish glass, hardly transparent owing to corrosive action
Height 42.6 cm.
Prague, Museum hlav. města Prahy

Pedestal foot, narrow cylindrical body ornamented with twenty-six horizontal rows of tiny, snake-like prunts. Above and below this decorated part, a ring has been applied.

German, first half of the 15th Century.

Reference: Franz Rademacher: *Die deutschen Gläser des Mittelalters*, Berlin 1963, plate 38b.

103. Krautstrunk

Dark green glass
Height 10.5 cm.
Leipzig, Museum des Kunsthandwerks

Convex beaker with twelve large applied drops, drawn upward to a point. Crinkled foot-ring and spreading lip.

German, c. 1500.

104. Stangenglass

Green glass
Height 19.5 cm.
Hamburg, Museum für Kunst und Gewerbe

Spreading foot, narrow cylindrical body and tall spreading

lip; decorated with six vertical rows of applied drops drawn out horizontally to a point.

German, c. 1500.

Reference: Franz Rademacher, *Die deutschen Gläser des Mittelalters*, Berlin 1963, plate 51.

105. Nuppenbecher with owner's inscription

Bluish-green glass with applied drops and blue circuit
Height 19 cm.
Leipzig, Museum des Kunsthandwerks

Crinkled foot-ring and conical kick in base, body widening slightly upwards and decorated with five rows of large drops. Blue thread some distance below the rim. A diamond-scratched inscription of later date referring to the then owner of the beaker is visible on the plain area beneath the rim: Hanns Sebastian Neithart von und zu Baustetten anno 1640 den 5 Martzii.

German, beginning of the 16th Century.

Reference: *Kunsthandwerk und Plastik aus Deutschland im Museum des Kunsthandwerks Leipzig*, edited by Anneliese Hanisch, Leipzig 1961, plate 8.

106. Römer

Dark green glass
Height 12 cm.
Eisenach, Thüringer Museum

Core-wound foot, hollow cylindrical shaft with raspberry prunt, a circuit of milled trailing beneath the spherical (cracked) bowl.

German, beginning of the 17th Century.

107. Nuppenbecher

Pale, bluish-green glass
Height 22 cm.
Nuremberg, Germanisches Nationalmuseum

Toothed foot-ring, cylindrical body with four rows of applied drops drawn upwards to a point, tall lip, widening upwards.

German, beginning of the 16th Century.

108. Mallet-shaped (Bocksbeutelform) bottle

Dark olive-brown glass
Height 23 cm.
Eisenach, Thüringer Museum

Hemispherical body with high projecting kick and tall, chimney-like neck. Glass circuit beneath the opening. The *Bocksbeutelform* is the traditional shape for the containers of Steinwein (wine from the Main area in Franconia).

German, 17th Century.

Reference: Walter Dexel, *Deutsches Handwerksgut*, Berlin 1939, fig. page 434

109. Ribbed spirit-flask

Clear, pale-green glass
Height 24 cm.
Eisenach, Thüringer Museum

Mould-blown bottle with smooth, vertical ribbing and projecting kick. Small opening and pewter screw-top.

German 16th Century.

Reference: Walter Dexel, *Deutsches Handwerksgut*, Berlin 1939, fig. page 432

110. Oviform bottle

Light green glass, with impurities, showing bubble texture
Height 28 cm.
Eisenach, Thüringer Museum

Oviform bottle with kick projecting slightly, smooth outline, and lead mount at the opening.

German, 16th Century.

111. Bottle with spiral trail

Rough, bluish-green glass
Height 23 cm.
Eisenach, Thüringer Museum

Body, inverted pear-shape with projecting kick. Opening with bulbous rim. Spiral trail round the neck.

German, 16th–17th Century.

Reference: Walter Dexel, *Deutsches Handwerksgut*, Berlin 1939, fig. page 434

112. Decanter derived from the Kuttrolf

Purple-tinged glass
Height 22 cm.
Eisenach, Thüringer Museum

Small foot; the lower body is large and spherical and is connected to the upper body, which is smaller and also spherical, by five tubes. Notched trailing on both parts.

German, 17th Century.

113. Ribbed bottle with pinched neck

Pale bluish glass, mould-blown
Height 24 cm.
Eisenach, Thüringer Museum

Deeply ribbed, mould-blown body with slightly projecting kick. Neck pinched to form four tubes. Funnel-shaped opening with wavy rim.

German, 16th–17th Century.

Reference: Anna-Elisabeth Liederwald, *Thüringische Gläser des 16. Jahrhunderts*, in: *Wissenschaftliche Zeitschrift der Friedrich-Schiller-Universität Jena*, Jena, 7, 1957/58, p. 360, fig. 20.

114. Four-tubed Kuttrolf

Pale yellowish-green glass
Height 17 cm.
Münich, Bayerisches Nationalmuseum

Wavy foot-ring; mould-blown body, rounded and coiled, with two milled trails encircling it; four short, spirally twisted tubes opening into the lip, which is inclined sideways.

German, 16th Century.

115. Four-sided decanter derived from the Kuttrolf

Clear glass
Height 31 cm.
Nuremberg, Germanisches Nationalmuseum

Square base, with a slight kick. Small upper and lower containers connected by one weak central and four corner tubes. Cylindrical neck.

German, 17th Century.

116. Wine jug

Bluish-green glass with pinched trailing
Height 30 cm.
Eisenach, Thüringer Museum

Wide, hollow foot, two-bulbed body and tall funnel mouth. Three diagonal pinched trails, and two zig-zag rings ornament the jug. Flattened handle.

German, 17th Century.

117. Daumenhumpen (Thumb glass)

Dark green glass
Height 21 cm.
Eisenach, Thüringer Museum

Sturdy foot, oviform body with six depressions into which finger and thumb were inserted. Notched trailed ring below the narrowing lip, and above the foot. The Daumenhumpen is shown in a copper engraving of 1554, "Man with Humpen", by Hans Lautensack, in the Staatliche Kunstsammlung, Weimar.

German, 16th–17th Century.

Reference: Anna-Elisabeth Liederwald, *Thüringische Gläser des 16. Jahrbunderts*, Wissenschaftliche Zeitschrift der Friedrich-Schiller-Universität Jena, Jena 1957/58, 7, No. 2/3, p. 359, fig. 15.

118. Ring-glass (German also *Ringelglas*)

Colourless, clouded glass
Height 14 cm.
Nuremberg, Germanisches Nationalmuseum

Tall, core-wound foot, flute-shaped also with milled spiral trail, and four rings hanging from angular loops.

German, 16th Century.

119. Small ewer

Pale green glass with impurities
Height 15 cm.
Eisenach, Thüringer Museum

Rounded body with slightly projecting kick and long chimney-like neck. Curving spout with wide base, small curving handle, bulbous where it joins the neck.

German, 16th Century.

Reference: Anna-Elisabeth Liederwald. *Thüringische Gläser des 16. Jahrbunderts*, in: *Wissenschaftliche Zeitschrift der Friedrich-Schiller-Universität Jena*, Jena 1957/58, 7, No. 2/3, p. 357, fig. 4.

120. Passglas

Colourless imperfect glass with circuits
Height 26 cm.
Leipzig, Museum des Kunsthandwerks

Cylindrical glass with spreading foot, high conical kick, and six horizontal milled trails, the fourth and fifth applied spirally. Rim smoothed out at the glory-hole.

German, 16th–17th Century.

121. Phallus glass

Green glass with mould-blown pattern
Length 25 cm.
Nuremberg, Germanisches Nationalmuseum

Hollow vessel with funnel-shaped opening.

German, 16th Century.

122. Trick glass in the form of a bear

Dull colourless glass, partly blown into a mould
Height 17 cm.
Nuremberg, Germanisches Nationalmuseum

Hollow, twisted body with hollow legs, arms and head applied. Funnel-shaped opening emerging from the animal's back.

German, 17th Century.

123/124. The Mainz Dean and Chapter Glass

Light, bluish-green glass with rich diamond point angraving
Height 32.5 cm.
Munich, Bayerisches Nationalmuseum

Broad stem with applied drops. Large bowl completely covered with diamond point engraving. The design consists of a view of Mainz in the year 1617, the arms of Archbishop Johann Schweikart von Kronberg (1604 to 1626) and the arms and initials of the members of the Cathedral Chapter. The inscription below the rim reads: "Celsitudo atque Nobilitas Florentissimae Metropolitanae Ecclesiae et Civitatis Moguntinae, ut es Anno 1617 constitu". The glass bears the signature: "I.R. fecit, 1617."

Netherlandish, 1617.

Reference: Ludwig F. Fuchs, *Die Glaskunst im Wandel der Jahrtausende*, Darmstadt 1956, p. 28 and fig. 19.

125. Armorial Humpen

Colourless glass with enamel decoration
Height 39 cm.
Munich, Bayerisches Nationalmuseum

Cylindrical vessel with only slightly curving walls, projecting kick, applied foot-ring and four-tiered cover terminating in a knop. As decoration, two coats of arms of the Palatinate, with the inscription "Otto Heinrich Pfaltzgrave bey Rhein-Dorothea Maria Pfaltzgrevin bey Rhein geborene Herzogin zu Würrttenberg". Between the arms the date 1596. Below the gemmed border the letters D.T.R.H. (Deum time regen honora).

Southern German, 1596.

Reference: Alice Bethe-Kränzner, *Emailglas*, Reallexikon zur deutschen Kunstgeschichte, 49, Stuttgart 1959, col. 73, fig. 4.

126. Humpen of the Magdeburg Cathedral Chapter

Pale green glass with enamel painting
Height 29 cm.
Leipzig, Museum des Kunsthandwerks

Slightly curving walls, and hollow applied footring. Cover not extant. Decorated area divided into two zones by gemmed borders. Arms of the twelve members of the Cathedral Chapter, and in the upper zone an image of St. Mauritius, with the date 1594.

Saxony, 1594.

References: *Kunstmuseum der Deutschen Demokratischen Republik, Mitteilungen und Berichte, Vol. 1*, 1957, fig. 63; for a further glass of this type (undated) see Robert Schmidt, *Das Glas*, Berlin 1912, fig. 84.

127. Humpen with equestrian figure of Gustavus Adolphus

Colourless glass with enamel painting
Height 17.5 cm.
Leipzig, Museum des Kunsthandwerks

Folded foot-ring and projecting kick. Cylindrical walls decorated with the equestrian figures of Gustavus Adolphus and Johann Georg with the inscriptions "Gustavus Adolphus König in Schweden" and "Iohann Georg. Churfürst zu Sachsen" and the date 1634. Between the figures, lily-of-the-valley ornament. Borders of plain gold stripes between rows of white enamel dots and scalloped lines.

Franconia, 1634.

128. Humpen with "Peeping Tom" scene

Pale green glass with enamel painting
Height 32 cm.
Nuremberg, Germanisches Nationalmuseum

Slightly curving *humpen*, with three-bulbed finial on cover. On the walls, a picture of a lover, peeping through the keyhole at a naked maiden lying on a bed. On the reverse side the inscription:

"Wen der Wolff daß Maul Also leckt
sich die Jungfrauw im Bett streckt
So hätt der Wolff gern ein Lam
undt die jungfrauw einen lieben man
anno 1694"
("The wolf looks on with greedy eye,
The maiden on her bed doth lie,
The wolf would fain devour the lamb,
The maiden hungers for a man")

The metal and the scale-border indicate Hessian manufacture.

Hesse, 1694.

Reference: Robert Schmidt, *Das Glas*, Berlin 1912, p. 191; Walther Bernt, *Sprüche auf alten Gläsern*, Freiburg i. Br. 1928, p. 32

129. Humpen with allegory of the Treaty of Westphalia

Colourless glass with enamel painting
Height, including cover, 31.5 cm.
Leipzig, Museum des Kunsthandwerks

Projecting kick and applied footring, cylindrical walls, cover with overlapping rim and triple bulbed finial. Below the rim, gold border with curving lines of white enamel dots. The painting shows the Holy Roman Emperor joining hands with the King of France and the Queen of Sweden, to the left and right kneeling ecclesiastics and citizens. Above the figures, God the Father and angels in the clouds. Biblical quotations on bands, a prayer of thanks on reverse, an "Anno Domini 1654". The border indicates Franconian origin.

Franconia, 1654.

130. Reichsadlerhumpen

Pale green glass with coloured enamel painting
Height 29 cm.
Leipzig, Museum des Kunsthandwerks

Cylindrical vessel with footring and conical kick. Two-headed eagle with imperial orb and crossed sceptres and 50 coats of arms arranged in groups of four (the Quaternion system). Signed: Böhmen (Bohemia), 1654.

Bohemia, 1654

131. Ochsenkopfglas (Ox-head glass)

Light green glass with coloured enamel painting
Height 16 cm.
Halle, Staatliche Galerie Moritzburg

Beaker in thick glass with projecting kick. The painting shows a forested mountain, with an ox's head at the summit. The rivers Eger, Saale, Main, and Naab issue from the foot of the mountain. Forest animals are seen among the trees, and a padlock and chain encircle the top of the mountain. Inscription on reverse, and in front the date 1722.

Fichtelgebirge, 1722.

132. Hallorenglas

Pale green glass with colourful enamel painting
Height 28 cm.
Halle, Staatliche Galerie Moritzburg

Club-shaped vessel divided into four horizontal zones, showing respectively a panorama of the town of Halle, a triple-gabled building, the salters' procession and the arms of the guild of salters between two apprentices. Dated 1681.

Saxony, 1681.

133/134. Beaker on three feet

Colourless glass with Schwarzlot (black) and translucent enamel painting
Height 10.8 cm.
Leipzig, Museum des Kunsthandwerks

Cylindrical beaker on three hollow ball feet. The painting, after Callot, shows a horse drawing a high two-wheeled cart, yokels, women and children. On a tree trunk the signature S.

Signed piece by Johann Schaper, Nuremberg, c. 1665.

Reference: *Kunsthandwerk und Plastik aus Deutschland im Museum des Kunsthandwerks Leipzig*, edited by Anneliese Hanisch, Leipzig 1961, plate 27.

135. Wine glass with pear-knopped stem

Colourless glass
Height 32.5 cm.
Halle, Staatliche Galerie Moritzburg

Flat foot, solid stem, with two annular knops at the top, and two at the bottom, and two hollow pear-knops, separated by a single annular knop. Conical bowl.

Holland, 17th Century.

Reference: *Schönes Glas, Staatliche Galerie Moritzburg, Halle, Exhibition Catalogue*, Halle 1957, No. 117.

136. Tall bowl, diamond-point engraved

Colourless lead-glass
Height 9.8 cm.
London, Victoria and Albert Museum
© Crown Copyright

On the bowl the arms of Butler Buggins (1646?–1690) of North Cray, Kent and Winifred Burnett his wife, whom he married on the 16th July 1676: among foliage a helmet, and above a bird with dragon's wings.

English, probably from the Savoy Glasshouse of George Ravenscroft, c. 1676.

137. Glass with diamond-point engraving

Colourless glass with a slight green tinge
Height 21 cm.
London, Victoria and Albert Museum
© Crown Copyright

Flat foot with foliage engraving, hollow fluted bulb between two ring knops; diamond engraving on the straight-sided bowl: in the upper portion a stag, a unicorn and two hounds; in the central area the inscription "John-Jone Dier 1581" and the arms of Queen Elizabeth. Leaf motifs in the lower part.

English, attributed to G. Verzelini, 1581.

Reference: Robert Schmidt, *Europäisches Glas, Die Sammlung Wilfried Buckley*, Berlin 1927, plate 83.

138. Goblet with portrait of man

Colourless lead glass
Height 25 cm.
Hamburg, Museum für Kunst und Gewerbe

The bowl of the glass shows a portrait of a man lighting his pipe, stipple engraved by Frans Greenwood, whose signature is clearly visible at the base of the bowl.

English glass, Newcastle-upon-Tyne, engraved in Holland, 1746.

139. Glass showing putti drinking wine

Colourless lead glass
Height 17 cm.
Halle, Staatliche Galerie Moritzburg

Another example of stiple engraved glass. The delicate engraving gives charm to this otherwise rather heavy-looking glass.

Holland, David Wolff, c. 1790.

140. Bottle with trailed thread decoration

Purple glass
Height 14 cm.
London, Victoria and Albert Museum
© Crown Copyright

Depressed, globular body with long vertical ribbed neck, and applied ring. Ribs extending from shoulder to form a reticulated pattern on the body.

England, c. 1675, probably from the Savoy glasshouse of George Ravenscroft.

141. Ruby-glass bottle

Ruby-red with ribbing, engraving and ormolu mount
Height 35 cm.
Dresden, Grünes Gewölbe

Tear-shaped bottle mounted on a foot, and with top, and chain. Cut flower-decoration on the spaces between the grooves of the ribbing.

Southern German, 17th Century.

Reference: Compare similar bottles in Ignaz Schlosser, *Das alte Glas*, Brunswick 1956, fig. 93.

142. Ruby-glass beaker mounted on silver-gilt foot

Height 12 cm.

Dresden, Grünes Gewölbe

Smooth beaker on a base supported by three ball feet.

Potsdam, end of the 17th Century.

143. Large covered goblet

Ruby-glass
Height 31 cm.
Eisenach, Thüringer Museum

Wide domed foot, broad stem with compressed ball knop, large, tallish bowl and cover with plain, oviform finial.

Probably Potsdam, 19th Century.

144. Group of musicians made at the lamp

Hollow white glass
Height 8–10 cm.
Lauscha, Museum für Glaskunst

Five Bohemian musicians, three with guitars, and a lamp-post. The cold painting has in parts flaked off.

Thuringia, Lauscha, end of the 18th Century (?)

145. Lamp-blown centrepiece of fountain and birds

Colourless and coloured glass
Height 40 cm.
London, Victoria and Albert Museum
© Crown Copyright

Colourless glass fountain, birds in coloured and spun glass, trees also in coloured glass.

England, middle of the 19th Century.

146. Glass with allegorical figures

Colourless, imperfect glass with wheel engraving
Height 24 cm.
Prague, Národní Galerie

Beaker-shaped glass on high folded foot. Engravings of "Potestas", "Nobilitas" and "Liberalitas" surrounded by flowers and insects. Signed C. Leman F. 1605. The figures are after copper engravings by the Flemish artist Johann Sadeler, who received privilege for his engravings from the Emperor Rudolf II.

Caspar Lehmann, 1605.

Reference: Robert Schmidt, *Das Glas*, Berlin 1912, fig. 122; F. X. Jiřík, *České sklo*, Prague 1934, plate XVIII, fig. 42 and 43.

147. Covered goblet with hollow stem

Clouded, yellowish glass with polished and unpolished wheel engraving
Height 52.3 cm.
Leipzig, Museum des Kunsthandwerks

Wide, folded foot, hollow stem with one ball and twelve discs. Cover with two hollow ball knops and multiple collars. Engraving of the Prodigal Son with the four scenes: Leave-taking, Carousing, the Swineherd, and Return, separated by tall trees. On the cover, engraved landscape.

Attributed by Erich Meyer-Heisig to Georg Schwanhardt the Elder (c. 1665); Annegrete Janda-Bux suggests the Thuringian Master IH, c. 1710.

Nuremberg glass with Thuringian engraving, c. 1710.

References: Annegrete Janda-Bux, *Der Thüringer Glasschnitt im 17. und 18. Jahrhundert*, Leipzig, Thesis 1962; Erich Meyer-Heisig, *Der Nürnberger Glasschnitt des 17. Jahrhunderts*, Nürnberg 1963, WT 49.

148. Covered goblet with floral decoration

Colourless glass with polished and unpolished wheel engraving
Height 23.5 cm.
Leipzig, Museum des Kunsthandwerks

Flat foot with leaf-garlands, cut stem with red and green spiral threads, facet-cut pointed cover with minute flower and leaf patterns and two areas with figures of lions.

Bohemia, beginning of the 18th Century.

149. Goblet with arms of Count Schaffgotsch

Clear, colourless glass with cutting in high relief
Height 20 cm.
Prague, Národní Galerie

Flat, wide foot, solid pillar stem with upper part enveloped in cut foliage. Conch-shaped bowl with rich leaf decoration and arms of Count Schaffgotsch.

Silesia, Hirschberg Valley, c. 1690.

References: F. X. Jiřík, *České sklo*, Prague 1934, plate XXIII, fig. 51 and 52; J. R. Vávra, *Das Glas und die Jahrtausende*, Prague 1954, fig. 190.

150. Covered goblet with view of Leipzig

Violet-hued glass, with *Hochschnitt* and *intaglio* engraving
Height without cover 21.5 cm.
Leipzig, Museum des Kunsthandwerks

Angular foot with *Laub und Bandelwerk* engraving (formal strap-work and foliate patterns). Facetted rosette under foot. Facetted baluster stem, conical bowl with palmette foliage in the lower part, and on facing sides. In between, a view of Leipzig with the inscription "Es lebe die Berühmte Handelsstadt Leipzig" (Long live the famous trading town of Leipzig). On the other side a Rococo scene of a lady and her lover. On the rim, shell scroll-work, fruit and foliage. Small landscapes on the remaining areas.

Silesia, c. 1760.

151. Covered goblet with Venus and Adonis motif

Colourless glass with cameo-relief engraving
Height 43.5 cm.
Arnstadt, Schlossmuseum (Castle Museum)

Flat foot with solid ball and baluster stem, conical bowl, domed cover with pointed finial. Foliage frieze engraved on the foot. On the bowl, a scene with Venus and Adonis beneath tall trees. Venus, seated on a tree stump, lays her hand on Adonis's hip, and he lets his right hand rest on her shoulder. Cover engraved with landscape, ruins and small figures.

Thuringia, signed I.H. (Heinrich Jäger or I. Hartmann), c. 1715–1720.

Reference: Annegrete Janda-Bux, *Der Thüringer Glasschnitt im 17. und 18. Jahrhundert*, Leipzig, Thesis 1962, Catalogue No. 160.

152. Two engraved glasses

Lead-crystal glass
Height c. 13 cm.
London, Victoria and Albert Museum
© Crown Copyright

a) Glass with conical bowl, and engraving of Prince Charles Edward, the Young Pretender, and air-twist stem with two knops.

b) Bucket-shaped bowl, rose motif engraving and double-knopped air-twist stem.

England, 18th Century.

153. Candlestick

Opaque-white glass
Height 30 cm.
London, Victoria and Albert Museum
© Crown Copyright

Wide domed foot, spirally ribbed shaft; tall nozzle and foot enamel painted.

England, c. 1760.

154. Covered goblet with representation of Neptune

Colourless potash-lime glass with rich cutting and engraving
Height 41 cm.
Hamburg, Museum für Kunst und Gewerbe

Scale cutting on foot; baluster stem with scale and diamond pattern. Cylindrical facetting on the lower part of the bowl, above this shallow eyelid facets, and circular facets on the rim. This decoration is repeated on the cover. On the bowl a representation of Neptune with trident and flowing urn in a woody landscape

Potsdam-Zechlin; unsigned piece by Elias Rossbach, c. 1720

155. Wineglass with Silesian stem

Colourless lead-crystal
Height c. 17 cm.
London, Victoria and Albert Museum
© Crown Copyright

Folded foot, Silesian stem, the shoulder moulded with the words "God save King George"; plain bowl with thick base.

English, c. 1715.

156. Wine glass with gilt decoration

Colourless glass
Height 17.5 cm.
London, Victoria and Albert Museum
© Crown Copyright

Flat foot, air-twist stem double knopped. On the wall of the slightly bell-shaped bowl in a frame of rocaille ornament is the inscription "Families Friends and Favourites".

English, c. 1750.

157. Glasses with engraved decoration

a) Drinking glass with engraved decoration
Colourless lead-crystal with a slight yellow tinge
Height 22 cm.
Corning, New York, The Corning Museum of Glass

Short, hollow, knopped stem with "George Trisler" and the date 1793 on the bowl among foliage ornament.

North America, John Frederick Amelung Glassworks, New Bremen, Maryland 1793.

b) Covered glass with engraved decoration
Colourless lead-crystal
Height 28.8 cm.
Corning, New York, The Corning Museum of Glass

Rectangular foot, conical bowl, cover with finial. On the bowl a representation of Tobias and the Angel between rocaille motifs, surrounded by the inscription: "Happy is he who is blessed with virtuous children. Carolina Lucia Amelung. 1788."

North America, John Frederick Amelung Glassworks, New Bremen, Maryland, 1788.

c) Bottle with engraved decoration
Colourless glass tinged slightly greyish-green
Height 17.2 cm.
Corning, New York, The Corning Museum of Glass

Rounded body with short neck and slightly thickened rim. On the wall "F. Stenger 1792" among floral motifs.

North America, John Frederick Amelung Glassworks, New Bremen, Maryland, 1792.

158. Tankard with painted decoration

Opaque-white glass
Height 11.5 cm.
London, Victoria and Albert Museum
© Crown Copyright

Cylindrical tankard showing painted landscape with youth carrying stick and basket, dressed in knee-breeches and feathered hat.

England, c. 1760.

159. Cut-glass dish

Diameter c. 40 cm.
London, Victoria and Albert Museum
© Crown Copyright

The cut design consists of a central rosette, the points of which indicate the division of the plate into nine sections. Star motifs form the remaining decoration. Raised rim.

England, c. 1770.

160. Zwischengoldglas with coloured painting

Colourless glass with facetting
Height 8 cm.
Leipzig, Museum des Kunsthandwerks

Facetted beaker with a stag-hunting scene in red, green and brown paint, red and green foliage decoration, and acanthus friezes. On the base a gilt riding scene.

Bohemia, c. 1730.

161. Zwischengoldglas with hunting scene

Colourless glass with facet-cutting
Height 8.5 cm.
Halle, Staatliche Galerie Moritzburg

Facet-cut poly-angular beaker. There is a hunting scene (rider with lance) round the beaker, bordered by two acanthus-friezes. The engraving is executed on gold-leaf on the interior and silver-leaf on the exterior surface. Sealed joint of the two glasses round the rim.

Bohemia, about 1735.

162. Glass with gilt monogram

Colourless glass with facetting and sealed-in double wall
Height 11 cm.
Leipzig, Museum des Kunsthandwerks

Cylindrical glass with almond- and lentil-shaped facetting round the base. Red gilt medallion with the monogram A.W., surrounded by silver and gold floral wreath. Reverse of the medallion, silver inscription on red: "Wer bey Leerung dieses Bechers, seine Freunde liebt und ehrt, dem wünsche ich, daß sich das Glücke tausendfach bey ihm vermehrt. ("Whosoever empties this glass, loving and honouring his friends, I wish that his happiness may increase a thousandfold".) Mildner fec. a Gutenbrunn, 1797." In the bottom of the glass, *Zwischenglas* image of St. Agnes with a lamb and the inscription: "Sanct Agnes V., et. M." Base, silver gilt with gilt rosettes.

Austria, Gutenbrunn, Johann Josef Mildner, 1797.

163. Glass with view of Dresden

Colourless glass with transparent enamel painting
Height 10.5 cm.
Leipzig, Museum des Kunsthandwerks

Footless beaker. View of Dresden with the Hofkirche, Elbe bridge and small figures of townspeople. Below right of the picture the signature "Mohn", and left "C.v.S. 1815". Border of leaves and larkspur flowers below the rim. The plan for the decoration was applied to the glass as a transfer print. C.v.S. (C. v. Scheid) was a pupil and collaborator of S. Mohn.

Dresden, signed piece by Samuel Mohn, c. 1810.

Reference: Gustav E. Pazaurek, *Gläser der Empire- und Biedermeierzeit* Leipzig 1923, p. 171 and fig. 150.

164. Glass showing St Stephen's Cathedral, Vienna

Colourless glass with cutting, gilding and translucent enamel painting
Height 11.5 cm.
Leipzig, Museum des Kunsthandwerks

Flared beaker with ribbed, gilt-ridged foot. Gold acanthus design frieze below rim. Scene of St. Stephen's Cathedral, executed mainly in sepia tones, surrounded by border of corn-ear motif. On reverse, the inscription: "Domkirche zu St. Stephan in Wien". Star-shaped cutting under the foot.

Vienna, Anton Kothgasser, c. 1825.

Reference: Gustav E. Pazaurek, *Gläser der Empire- und Biedermeierzeit*, Leipzig 1923, p. 193.

165. Glass showing the ages of man

Colourless glass with slight yellow tinge, cut and engraved
Height 11.5 cm.
Leipzig, Museum des Kunsthandwerks

Foot deeply incised all round and forming triangles which are criss-cross cut. Cylindrical body engraved with the ages of man. Beneath the flight of steps, a small scene showing the christening drive and the funeral procession. The visible inscriptions read as follows: "10 a boy, 20 a youth, 30 a man, 40 a success, 50 the turning point, 60 onset of old age."

German, c. 1815.

166. Sweetmeat bowl and cover

Colourless, slightly greyish cut glass
Height 27.5 cm.
Leipzig, Museum des Kunsthandwerks

Massive round foot star-cut in base. Lower part of the body and stem facet-cut, body with cut relief diamonds. Facet and diamond relief cutting in alternating bands on the cover and finial.

Northern German, c. 1820.

167. Pear-shaped ewer showing Cupid and Psyche

Cut lead-crystal
Height 30.5 cm.
Leipzig, Museum des Kunsthandwerks

Plain foot, pear-shaped body, tall ringed neck and trefoil opening with long handle attached. On the body of the vessel, an engraving of Cupid, about to release his bolt, and Psyche, bound to a tree. Below, a frieze in the "laufenden Hund" (running hound) pattern.

English lead crystal and German engraving, c. 1850.

168. Glass with engraving of Venus

Lead-crystal glass with engraving, polished and unpolished
Height 8.5 cm.
Hamburg, Museum für Kunst und Gewerbe

Venus is shown, seated in a chariot drawn by two swans. A dove is perched on each of her wrists. A flower frieze ornaments the flared rim.

Paris, Charpentier, c. 1810.

References: Franz Adrian Dreier, *Geschnittene Gläser von Charpentier*, *Glastechnische Berichte*, 34, Frankfurt/M. 1961, p. 282ff., fig. 1; Gustav E. Pazaurek, *Gläser der Empire- und Biedermeierzeit*, Leipzig 1923, p. 40, fig. 21.

169. Goblet

Lead-crystal glass
Height 36 cm.
Munich, Bayerisches Nationalmuseum

Relatively small foot with radial cutting, hexagonal stem and large bell-shaped bowl richly decorated with formal high relief and *intaglio* engraving. Cut beading on rim.

Ireland, beginning of the nineteenth century.

170. Mould-blown vessels

a) Mould-blown bottle, "pitkin Type"
Transparent green bubbled metal
Height 16.5 cm.
Corning, New York, The Corning Museum of Glass

Rounded body with short neck, double moulded.
(After being blown into a finely ribbed mould, the glass bubble was swiftly revolved and then blown into a second, more widely ribbed mould).

North America, early 19th century.

b) Mould-blown bottle, known as a "Grandfather"
Light amber-coloured glass
Height 22.4 cm.
Corning, New York, The Corning Museum of Glass

Rounded body with short widening neck and double-moulded ribbed decoration. North America, attributed to Ohio, probably Zanesville Glassworks, first half of the 19th century.

c) Mould-blown sugar bowl
Transparent light amber-coloured glass
Height 16 cm.
Corning, New York, The Corning Museum of Glass

Wide foot-ring, funnel-shaped, vertically ribbed bowl narrowing below the dish-like rim.

Double domed with slight spiral ribbing.

North America, possibly Zanesville Glassworks, Ohio. c. 1815–1830.

171. Sugar bowl and jug

a) Sugar bowl
Green glass
Height 9.5 cm.
Corning, New York, The Corning Museum of Glass

Domed foot, wide rounded bowl with two nipped and knotted handles. Domed lid with finial. North America, Southern New Jersey, possibly Wistarberg or Glasburg, 18th century.

b) Jug with trailed decoration
Colourless glass
Height 18 cm.
Corning, New York, The Corning Museum of Glass

Wide foot, rounded body with tall wide neck and curving handle. Fine trailed threads round the neck. On the body garland-like trailing. The jug belongs to a type known as the McKearin Type 1.

North America, attributed to the Lancaster or Lockport Glassworks, New York, c. 1850.

172. Rosenwasserflasche

Cobalt-blue glass, blown into a mould
Height 39 cm.
Hamburg, Museum für Kunst und Gewerbe

Foot-ring, high kicked base, globular body with long S-shaped neck and vertical mouth. A fine spiral ribbing ornaments throat and body.

Persia, probably Shiraz, 18th century.

173. Ewer

Dark green glass
Height 24 cm.
Berlin, Staatliche Museen, Islamisches Museum

High kicked base with wide applied foot-ring; tear-shaped body, bulge at throat and funnel-shaped opening. Widely curving handle. Tall curving spout with pincered wing-like appendages.

Persia, 17–18th century.

174. Vase in Persian style

Olive-green glass with trailing
Height 17.5 cm.
Eisenach, Thüringer Museum

Round foot, low bulging body and tall funnel neck with trailed thread decoration. Thick, twisted trailing round the lower part of the neck and, extending from this, four handles drawn down along the body in pinched trails. The late

Persian style in which the bottle is made does not exclude the possibility that it was made at a German glass-house, probably in Thuringia, for the Persian market. There are records of such orders to Bohemian manufacturers. A very similar bottle is attributed to Andalusian workshops by A. W. Frothingham.

Probably Thuringia, 19th Century.

References: Compare similar piece in *Glas, Katalog des Kunstgewerbe-museums der Stadt Köln*, edited by Brigitte Klesse, Cologne 1963, no. 563; and Alice Wilson Frothingham, *Hispanic Glass*, New York 1941, fig. 64.

175. Bowl

Opaque white glass with red cut overlay
Diameter 24.5 cm.
Berlin, Staatliche Museen, Ostasiatische Sammlung

Red foot-ring, wide rimmed bowl. Decoration of plum blossom and birds cut from the red overlay.

China, c. 1950.

176. Decorated bottle

Opaque white glass with red cut overlay
Height 19.5 cm.
Hamburg, Museum für Kunst und Gewerbe

Mallet-shaped vessel. On the body, a dragon flying over water. On the neck, clouds and bats in flight.

China, 18th Century.

Reference: Martin Feddersen, *Chinesisches Kunstgewerbe*, Berlin 1939, fig. 154.

177. Snuff bottle

Opaque whitish glass with red cut overlay
Height 10.5 cm.
Hamburg, Museum für Kunst und Gewerbe

Round, laterally flattened bottle with small foot-ring, short neck, and hemispherical stopper. The decoration, on a dull white background, consists of the creatures of the zodiac. On the neck, simple foliage decoration.

China, 18th Century.

Reference: Martin Feddersen, *Chinesisches Kunstgewerbe*, Berlin 1939, fig. 155.

178. Snuff bottle

Colourless glass with painting on inner surface
Height 9.5 cm.
Berlin, Staatliche Museen, Ostasiatische Sammlung

Shallow foot-ring, rounded bottle with short neck. The front view shows two riders.

China, 18th Century.

179. Tall vase

Dark purplish glass with gold mount on rim
Height 36.5 cm.
Berlin, Staatliche Museen, Ostasiatische Sammlung

Baluster-shaped vase without decoration. Tall vase with rounded shoulders and short wide neck.

China, 18th Century (Ch'ien-lung period).

180. Vase of cut overlay glass

Colourless, wine-red and yellow glass, with deep and shallow cutting, engraving and acid etching respectively
Height 32 cm.
Leipzig, Museum des Kunsthandwerks

Tall, curved vase with rim folded inwards. Decoration: pansy leaves and flower in the lower region, in dark colours on a deep wine-red background. A lightening of the colours towards the middle into yellowish tones on a white background. Pale wine-red background in the upper part. Signed: Gallé.

France, Émile Gallé, Nancy, c. 1900.

181. Vase with clematis-flowers

Yellowish-green and brownish-purple glass
Height 13.5 cm.
Halle, Staatliche Galerie Moritzburg

Heavy rounded foot, slender vase with small opening. Clematis-flower and -leaf decoration.

France, Émile Gallé, Nancy, c. 1900.

182. Vase of cut overlay glass

Multi-coloured overlay glass
Height 64 cm.
Owned by Klaus Beyer, Weimar

Wide, hollow foot, truncheon-shaped vase, shouldered and with a short neck. Decoration: lake landsape at dusk with tall trees. Foot black, trees dark brown, sky yellow to reddish, landscape in shades of green. Signed: "Daum Nancy".

France, Daum frères, Nancy, c. 1900.

183. Vase with inlaid and trailed thread decoration

Opaque blue, green and purple iridescent glass, red inner surface showing through
Height 9.5 cm.
Leipzig, Museum des Kunsthandwerks

Footless, squat bulbous vase with short smallish neck. Thread inlay in spiral patterns. Trailing in a twig-like design. Signed underneath: "L.C.T."

U.S.A., Louis Comfort Tiffany, New York, c. 1900.

184. Onion-shaped vase

Red, yellow and brown glass
Height 34 cm.
Hamburg, Museum für Kunst und Gewerbe

Small onion-shaped body and long neck, widening gradually into a flower-shaped opening.

185. Tulip-shaped glass

Coloured glass, made at the lamp
Height 32 cm.
Hamburg, Museum für Kunst und Gewerbe

Stem in blue glass with spiral twist in the middle. Two lanceolate leaves in copper-green glass attached to stem. Tulip-shaped bowl with metallic surface produced by lustre flashing. Signed on the thin foot: "C. Köpping."

Germany, Karl Köpping, Berlin, c. 1900.

Reference: Compare similar glasses in Gustav E. Pazaurek, *Moderne Gläser,* Leipzig, without date, fig. 2.

186. Bowl with inward curving rim

Purple and green lustre glass with trailed decoration
Diameter 20 cm.
Leipzig, Museum des Kunsthandwerks

Rounded bowl with slightly projecting base and wavy rim.

Bohemia, manufactured by Josef Pallme, Steinschönau, c. 1900.

187. Beaker with Broncit decoration

Colourless glass, acid etched
Height 10 cm.
Prague, Národní Galerie

Cylindrical beaker divided into 27 equal zones, each containing a medallion with stylised flowers.

Vienna, Josef Hoffmann, 1912.

References: Gustav E. Pazaurek, *Kunstgläser der Gegenwart,* Leipzig 1925, p. 153; A. S. Levetus, *Art and crafts at the Austrian Museum for Art and Industry, Vienna, The Studio,* London, Vol. 55, fig. p. 32.

188. Bowl with Broncit decoration

Clear glass, cut and acid etched
Height 8 cm.
Prague, Národní Galerie

Many-sided bowl, basically oval in shape, with straight walls and decorated with a geometrical pattern and medallions showing various animals.

Vienna, J. and L. Lobmeyr, designed by Urban Janke, Blottendorf, 1912.

189. Tumbler

Lead crystal glass, facet-cut
Height 12 cm.
Leipzig, Museum des Kunsthandwerks

Conical tumbler with six facet-cut sides, hexagonal base, and round rim.

France, Cristalleries de Baccarat, c. 1900.

190. Glass sculpture – hyaloplastic – (Resting Ox)

Lead crystal glass, moulded and cut
Length 15 cm.
Leipzig, Museum des Kunsthandwerks

The ox, its head inclined towards the left, rests on a rectangular base.

France, Cristalleries de Baccarat, 1927.

191. Tall bowl

Yellow
Height 18 cm.
Leipzig, Museum des Kunsthandwerks

Small, thick foot-ring and tall curved bowl. The apparent impurities in the glass are intentional, the aim being to produce a vessel of antique appearance.

England, J. Powell & Sons Ltd., London, 1927.

References: *Europäisches Kunstgewerbe 1927, Berichte über die Ausstellung,* published by Städtisches Kunstgewerbemuseum zu Leipzig, Leipzig 1928, fig. 96.

192. Vase

Sea-green
Height 25 cm.
Leipzig, Museum des Kunsthandwerks

Slightly concave ground base, tall, curved body, mould-blown to produce a scale-like pattern, and wide rim.

England, J. Powell & Sons Ltd., London, 1927.

193. Beaker-shaped vase

Pale green glass
Height 12 cm.
Leipzig, Museum des Kunsthandwerks

Solid foot, bowl widening upwards, the wall becoming thinner towards the rim. Marked "Orrefors F.V. 1742" on the base.

Sweden, Orrefors Glasbruk A.B., Orrefors, 1937.

194. Wine glass

Smoke-coloured glass
Height 23.5 cm.
Leipzig, Museum des Kunsthandwerks

Wide conical foot drawn upwards into a stem, bell-shaped bowl. Leaf-decoration melted on to the lower part of the bowl, the stalk twisted round the stem.

Sweden, Orrefors Glasbruk A.B., Orrefors, 1930.

195. Tall bowl with dancing maidens

Pale blue glass with unpolished cutting
Height 16 cm.
Leipzig, Museum des Kunsthandwerks

Foot smaller than base of bowl. Bowl slightly bell-shaped, engraved with angel performing act of sacrifice and dancing maidens with veil draperies. On foot and rim friezes of acanthus-like leaves. Marked "Orrefors Simon Gate 310." 1927. H. Bayer.

Sweden, Orrefors Glasbruk A.B., Orrefors 1927.

196. Bowl with matt surface

Colourless glass
Height 9.5 cm.
Leipzig, Museum des Kunsthandwerks

Hemispherical bowl with small cut foot-ring. The external surface is cut in such a way as to obtain a semi-matt appearance, and strewn with fully-matt engraved spots. Signed "H.M." on the foot.

Germany, Hanns Model, 1937.

197. Shallow bowl depicting John the Baptist

Lead crystal with cutting in deep relief
Diameter 28.5 cm.
Leipzig, Museum des Kunsthandwerks

Bowl of thick glass with very deep cutting executed on the underside, polished and unpolished, representing John the Baptist. Signed "XXVI RS."

Germany, Richard Süssmuth, 1926.

Reference: *Europäisches Kunstgewerbe 1927, Berichte über die Ausstellung*, published by Städtisches Kunstgewerbemuseum Leipzig, Leipzig 1928, fig. 47.

198. Shallow bowl with cut motif

Lead crystal glass
Diameter 31 cm.
Leipzig, Museum des Kunsthandwerks

Thick glass. Kneeling woman cut into the underside.

Stuttgart, Kunstgewerbeschule, Klasse Wilhelm von Eiff, executed by Hans Klein 1927.

Reference: Compare similar piece in *Europäisches Kunstgewerbe 1927, Berichte über die Ausstellung*, published by Städtisches Kunstgewerbemuseum Leipzig, Leipzig 1928, fig. 73.

199. Bottle and Decanter

a) Mould-blown "Washington bottle"
Green glass with mould-blown decoration
Pint size
Corning, New York, The Corning Museum of Glass

Flat oval bottle with short neck. The mould-blown decoration shows the American eagle surrounded by sunrays, the motto *E Pluribus Unum*, and the letters T. W.D. (Timothy W. Dyott, a self-styled 'doctor' or patent medicine man who went into glass-making to keep himself supplied with medicine bottles). On the reverse a portrait of General Washington with name inscribed above. On the narrow side of the bottle the names Adams and Jefferson July 4 A. D. 1776 (a patriotic reference to the fact that Adams and Jefferson died exactly half a century after the signing of the Declaration of Independence).

North America, Philadelphia, Kensington Glassworks, 1826–1833.

b) Mould-blown decanter
Colourless glass
Height 25.7 cm.
Corning, New York, The Corning Museum of Glass

The moulding techniques in this decanter are of particular interest. The vertical ribbing was achieved by pattern moulding. The glass was then blown into a full-size mould to achieve the sunburst and diamond diapering. Extra vertical ribbing was obtained by a "blow-three-mould" technique. Spiral ribbing has been applied around the neck.

Eastern North America, c. 1820–1835

200. Jug

Colourless lead glass
Height c. 25 cm.
Corning, New York, Steuben Glassworks

A martini or water jug designed and manufactured for sale by Steuben. The handle is formed of two crystal loops converging at the deeply sheared rim. The Steuben number is 8077.

USA, Steuben Glassworks. Contemporary piece, still in production.

201. Flower bowl

Steel-blue glass with cut decoration
Diameter 17 cm.
Eisenach, Thüringer Museum

Thick walled bowl standing on narrow polished foot. Rounded rim with cut fishbone decoration.

Germany, Oberlausitzer Glaswerke, Entwurf Wilhelm Wagenfeld, 1951.

Reference: *Oberlausitzer Glaswerke, Catalogue*, Weisswasser 1951, p. 42, No. 4404.1.

202. Urn-shaped vase

Steel-blue glass
Height 56 cm.
Leipzig, Museum des Kunsthandwerks

Wide-shouldered urn-shaped vase with flat handles applied.

Germany, Oberlausitzer Glaswerke, designed by Wilhelm Wagenfeld, 1940.

Reference: Fritz E. Hellwag, *Wilhelm Wagenfeld, Werkstattbericht 4*, published by Kunst-Dienst, Berlin 1940, fig. p. 23.

203. Ewer

Pale blue glass
Height 25 cm.
Leipzig, Museum des Kunsthandwerks

Rounded body, applied footring; short slender neck opening into a flattened lip. Tall curving handles. Signed underneath: "Venini Murano."

Italy, design by Paolo Venini, Murano, 1937.

204. Bottle with matt surface

Greyish-blue glass with ground surface
Height 27 cm.
Munich, Die Neue Sammlung

The bottle is angular in line with wide shoulders and short neck. Ball stopper.

Italy, design by Paolo Venini, Murano, 1958.

205. Flask in the *filigrana* technique

Amethyst-coloured *filigrana* and colourless glass
Height 40 cm.
Munich, Die Neue Sammlung

Tall tear-shaped bottle with *latticino* decoration. Base in clear glass. Acorn-shaped *latticino* decorated stopper.

Italy, design by Paolo Venini, Murano, 1959.

Reference: *Glass 1959, The Corning Museum of Glass, Exhibition Catalogue*, Corning, New York, 1959, fig. 192.

206. *Fazzoletto* bowl in the *sanfirico* technique

Colourless glass with white interlaced *latticino* work
Height 27 cm.
Munich, Die Neue Sammlung

Footless bowl with irregular folding. *Latticino* bands in two patterns.

Italy, design by Paolo Venini, Murano, 1952.

Reference: *Glas der Gegenwart – Baccarat, Orrefors, Venini, Gläser der Sammlung August Warnecke, Hamburg, Exhibition Catalogue*, essay by P. W. Meister, Hamburg, without date, fig. p. 47.

207. Multi-coloured vase

Colourless, light brown and steel-blue glass with matt surface
Height 14 cm.
Munich, Die Neue Sammlung

Italy, design by Paolo Venini, Murano, 1958.

208. Shouldered bottle with matt surface

Dark moss-green glass with colourless overlay and matt surface
Height 42 cm.
Munich, Die Neue Sammlung

Thick glass, tall, shapely bottle with sloping shoulders and chimney-shaped neck.

Italy, design by Paolo Venini, Murano, 1958.

209. Large bowl

Purplish lead crystal glass
Diameter 50 cm. (base elliptic)
Munich, Die Neue Sammlung

Italy, Ernesto Seguso, designed by Flavio Poli, Murano, 1958.

Reference: Similar bowl: *Glass 1959, The Corning Museum of Glass, Exhibition Catalogue*, Corning, New York 1959, fig. 182.

210. Four-coloured vase

Colourless, violet, blue and green glass
Height 34 cm.
Munich, Die Neue Sammlung

The vase is elliptical in cross-section.

Italy, Ernesto Seguso, Murano. Designed by Flavio Poli, 1958.

References: Gio Fonti, *Alta fedeltà. Gläser von Flavio Poli*, in Domus, Mailand 1964, 410, p. 50–52; Hans Heilmaier, *Kunstgläser aus der Manufaktur Ernesto Seguso nach Entwürfen von Flavio Poli, Die Kunst und das schöne Heim*, 54, München 1956, p. 300–303.

211. Squat bottle of speckled glass

White, grey and blue glass
Height 14.3 cm.
Munich, Die Neue Sammlung

Squat cylindrical bottle with rounded base and shoulders. Short, broad neck and thick, ring-like rim.

Holland, N.V. Koninklijke Nederlandsche Glasfabriek, Leerdam, 1959.

212. Bowl in mosaic-glass

Colourless, dark brown, blue and white glass
Diameter 12.5 cm.
Munich, Die Neue Sammlung

Italy, design by Paolo Venini, Murano, 1958

213. Vase with air-bubble decoration (Ariel glass)

Colourless and dark purplish glass
Height 16.4 cm.
Hanover, Kestner Museum

Tear-shaped vase in purplish glass with colourless overlay thickened at the base. Decoration in ariel technique (control of air-bubbles to form design), of a man serenading in a gondola with star motifs, girl's head and flowers.

Sweden, Orrefors Glasbruk A.B., Orrefors, designed by Edvin Öhrström, 1957.

214. Flower vase with overlay reticulated pattern

Greyish-green and colourless glass.
Height 20 cm.
Hanover, Kestner Museum

Tear-shaped vase, with inlaid *latticino* work. Thick plain foot.

Sweden, Orrefors Glasbruck A.B., Orrefors, designed by Sven Palmquist, Orrefors, 1953.

Reference: *Venini-Murano und Orrefors-Schweden, Kestner-Museum Hannover, Exhibition Catalogue*, edited by Christel Mosel, Hannover 1957, cat. No. 171.

215. Bottle with two superimposed layers

Greenish-grey and colourless glass
Height 24 cm.
Hanover, Kestner Museum

Tear-shaped vase with long neck and thick overlay, extremely thick round body and base. Rim smoothed at the furnace. Flat base.

Sweden, Orrefors Glasbruk A.B., Orrefors, designed by Nils Landberg, Orrefors, 1956.

References: *Venini-Murano und Orrefors-Schweden, Kestner-Museum Hannover, Exhibition Catalogue*, edited by Christel Mosel, Hanover 1957, cat. No. 132.

216. Slender vase

Colourless vase, acid-etched matt surface
Height 31 cm.
Munich, Die Neue Sammlung

Round foot, long stem widening slightly towards the top, bowl of exaggerated tulip-shape.

Sweden, Reijmyre Glasbruk, Reijmyre, 1958.

217. Water set

Colourless and smoke-coloured glass
Munich, Die Neue Sammlung

Jug: the shape resembles two cylinders, the smaller one forming the top half and drawn out into a lip. Applied handle, round in cross-section. High projecting kick. Glasses: again double cylinder shape, the larger one this time forming the upper part.

Finland, Notsjö Glasbruk, Notsjö, 1958, designed by Kaj Franck.

218. Bottle

Red and manganese-coloured glass
Height 20 cm.
Munich, Die Neue Sammlung

Bottle of exotic shape with lower part cylindrical, central part bulbous and tall neck with widening rim. Large ball stopper.

Finland, Notsjö Glasbruk, Notsjö, 1959.

219. Two cylindrical vases

Amethyst-coloured, dark blue and colourless glass, double-cased
Heights 17.5 and 30 cm.

Munich, Die Neue Sammlung

The upper-half mirrors the lower part in each vase; dividing "floor" in colourless glass.

Finland, Karhula littala Glasbruk, designed by Timo Sarpaneva, 1957.

Reference: *Glas, Gebrauchs- und Zierformen aus vier Jahrtausenden, Die Neue Sammlung, Munich, Exhibition Catalogue*, 1959, No. 95 and 96 with fig.

220. Vase

Dark steel-blue glass
Height 17 cm.
Munich, Die Neue Sammlung

Double conical shape, thick glass. Opening smoothed at the furnace.

Denmark, Holmegaards Glasværk, Holmegaard and Copenhagen, 1959.

221. Brandy bottle in the style of a Kuttrolf

Light greenish-blue glass with clear glass stopper
Height 26.5 cm.
Leipzig, Museum des Kunsthandwerks

Footless vessel, its upper and lower parts linked by five pincered tubes. Short neck with flat rim. Ball stopper.

Denmark, Kastrup-Glasværk, Copenhagen, 1960.

222. Two cylindrical vases

Dark bluish-green, rather transparent green
Height 37 cm.
Munich, Die Neue Sammlung

Denmark, Holmegaards Glasværk, Holmegaard and Copenhagen, 1958.

223. Bowl

Lead crystal glass
Diameter 27 cm.
Munich, Die Neue Sammlung

Wide bell-shaped bowl with thick foot.

England, J. Powell & Sons Ltd., London, 1958.

224. Dish

Light steel-blue glass
Diameter 32 cm.
Munich, Die Neue Sammlung

Thick foot, body small in diameter widening gradually. Very wide rim with the edge curving inwards.

Holland, N.V. Kononklijke Nederlandsche Glasfabriek Leerdam, 1958.

225. Vase

Glass with marbled effect
Height 17 cm.
Munich, Die Neue Sammlung

Footring in coloured glass, cylindrical vase of light and dark mottled glass with enclosed air-bubbles and irregular stripes.

Holland, N.V. Kristalunie Maastricht, 1958.

226. Parts of a drinking service

Colourless, very thin blown glass
Height: carafe 29.5 cm., wine glass 18,5 cm.
Munich, Die Neue Sammlung

Compressed cylindrical carafe on slender stem and flat foot, with tall neck and stopper with thread-like finial and tiny ball. Wine glass on a slightly wide foot, very tall thin stem, and with flattish conical bowl. Carafe executed after a design by Oswald Haerdtl, Vienna, dating from 1924. Wine glass designed by Stefan Rath, Vienna, 1954.

Austria, Glasmanufaktur J. & L. Lobmeyr, Vienna.

Reference: Robert Schmidt, *100 Jahre österreichische Glaskunst*, Vienna 1925, plate 28; Stefan Rath, *Lobmeyr*, Vienna 1962.

227. Vase

Steel-blue glass, cut
Height 32 cm.
Prague, Národní Galerie

Tall vase with convex silhouette, cut in a flat plane in front and behind. Extremely thick glass with a very narrow opening and ground top.

Czechoslovakia, Borské sklo glass-house, Nový Bor, designed by Pavel Hlava, 1959 (Prof. Pavel Hlava, born 1924, trained at the Prague College of Applied Arts, now employed by the Institute for Household Design, Prague).

Exhibition Catalogue, edited by Alene Adlerová, Leipzig 1964, No. 21.

228. Two-layer vase

Purple glass, with blue overlay
Height 50 cm.
Prague, Národní Galerie

Slender, two-bulbed vase

Czechoslovakia, Borské sklo, Glashütte Chribska, designed by Josef Hospodka, 1960 (Prof. Josef Hospodka, born 1923, trained at the Academy of Applied Art, Prague, is Director of the School for Apprentices at the Chribska Glassworks).

Reference: *Tschechoslowakisches Glas, Museum des Kunsthandwerks Leipzig, Exhibition Catalogue*, essay by Alena Adlerová, Leipzig 1964, No. 30.

229/230. Plate with sand-blast engraving

Lead-crystal glass
Diameter 36.2 cm.
Prague, Národní Galerie

Plate with slightly raised rim. Grill-like decoration. The cuts are about 10 mm. deep.

Czechoslovakia, designed and executed by Ladislav Oliva, 1959.

References: *Tschechoslowakisches Glas, Museums des Kunsthandwerks Leipzig, Exhibition Catalogue*, essay by Alena Adlerová, Leipzig 1964, No. 60; *Glass 1959, The Corning Museum of Glass, Exhibition Catalogue*, Corning, New York 1959, fig. 34.

231. Vase decorated with sand-blast engraving

Lead-crystal glass
Height 34 cm.
Prague, Národní Galerie

Tall straight-sided vase, narrowing slightly towards the top. Deep central band of decoration consisting of irregular ribbon-like motifs running vertically.

Czechoslovakia, Ladislav Oliva, 1960.

Reference: René Roubíček, *Ladislav Oliva*, in: *Tschechoslowakische Glasrevue*, XIX, Prag 1964, No. 9, p. 274–77.

232. Glass sculpture

Colourless glass with light brown prunts
Height 24 cm.
Prague, Národní Galerie

Sperical body with small prunts and eight hollow tentacle-like appendages. Free hand-work.

Czechoslovakia, National Glasswork Borské sklo, Nový Bor, design by René Roubíček, 1960 (Prof. René Roubíček, born 1922, received his artistic training at the Academy of Applied Arts in Prague; he is now chief supervising artist at the glassworks Borké sklo).

233. Lustre-decorated vase

Colourless glass with blue and red lustre decoration
Height 27 cm.
Prague, Národní Galerie

Lustre painting on the cylindrical body, depicting grotesque bird forms.

Czechoslovakia, Franticek Tejml, 1960.

Reference: *Tschechoslowakisches Glas, Museum des Kunsthandwerks Leipzig, Exhibition Catalogue*, essay by Alena Adlerová, Leipzig 1964, No. 79.

234. Vase with engraved line pattern

Colourless glass
Height 21.5 cm.
Prague, Národní Galerie

The network design is composed of thin horizontal, vertical and diagonal lines.

Czechoslovakia, Jiři Harčuba, Prague, 1960.

235. Hollow bowl with deep facetting

Lead-crystal glass
Diameter 45 cm.
Prague, Národní Galerie

Irregularly shaped bowl with deep irregular facetting.

Czechoslovakia, Borské sklo, Nový Bor, design by Miluše Roubíčkova, 1958.

Reference: XII *Triennale di Milano 1960, Esposizione Cecoslovaca, Exhibition Catalogue*, No. 240; *Tschechoslowakisches Glas, Museum des Kunsthandwerks Leipzig, Exhibition Catalogue*, essay by Alena Adlerová, Leipzig 1964, fig. 5.

236. Jug

Smoke-coloured glass
Height 13.5 cm.
Munich, Die Neue Sammlung

Squat round jug with slightly flared mouth, horizontal rim, small spout and prominent handle.

Germany, Glashütte Theresienthal, design by Karl Baumann, 1958.

237. Tall jug

Brown glass
Height 22.3 cm.
Munich, Die Neue Sammlung

Barrel-shaped jug with slanting rim and upward-curving spout, balanced by a sturdy handle.

Germany, Gralglashütte, Dürnau-Göppingen, design Heinrich Löffelhardt, 1954.

Reference: Bernhard Siepen, *Gralglas – ein Leistungsbegriff*, in: *Die Kunst und das schöne Heim*, 55, Munich 1957, p. 34–37.

238. Vase in alabaster-like metal

Lamp-blown glass
Height 15 cm.
Leipzig, private collection

Flattened base, tall diabolo-shaped vase.

Germany, designed by Ilse Decho, Leipzig, 1960.

239. Vase with cut decoration

Bluish-green glass with colourless casing
Height 20,8 cm.
Leipzig, Museum des Kunsthandwerks

Cylindrical in shape with wedge-shaped cutting forming window-like pattern.

Germany, Ilse Scharge-Nebel, Halle, 1964. (Ilse Scharge-Nebel, born 1904, trained at the Akademie für Kunstgewerbe, Dresden, working in Halle (Saxe-Anhalt) as artist in glass).

References: *Kunsthandwerk im Grassimuseum 1965, Museum des Kunsthandwerks Leipzig, Exhibition Catalogue*, publ. by Fritz Kämpfer, Leipzig 1965, Plate 84, Collection of writings on I. Scharge-Nebel: *Ilse Scharge-Nebel, Otto Scharge, Günther Laufer, Museum des Kunsthandwerks Leipzig, Exhibition Catalogue*, publ. by Fritz Kämpfer, Leipzig 1963.

240. Table glasses

Colourless glass
Height 12 cm.
Weimar, Hochschule für Architektur

A set of five glasses of equal height, each having slim bowl tapering to rounded bottom, slender, stem.

Germany, designed by Horst Michel, Weimar, 1964 (Professor Michel is director of the Institute of Interior Decoration in the School of Architecture at Weimar).

241. Blue glass vase with colourless insertions

Lamp-blown glass
Height 29.5 cm.
Leipzig, Museum des Kunsthandwerks

Tall cylindrical vase in eight sections, each section separately blown. Decorated with an abstract ribbon-like pattern running horizontally.

Germany, Albin Schaedel, Arnstadt 1962.

Reference: *Kunsthandwerk im Grassimuseum 1964, Museum des Kunsthandwerks Leipzig, Exhibition Catalogue*, edited by Fritz Kämpfer, Leipzig 1964, fig. 21.

242. Table glasses

Colourless and light grey glass
Height 7 to 13 cm.
Munich, Die Neue Sammlung

Heavy colourless foot in each case and simple curved bowl.

Germany, Gralglashütte Ltd., Dürnau-Göppingen, 1959.

243. Drug jars

Green and brown glass
Height 22 cm.
Munich, Die Neue Sammlung

Germany, Vereinigte Farbglaswerke Zwiesel, design by Heinz Löffelhardt, 1958

List of Museums

ACID-ETCHING: to make the surface of glass matt by treating it with a mixture of potassium fluoride and hydro-chloric acid (e.g. 100 parts of water, 10 parts of potassium fluoride and 1 part hydrochloric acid). The parts not to be affected are covered up with wax paraffin or colophon; a graded etching can also be achieved. The invention of this technique has been doubtfully ascribed to Heinrich Schwan-hardt (q.v.). There is a Nuremberg glass panel with an acid-etched inscription dated 1686.

Since Egermann (q.v.) the so-called colour-etching tech-nique was used in Bohemian glass: a thin layer of coloured glass different from the one of which the vessel was made was applied to the outer surface (flashing or casing), which was then etched, so that the subject of the etching appear-ed in clear glass.

AGATE: a precious stone, often with curious markings or with colours in layers or bands. Imitated in glass and known as *Schmelzglas* or sometimes as "calcedonio glass".

AGRICOLA, (Latinised from of the original *Bauer*), GEORG: born in Glauchau, Saxony, on March 24th, 1490, and died at Chemnitz on November 21st, 1555. In the course of his life he was headmaster in Zwickau, physician in the Joachimstal, and Mayor of Chemnitz. He is acknowledged as "the father of mineralogy", his most famous work being *De re Metallica, libri XII*, a treatise on mining and metallurgy published at Basle in 1556. The twelfth book deals with glass and contains descriptions of different manufacturing tech-niques.

Reference: Georgius Agricola, *Zwölf Bücher vom Berg- und Hüttenwesen*, transcribed into modern German by Carl Schiffner, Düsseldorf 1953.

ALABASTRON: ancient Egyptian cylindrical vessel with a rounded base and a broad rim. Two small handles were used for a chain or a string. Originally made of alabaster, it was used for cosmetic purposes, but was later exclusively used for putting into graves as provision for after-life. [Fig. 4]

ALTARE: Italian glasshouse near Genoa, founded probably in the XIth Century, always a rival of Venice. Whereas the emigration of glass-makers was regarded as a severe crime at Murano and punished as such, the Altarists had to work abroad temporarily, as it was laid down in the constitution of their *Universita dell' arte vitrea* in 1495. They founded glass-works in France and in the Netherlands. Thus indirectly they caused the rapid spread of the *façon de Venise*, especially since one has to assume that among them were numerous glass-makers who originally came from Murano.

Reference: Giovanni Mariacher, *Edle Gläser von der Antike bis Murano*, Munich 1962.

AMERICAN GLASS: The first glasshouse in the United States of America was founded in Jamestown, Virginia in 1608, but did not exist for very long. The actual development starts with the foundation of both glassworks in Wistarburg

in New Jersey by the German Caspar Wistar in the middle of the eighteenth Century, and in Manheim in Pennsylvania by the German Heinrich Wilhelm Stiegel towards the end of the same century. In both places a European influence prevails, although in a simpler and utilitarian way. Especially the everyday glasses of the Wistar works determine the American utility-style. In the first half of the nineteenth century, in about 1827, the celebrated dip-moulded glass, best seen in bottles, was succeeded by pressed glass. Tiffany's experiments (q.v.) strongly influenced Europe, especially Germany, Bohemia and Austria. Recently a tremendous search for new possibilities in the art of glass-making has been evident everywhere, especially in the fields of glass sculpture and the production of mosaic glass. [Figs. 157, 170, 171, 183, 184]

Reference: *Amerikanisches Glas aus drei Jahrbunderten*; Exhibition arranged by the Amerikahäuser in Germany; catalogue published by the Corning Museum of Glass, Corning, New York, 1955. McClinton, *American Glass*, Cleveland 1950: McKearin, *American Glass*, New York 1941.

AMPHORA: Ancient vessel for wine or oil. The form was first created in Egypt but later developed to its utmost refinement in Greece. It consists of a flat base and a slightly shouldered body, connected by two handles with a wide neck which is crowned by a distinct rim. The vessel is widest in the upper third. In its rational structure and grace-ful shape the amphora exemplifies the classical vessel. [Figs. 3, 6, 29]

ANCIENT GLASS: From the beginning of glass-making to about the fifteenth century A.D. It comprises glass from Egypt, Mesopotamia, Babylon, Syria, Rome and the Rheno-Romanic glass up to the onset of Frankish culture in the west and Islamic culture in the east.

References: Anton Kisa, *Das Glas im Altertume*, 3 Vols., Leipzig 1908; Federic Neuburg, *Antikes Glas*, Darmstadt 1962; Ancient glass technique: William E. S. Turner, *Die Leistungen der alten Glasmacher und ihre Grenzen*, in: *Glastechnische Berichte*, Frankfurt a. M., 30. Vol. 7, pp. 257–265 (1957); Waldemar Haberey, *Der Werkstoff Glas im Altertum*, in *Glastechnische Berichte*, Frankfurt a. M., 30: Vol. 12, pp. 505–509 (1957) and 31: Vol. 5, pp. 188–194 (1958).

APOSTLE GLASS: Enamelled *humpen* (q.v.) depicting the twelve Apostles. They were inspired by contemporary ceramic productions, especially the Kreussen *Apostelkrüge*, and were in use in Germany from the end of the sixteenth into the seventeenth Century.

ARIELGLASS: Manufacturer's name for two-layered glass embellished by figure-like air-bubbles. The technique was invented by Edvin Öhrström of the Orrefors Glassworks in Sweden. [Fig. 213]

ARYBALLOS: Ancient Greek globular bottles for cosmetic oils and balms. The small bottle, usually made of clay, was intended for daily use and carried around suspended on a string or chain.

AVENTURINE GLASS: Glass with inclusions of glittering metallic particles. It was made in Venice in the seventeenth and eighteenth centuries and the process was kept secret. The particles consist of metallic copper which is chemically produced when forge-scales and copper-oxide are added to the glass mixture. Pettenkofer re-invented the process during the second half of the nineteenth century.

BACCARAT: French town in the department Meurthe et Moselle, site of the glassworks *Compagnie des Cristalleries de Baccarat, Paris*. The foundation of the first glasshouse was laid in 1765. Since 1816 it has been owned by d'Artiques. They produce lead-crystal in the English fashion. The glasshouse is still one of the leading French glass manufacturers. [Fig. 189, 190]

Reference: James Barrelet, *La Verrerie en France*, Paris 1953; *Glas der Gegenwart, Baccarat, Orrefors, Venini*, Exhibition catalogue edited by August Warnecke, Hamburg, without date.

BALSAMARIUM: Ancient small container, usually in the form of a bottle, for cosmetics, balms, or fragrant oils. Because they were often found in tombs, they were popularly termed tear-bottles. Special forms of balsamaria are the amphora (q.v.), Lekythos (q.v.), Aryballos (q.v.), Alabastron (q.v.). Twin balsamaria are often to be found; they are usually looped or handled. [Figs. 4, 14]

BEADS: They were of importance in ancient glass-making and originated in Egypt. From the time of the VI Dynasty spirally twisted polychrome beads had been known. Beads were also made in Tell el-Amarna. Since about 1000 B.C., the so-called eye-beads had been made; after the seventh century B.C. beads with zig-zag patterns appear; the so-called mask-beads were made after the fifth century B.C., and millefiori-beads came into being after the third century B.C. Aggrybeads are many-layered, short, ribbed glass-canes, the ends of which were obliquely cut, thus producing a fancy zig-zag pattern.

The age-old manufacture of beads was brought to life again by the glass-makers of Venice. During the Biedermeier period, small cylindrical beads were employed in making embroidered miniature mosaics. Later, in the nineteenth century, short tube-shaped beads (bugle beads; German: *Schmelzperlen*) were in fashion; they were also used for making curtains later in the *Jugendstil* period. [Fig. 5]

Reference: Frederic Neuburg, *Antikes Glas*, Darmstadt 1962; Gustav E. Pazaurek, *Glasperlen und Perlenarbeiten aus alter und neuer Zeit*, Darmstadt 1911.

BEINGLAS: Semi-opaque white glass produced by adding the ashes of calcined bones to the mixture. Mainly of Bohemian and Thuringian manufacture, it was produced in large quantities in the second half of the eighteenth and the first half of the nineteenth century, largely influenced by porcelain. This opaque glass was usually decorated by enamel pigment.

In Bohemia it was often cased and cut. Beinglas is not identical with the so-called milk-glass, the Italian *lattimo* or *latticino*, the colouring of which results from tin oxide. This has been produced in Venice since the sixteenth century. *Beinglas* is, however, related to the so-called opal-glass, which is also made with the help of bone ashes or hartshorn; the degree of opalescence depends on the ratio of ingredients in the glass-mixture. Anton Neri (q.v.) has described how to make a peach-blossom coloured opal glass.

BERKEMEYER: Dutch drinking glass of the seventeenth century. Similar to the *Römer* but with a cylindrical lower part and a bulging bowl.

BIEDERMEIERGLÄSER: German and Bohemian glasses peculiar in style to the first half of the nineteenth century. Partly influenced by the heaviness of English lead-glasses, the form, especially the feet, becomes bold and massive. In the beginning of the period facetting is predominant. Later a subtle and refined form of engraving flourishes (Dominicus Bimann, q.v.). Along with it coloured glass becomes fashionable: Hyalith glass, (q.v.); Lithyalin (q.v.); surface staining (q.v.); etc. Entirely new types of glasses came into being e.g. Friendship-glasses, commemorative glasses, *Badegläser* etc. (v. Kothgasser, Mohn). [Figs. 162 – 168]

Reference: Hermann Trenkwald, *Gläser der Spätzeit (um 1790-1850)*, Vienna 1923; Gustav E. Pazaurek, *Gläser der Empire- und Biedermeierzeit*, Leipzig 1923.

BIMANN, DOMINIC: Bohemian glass engraver, born at Neuwelt in the Bohemian part of the Riesengebirge in 1800, died 1857. He is the most important engraver of the Biedermeier period. His outstanding merit rests in his achievements in portrait engraving. Unlike the miniature painters, he executed his commissions mainly in the famous spas of Western Bohemia, especially at Franzensbad where he took up residence during the watering season. Therefore his glasses are widely scattered, and many of his works went to Russia. Characteristic objects of the crafts of the Biedermeier period are engraved roundels executed by him.

Reference: Gustav E. Pazaurek, *Gläser der Empire- und Biedermeierzeit*, Leipzig 1923: Julius Streit and Otto Lauer, *Dominik Bimann: Lebensbericht und Meisterarbeiten des besten Porträtgraveurs*, Schwäbisch Gmünd 1958.

BLANKÄTZUNG: Method of polishing crystal glass with a chemical solution. This is deeper than polishing by hand. The solution consists of one part hydrochloric acid, one part water and two parts sulphuric acid.

BOHEMIAN AND SILESIAN GLASSMAKING: The art of glass-making in Bohemia reached a climax after the invention of potash-lime glass around the year 1685. It was allegedly invented by Michael Müller, a master craftsman at the glasshouse of Winterberg in South-West Bohemia. It flourished until the middle of the eighteenth century.
To distinguish properly between Silesian and Bohemian glass-making is hardly possible, since the areas overlap.

It started with goblets, engraved in high relief, from the Hirschberg Valley in Silesia from about 1680 until 1690. At the turn of the century the Bohemian goblets with facet-cutting and flower- and fruit- ornamentation take the lead. They again are succeeded by Bohemian wine-glass-shaped goblets with a delicate formal foliage decoration. After 1725 the Silesian side of the Riesengebirge dominates the scene with goblets, the decoration of which begins with heavy formal foliage and gradually develops into the *rocaille*.

Flanked by these ornaments, scenes, towns or landscapes are depicted. Besides goblets, sweetmeats in the shape of small boats were made. The period between 1680 and the middle of the nineteenth century is also marked by the flourishing Bohemian glass trade; in many places all over the globe Bohemian glass companies were established. [Figs. 148–150, 160, 161]

Reference: Edmund Schebek, *Böhmens Glasindustrie und Glashandel*, Prague 1878; J. R. Vavra, *Das Glas und die Jahrtausende*, Prague 1954

BRANDENBURG GLASS: The main Brandenburg glass-houses were Krimnitz, Marienwalde, Drewitz, Potsdam, and Zechlin. Until the beginning of the seventeenth century Brandenburg depended on the import of glass from Bohemia, Saxony, Thuringia and Schleswig-Holstein. In 1602, under the patronage of the Elector Joachim Friedrich, the first Brandenburg glasshouse was founded near Krimnitz. It was moved to Marienwalde in the year 1607 where it existed till 1825. From 1653 to 1792 there existed a second glasshouse at Krimnitz. These early Brandenburg glass-houses usually produced drinking glasses, window-panes and enamelled glass. The products were very similar to Bohemian glass, since the craftsmen were recruited from Bohemia. With the foundation of the Potsdam glasshouse near Drewitz by the Elector Friedrich Wilhelm in 1674, begins the really important period of glassmaking in Brandenburg (see Potsdam). [Fig. 154]

Reference: Robert Schmidt, *Brandenburgische Gläser*, Berlin 1914.

BRONCIT-DECORATION: A method of glass-decoration with a blackish matt paint application usually in geometrical patterns; designed by Josef Hoffmann (q.v.) around 1910, and executed by the Viennese glass-manufacturers Lobmeyr (q.v.). This decoration forms one of the elements of the style of the Wiener Werkstätte (Vienna Crafts Centre). [Figs. 187, 188]

BUTZENSCHEIBE = BULL'S-EYE-GLASS: Palm-sized flat glass disc with a central boss ("the bull's eye") on one side, produced by rapid rotation of an opened glass sphere on the iron in the furnace.

BYZANTINE GLASS: Glass from Constantinople (Byzantium), continuation of the tradition of the ancient art of glass-making and further development of some branches of it, e.g. the decoration of glass in gilt and enamel pigment. Also noteworthy are Byzantine glass mosaics. The Em-

peror Constantine decreed in 337 A.D. that glass-makers (*vitriarii*) were to be exonerated from all public duties. In the sixth century A.D. numerous Jewish glassmakers lived in Constantinople. The Venetian art of glass-making was strongly influenced by Byzantine glass. After the conquest of Constantinople in 1224 Byzantine glass-makers worked in Venice.

Reference: Frederic Neuburg, *Antikes Glas*, Darmstadt 1962.

CÁNTARO: Spanish, special vessel with an apical circular handle and two spouts pointing in opposite directions, one short and wide for filling the vessel, and one long, slightly curved and tapering for pouring out the liquid. In use from the seventeenth to the nineteenth century. [Fig. 93]

CASED OR FLASHED GLASS: The superimposing of a layer of contrasting coloured glass onto the glass bubble before blowing. In ancient glass this was only a preliminary to the cameo-carving executed on the vessel, and not a decorative technique in itself. The outer coloured layer was cut away to produce a relief pattern, and the skilful craftsman was able to achieve an effective gradation of tone. The technique of cameo-carving cased glass was developed to its height in Alexandria and Rome during the time of the Roman Empire. The craftsman has in many cases attempted to reproduce the effects of layered gem-stones, such as onyx. The Portland Vase is a supreme example of this technique.

The cutting was much simplified in the nineteenth century, so that the superimposed layer was left very thin (flashed) and engraved in flat patterns. The casing of glass is important in Chinese work, (as shown by the snuff bottles), and from this Gallé drew the inspiration for his *verres doublés*.

In more recent glass-work, brighter, thicker layers of glass are superimposed on darker and thinner layers, with attractive results. Efforts are being made in Czechoslovakia to give a new lease of life to the cut-cased glass (Karel Wünsch in Nový Bor). [Figs. 175–178, 180, 181]

CHARPENTIER: French goldsmith and engraver of the beginning of the nineteenth century. Five glasses engraved by this artist are known. The engraving is in each case of extreme subtlety, reproducing in the most delicate detail the tiniest flowers in the garland ornament and the fine curls on the heads of his figures. The name of the engraver was imprinted on a case containing a glass. We learn that Charpentier was a "graveur sur pierres et sur tous metaux. Il grave les cristaux dans un nouveau genre ..." ("engraver of precious stones and all metals. He engraves crystal in an entirely new style ..."). This last sentence no doubt refers to English lead-crystal or English lead-crystal style of cutting.

The engraver's widow, Madame Desarnaud-Charpentier, received a gold medal at the Paris Industrial Exhibition of 1819 for her exhibits. It was stated in the *Annales de l'Industrie Étrangère ou Mercure Technologique* that she obtained her raw material from the Établissement d'Antigues. This establishment, which produced lead glass in the English fashion, was founded in Vonêche near Brussels in 1802, and was later, after the setting-up of subsidiary glass-houses in Baccarat and Val-Saint-Lambert, in a position to make the French glass-industry independent of English lead-crystal importation; it had been reliant on foreign materials throughout the previous century. [Fig. 168]

CINERARY URNS: Spherical or ovate glass-urns, usually with a broad rim. The cover has two erect loop handles. They originated from Greek clay vessels (Hydria) and were used at first for storage purposes and later as burial urns. The earliest burial urns known date from the time of the first Roman Emperor, the latest from the middle of the third century A.D. They were found in large numbers in burial grounds, especially in Gaul and the Rhineland. [Fig. 23]

"COMBED" DECORATION: This type of decoration is principally associated with ancient Egyptian glass. Threads of coloured glass were pressed onto the glass vessel whilst it was still hot, and these were then "combed" or "tooled" into zig-zag, feather and other patterns. [Figs. 1, 3]

CROWN GLASS: Flat sheets of glass for the making of windows etc. A blown bubble of glass was cut open, rapidly rotated and reheated from time to time until it formed a flat disc on the iron. This process gave the familiar bull's-eye window panes of the Middle Ages.

CRYSTAL GLASS: The word crystal is derived from the Greek *Krystallos*, that is, "clear ice", rock-crystal, hence its use in referring to very clear transparent glass. Venetian glass of the sixteenth century was known as *crystallo* because of its contrast with the green *Waldglas* (q.v.). In the seventeenth century, use of the term was extended to embrace the Bohemian potash-lime crystal glass. Subsequently it was applied to English lead-crystal which was introduced, very successfully, onto the market in the eighteenth century. Today high quality cut glass is generally meant when the term is used, and lead-crystal must contain at least 18% lead oxide.

CRYSTALLO-CERAMIE: Otherwise known as "sulphides". Reliefs (mainly portraits) moulded from a soft paste of porcellaneous, glass or china clay content, then sculpted into fine detail, and fired. The resulting medallions were inserted into a bubble of glass from which the air was extracted, so that they were solidly lodged in the mass of glass. The process was perfected by Apsley Pellatt (q.v.) although he derived his knowledge from a French source. His brilliant flint-glass was excellent for this purpose, showing off the medallions to perfection, and the whole was further enhanced by the deep cutting of the heavy metal.

CULLET: Glass sherds which are re-used in the melting process.

CUTTING: Cutting of glass followed soon after the advent of glass-blowing. The age-old technique of cutting precious stones and rock crystal was transferred to glass. Glass cutting in ancient times reached its climax in the Cologne area in the third and fourth centuries A.D. The great revival took place in Bohemia and England in the seventeenth and eighteenth centuries. Some special patterns achieved by cutting are: facet cut, producing shallow diamond fashions; flute cresting, producing parallel hollowed or notched flutes; star cutting, producing diamond patterns of all sorts; curved cutting, producing shallow, circular or crescent-shaped slices.

For shallow facet-cutting a vertically rotating iron wheel, which is fed with emery or sand, is employed. The cut surface is then successively polished by a fine grained stone wheel, a wooden wheel and tripoli powder. [Figs. 38, 166, 235]

CZECHOSLOVAKIAN GLASS: Since 1918, glass produced in Czechoslovakia has been known by this term, although Czechoslovakian literature includes under it the earlier Bohemian glass. To complicate the issue still further, outside Czechoslovakia modern products are often referred to as "Bohemian". The contemporary Czechoslovakian glass industry is aware of its long tradition and continues to use classical techniques of glass cutting and engraving to a greater extent than most other countries, although adapting these techniques to the modern idiom. Some 100 designers, most of them ex-students of the Prague School of Art, are active at the present time, involved with both industrial and art glass. [Figs. 227-235]

References: F. X. Jiřík, *České Sklo*, Prague 1934; Museum des Kunsthandwerks Leipzig, *Tschechoslowakisches Glas*, Exhibition Catalogue (Text A. Adlerová), Leipzig 1964; *Tschechoslowakische Glasrevue*, monatl. Zeitschrift, Prague; J. R. Vávra, *Das Glas und die Jahrtausende*, Prague 1954; J. Raban, *Modernes Böhmisches Glas*, Prague 1963 (this work gives a list of names of most of the leading Czechoslovakian glass-designers).

DAUMENHUMPEN, DAUMENGLAS: Large cylindrical or barrel-shaped goblet with circular indentations (*Fingernäpfen*), most probably to give the hand a firm hold of the glass. [Fig. 117]

DAUM FRÈRES: The Daum brothers founded a glassworks in Nancy at the time of the Franco-Prussian war. Greatly influenced by Gallé (q.v.), they produced glass in his style, yet not lacking in characteristics of its own. The firm still exists, now known as the "Crystalleries de Nancy", producing, according to its tradition, glass which reflects the spirit of the times. [Fig. 182]

DECOLORISING: Decolorising always played an important role in the history of glass technique, since the sands used for glass-making almost always contained impurities, mostly traces of iron which gives the glass a greenish tint. The usual decolorising agent is oxide of manganese, the so-called glass-maker's soap. J. Kunckel (q.v.) in his *Ars vitraria*, when referring to Neri's first book, advises German glass-makers to use pyrolusite, that is oxide of manganese in a mineral form, as "soap" rather than the more expensive

Piedmontese manganese, though the method was said to be somewhat out of date. He regrets that he is unable to publish his new and much better recipe for making glass by adding carbonate of lime. Decolorising agents act either physically by chromatic neutralisation or chemically by releasing oxygen, e.g. arsenic; the greenish ferrous oxide is transformed into yellowish ferric oxide.

DIAMOND: The hardest precious stone known; chemically, pure carbon. Diamond splinters are used for diamond point engraving (line engraving and stipple engraving).

DIAMOND ENGRAVING: The glass surface is scratched with a diamond point. It was employed for "writing" the owner's name on a vessel from the fifteenth century onwards. Its use for artistic decoration started presumably in Venice. The usual ornaments consist of formal plant motivs such as scrolled foliage, large flowers or scroll-work. Shades were obtained by short parallel strokes. From Venice diamond engraving was taken over by glass-makers at Hall-in-the Tyrol. Here it was practised together with cold painting. Again borders of formal plant motivs are typical. The heyday of diamond engraving came in the second half of the sixteenth century. Later it was applied also in Bohemia, Silesia and the Electorate of Brandenburg. The artistic climax was reached in the Netherlands. Used on a very large scale it offered an alternative to the decoration in enamel pigment which was so fashionable in Germany. Glasses with engraved calligraphy were common; many such glasses with mottos and proverbs are still extant.

Among the improved Dutch diamond engravers the sisters Roemers of Amsterdam (Anna Roemers, 1583–1651 and Maria Tesselschade, 1594–1649) and Willem Jacob van Heemskerck of Leiden (1613–1692) are notable. In the eighteenth century the line-engraving was superceded by the delicate technique of stippling with a diamond point (David Wolff and Greenwood q.v.). Both line-engraving and stippling by means of the diamond point have been revived in our time and further developed into modern styles of decoration, especially by Ilse Scharge-Nebel. [Figs. 88, 105, 123, 124, 136, 137]

DIATRETA GLASS (VASA DIATRETA): Term given by J. J. Winckelmann to a small group of glasses of fourth century A.D. Rheno-Roman origin. These glasses consist of a solid vessel which is surrounded by a basket-like network of interlaced ornaments. The outer layer of ornaments is joined to the solid inner part of the cup-shaped vessel by short glass struts. In Roman literature the name *diatretum* was indiscriminately used for all glass vessels which were cut by the wheel, perhaps even for vessels cut out of precious stones. Many difficulties in the philological interpretation of ancient documents result from this remarkable confusion. There are conflicting opinions about the process of making *diatreta* glasses. Since Winckelmann it has been supposed that the vessels were made of one solid piece of glass which was then cut. While Anton Kiesa, Fritz Fremersdorf and

Otto Doppelfeld hold this view, other experts propose a different method. Wilhelm von Eiff thinks the glass was produced by moulding in two independent layers; according to K. Wiedmann the connecting rods were perhaps fused on by soldering; O. Knapp regards this question as unsolved and categorically denies the possibility of the design being undercut. More recent research (O. Doppelfeld) supports the theory that the *diatreta* glasses were produced by the cutting of a solid vessel; this opinion is founded on a passage of Roman literature (from a fragment of Oppian). There it is said that in the event of unsuccessful cutting of a *diatreton* vessel damages had to be paid. The craftsman was to be permitted to accept the work only on condition that he took no risk whatsoever. Doppelfeld concludes from this legal clause that the *diatreta* cutter was put into a privileged position. Nevertheless the question remains whether or not the term *diatreta* referred to all kinds of cut glass or to glasses in Winckelmann's sense. – So far twenty-six *diatreta* glasses have been found inclusive of fragments. The most up to date reports on the subject are given by Doppelfeld, Harden and Toynbee. [Figs. 41, 42]

References: J. J. Winckelmann, *Werke III*, p. 113; Anton Kisa, *Das Glas im Altertume*, Leipzig 1908, p. 621; Bruno Mauder, *Diatreten und ihre Herstellungsweise*, in: *Keramische Rundschau*, Berlin: No. 25, p. 321 (1932); Oscar Knapp, *Diatreten und ihre Herstellungsweise*, in: *Keramische Rundschau*, Berlin 40: No. 9, p. 116–117 (1932); Hans Eiden, *Diatretglas aus einer spätrömischen Begräbnisstätte in Niederemmel an der Mosel*, in: *Trierer Zeitschrift*, Trier, 19: p. 26–40 (1950); Karl Wiedmann, *Das römische Diatret, mit den Augen des Hohlglastechnikers gesehen*, in: *Glastechnische Berichte*, Frankfurt a. M. 27: p. 33–44 (1954); Oscar Knapp, *Über die Herstellung der spätrömischen Diatret-Gläser*, in: *Silikattechnik*, Berlin 5: p. 378–381 (1954); Otto Doppelfeld, *Das neue Kölner Diatretglas*, in: *Germania*, Berlin 38: p. 403–417 (1960); Otto Doppelfeld, *Das Kölner Diatretglas und die anderen Netzdiatrete*, in: *Gymnasium* Heidelberg, Vol. 68: p. 410–424 (1961), Otto Doppelfeld, *Das Diatretglas aus dem Gräberbezirk des römischen Gutshofs von Köln-Braunsfeld*, in: *Kölner Jahrbuch für Vor- und Frühgeschichte*, Berlin, 5: p. 7–34 (1960/61); D.B. Harden und J. M. C. Toynbee, *The Rothschild Lycurgus Cup*, in: *Archaeologia*, 97: p. 179ff. (1959).

DISEASED GLASS: The disintegration of all alkaline chalk-glass, that is, all ancient glass which is subjected to humidity, water, carbon-dioxide or acids in the soil.

The "disease" takes on two forms: 1. an even disintegration of the entire surface, with a thin layer of scales, producing the familiar iridescence of ancient glass, forms; 2. deeper corrosion in the wall of the vessel for reasons unknown, or at points where the vessel was damaged. Both types of decay lead eventually to the total disintegration of the vessel. The process involved consists of the extraction of the alkali in the glass and the consequent increase in the silicic content. The final result of the process is silicic acid with small quantities of titanium, aluminium and iron.

Sometimes faulty knowledge of the correct proportions of the ingredients used in making glass resulted in an excess of alkali, and a glass "that is unstable in composition. Such 'diseased' glass develops a network of fine interior cracks, a sour-smelling liquid forms on its surface and it eventually decomposes and crumbles. This defect in its early stages was known in England as 'crisselling'" Honey p. 4.

References: Fritz Kämpfer, *Kranke Gläser*, in: *Neue Museumskunde*, Berlin, 6 1963, p. 211–214; Gustav E. Pazaurek, *Kranke Gläser*, Reichenberg 1903; Rolf Wihr, *Glasverwitterung und Möglichkeiten ihrer Behandlung*, in: *Trierer Zeitschrift*, Trier 24.–26. 1956–58, No. 1.

DOLPHIN BOTTLES: Small ancient vessels with fused decoration resembling sea animals, usually dolphins. They are products of Roman glass-making and were mainly made in Italy, Gaul and the Rhineland. They were usually worn suspended from the belt by a bronze chain or string.

Reference: A. Kisa, *Das Glas im Altertume*, Leipzig 1908, p. 768.

DOUBLE-GLASS: A. An outer glass, which was usually without a bottom, was made to fit exactly round an inner one (see also *Zwischengoldgläser*). The process is described by J. Kunckel (q.v.), Vol. I part 2, chapter 27. The inner surface of the outer beaker is painted to resemble marble and delicately veined; to the outer surface of the inner beaker gold-leaf is applied. When the two are put together, the outside of the double-walled beaker appears marbled, and the inner gilt. B. Two superimposed vessels (beaker or wine glass) which were given as wedding or friendship glasses. In the collection of the Germanisches Nationalmuseum in Nuremberg, there is a seventeenth century double-glass consisting of two superimposed wine glasses. The cover of the lower is crowned by a smaller one. The inscription "Vivat des Herrn (master), Vivat der Frau (mistress)" indicates the purpose.

EGERMANN, FRIEDRICH, 1777–1864: An outstanding Bohemian glass-manufacturer of the Empire- or Biedermeierperiod, born at Blottendorf near Haida. He decorated many of his glasses by staining them with amber or ruby colours (*Silber lasur* and *Kupferrubinlasur*, also termed *Kupferrubinätze*). The flashing, which was applied with a brush, served as a subsitute for the more complicated overlay-glass. Moreover, Egermann is the inventor of the famous *Lithyalin*, a glass which aimed at imitating precious stones and was produced in shades of dark red-brown, grey-green, dark green to bluish-green, also veined or marked.

References: Gustav E. Pazaurek, *Gläser der Empire- und Biedermeierzeit*, Leipzig 1923; Jarmila Brožová, *Vor hundert Jahren starb der berühmte böhmische Glasmacher Friedrich Egermann*, in: *Tschechoslowakische Glasrevue* 1964; 7, p. 201–204, Prague 1964.

EIFF, WILHELM VON: Stone-and glass- cutter, born 1890 at Göppingen in Swabia, died 1943. From 1922 professor at the Kunstgewerbeschule (art school) Stuttgart. His training took him to Paris (Lalique), Vienna (Stephan Rath) and northern Bohemia (Lobmeyr). He may be regarded as the greatest glass-engraver of the twentieth century. Wilhelm von Eiff was the first to make use of the flexible drive for glass cutting. [Fig. 198]

Reference: Gustav E. Pazaurek, *Kunstgläser der Gegenwart*, Leipzig 1925.

ENAMELLED DECORATION: Powdered glass coloured with metal oxides is applied to the surface of glass vessels by means of an oily medium, and then fired at a temperature of 700 to 800 °C. The application, which has a strong lead content, fuses into the glass surface, and the result is a fixed, shiny decoration, translucent or opaque.

The technique of enamel painting was employed in Egypt at the time of the Roman Empire, and later in Syria and the Rhineland. Its greatest period may be said to be represented by the Islamic glasses from Mesopotamia and Syria, produced at centres such as Raqqa, Damascus, and Aleppo in the thirteenth and fourteenth centuries. During the fifteenth Venice developed her own style of enamelled decoration which was the inspiration for the numerous German enamel-painted glasses which were at their best in the seventeenth century. Armorial bearings were at first the most popular motif with German artists; their scope was wider from the end of the sixteenth century, although the well-known representations of the *Reichsadler-Humpen*, the *Kurfürsten-* and *Apostelglas*, and hunting scenes or *Familiengläser* (family glasses) were frequently repeated. Mention must also be made of the *Ochsenkopfgläser* of the Fichtelgebirge and the *Hofkellereigläser* of the Saxon courts. The most important centres of German enamel-painting were in the Bavarian Forest, in Bohemia, Silesia, Franconia, Thuringia, Hesse, Saxony and Brandenburg. It is sometimes difficult to attribute a glass to a certain place of manufacture, unless there is some distinct local feature, since they had so many ornamental elements in common. Some indication of origin is provided by the border just beneath the rim: Franconian artists often painted a frieze of overlapping arches or zig-zag pattern; on Bohemian glasses we usually see a border of enamel dots, and in Hesse, gold borders with white dots, or after 1670 plain gold borders. A Hessian characteristic is the yellow crown with the cypher of the Landgraf. Typical of Bohemia is a dark green or dark blue glass and vividly coloured enamels, whereas a light yellowish-green predominates in Franconian glasses. [Figs. 125-134]

ENGLISH GLASS: Mainly characteristic of it is the lead-crystal glass which was invented in England in the second half of the seventeenth century, and which was exported during the eighteenth century (see also flint-glass; lead glass; Ravenscroft). General history: the earliest glasshouses were founded by the Normans in the south of England in the thirteenth century, but there were few of them throughout the Middle Ages. Glass in the Venetian manner was produced in the late sixteenth and seventeenth centuries. Glass-making reached its height in England in the period from the end of the seventeenth century to the end of the eighteenth, when lead-crystal glass was being produced on a large scale. English glass of this period had a strong influence on the Continental product, particularly evident in the cutting of that time. English cut-glass was at its zenith at the end of the eigteenth century, and became the inspiration of Bohemian and German manufacturers. A shortage of wood compelled English glass-makers to employ coal as fuel as early as the beginning of the seventeenth century. English glasses of the eighteenth century are renowned for the excellence of their metal; the shapes are perhaps not so elegant as their Bohemian and German counterparts but rather more stout and practical; the decoration by engraving is also less refined.

Important present-day glass manufacturers are: James A. Joblin & Co, Ltd, Sunderland; James Powell and Sons Ltd, Wealdstone; Stuart and Sons, Wordsley, Stourbridge; the most important designers of art glass-making are: Mrs Phyllis Boissier, London (diamond engraving); Sheila Elmhirst, Ipswich (diamond engraving); John Hutton, London (engraving); Juniper Workshop and Edinburgh College of Art; Glass Design Department, Royal College of Art, London; Laurence Whistler, (diamond engraving). [Figs.136, 137, 140, 145, 152, 153, 155, 156, 158, 159, 167, 191, 192, 223]

FICHTELGEBIRGE GLASSES (FICHTELGEBIRGE = Fir mountains, Middle Germany): Large beaker-like vessels with enamel decoration which usually depicts the Ochsenkopf, the second highest peak of the mountain range. The earliest known specimen is dated 1656, the latest stems from the middle of the eighteenth century. They were made in the glasshouses of Bischofsgrün. The characteristic representation of the Ochsenkopf shows a steep, tree-covered hill, and on this the rebus of the mountain, an ox's head, the whole surrounded by a chain with padlock. Forest animals and the rivers Main, Naab, Saale and Eger, which have their sources in those hills, are also shown. [Fig. 131]

Reference: Thilde Ostertag, *Das Fichtelgebirgsglas, Beiträge zur fränkischen Kunstgeschichte*, Erlangen 1933.

FINNISH GLASS: The earliest known glasshouse was founded in 1793, and produced household glass from that date. The first artistic glass production dates from 1940. The main glasshouses are Karhula Iittala, the Notsjö and the Helsinki glassworks. Tapio Wirkkala (born 1915), Timo Sarpaneva (born 1926), Kaj Franck (born 1911), and Saara Hopea (born 1925) are the most notable designers. Finnish glass-making is not principally concerned with the production of decorative pieces alone, but with functional glass which embodies the highest artistic expression. Its designs reflect Scandinavian character. [Figs. 217–219]

FLINTGLASS: Term used for lead-glass since Ravenscroft, because calcined powdered English flint was used as silica supply. [Figs. 165–168]

FLUTE: Very tall, slender wine- or cider-glass (similar to the modern continental champagne-glasses but even slimmer) belong to the most typical Dutch glasses ranging from the sixteenth to the eighteenth century. [Fig. 77]

FONDI D'ORO: Shallow, ancient vessels; their bases were ornamented with a medallion of engraved gold-leaf which was covered by a layer of clear glass. They were made from the first until the fourth century A.D., originally in Alexandria and later in Rome, but from the third century onward also in Cologne where the technique reached its climax. Thematically they cover all aspects of life, e.g. portraits,

everyday scenes, Christian and Jewish symbolism etc. The most famous specimen which has come down to us is a dish which was found at the church of St Ursula in Cologne and is know kept in the collection of the British Museum. It was certainly made in a Cologne workshop of the fourth century.

Mutatis mutandis the same technique was adopted for the eighteenth century Bohemian *Zwischengoldgläser* and for the *Mildner glasses* of about 1800.

References: Fritz Fremersdorf, *Ein bisher verkanntes römisches Goldglas mit christlichen Wunderszenen in der Römischen Abteilung des Wallraf-Richartz-Museums Köln, in*: Wallraf-Richartz-Jahrbuch, N. F. Vol. I, 1930, p. 282–304.

FRANKISH GLASS (Merovingian glasses): comprises glass of the period from the 5th century up to about the year 700 A.D., when the custom of burying vessels with the deceased was discontinued. The glasses are confined to drinking vessels; bottles and ewers are almost unknown. The glasses are mostly characterized by the absence of foot or any practical base. Conical cups or bell cups are the most common forms. The rims were smoothed in the fire. The glasses are almost without exception of impure greenish or yellowish-green metal. The decoration consists solely of trailed threads or moulded ribs; cutting or engraving do not occur. [Figs. 46, 49]

Reference: *Glas und Schmuck der Römer und Franken*, Altertumsmuseum der Stadt Mainz, Exhibition catalogue, Mainz 1960.

FRENCH GLASS: A thriving industry was already established in Gallo-Roman times as well as during the Frankish or Merovingian period. Tradition has it that the Italian glasshouse of Altare (q.v.) was founded by Norman glassmakers. During the Middle Ages numerous glasshouses produced the so-called *verre de fougère*, which is similar to the German *Waldglas*. In the sixteenth and seventeenth centuries there is a notable influence from Venetian glass, because craftsmen from Murano and Altare were employed in many French glasshouses. Nevers adopts the technique of lamp-blown glass from Venice in the seventeenth and eighteenth centuries. In the seventeenth century France excels in the production of mirrors. Until the nineteenth century, however, French glass-making is of less importance than Bohemian and German. Both the adoption of English lead-crystal glass and the development of a refined cutting technique brings about a blossoming in the beginning of the nineteenth century. French glassmakers of the Art Nouveau period, most notably E. Gallé (q.v.) and Daum frères (q.v.) influenced Bohemian and Austrian glass to a large extent. The most important glass-manufacturers of to-day are: Cristalleries de Baccarat, Baccarat and Paris, founded 1765; Cristalleries Royales de Champagne, Bayel and Paris, founded 1666; Cristalleries de Saint-Louis, Paris, founded 1767; Cristalleries et Verreries Réunies de Choisy-le-Roi, founded 1821; Daum et Cie., Nancy, founded 1880; René Lalique et Cie., Paris, established 1909, and Les Gemmaux de France, Paris, founded 1953. [Figs. 168, 180–182, 189, 190]

Reference: James Barrelet, *La Verrerie en France*, Paris 1953.

FRIT: According to Theophilus (Book 2, Chapters IV-V) this term refers to the pre-heating of the glass ingredients until they become red hot, but do not melt or fuse, ("take it with an iron shovel and shake it onto the upper plate of the smaller compartment of the furnace, so that it becomes red hot. When it begins to get hot, turn it over immediately so that it does not become fluid or fuse in the heat"). Ch. V. "take up on a shovel the frit and fill all the crucibles with it". This process eliminates moisture from the material and reduces the development of gas in the melting process, and thus a glass with fewer impurities is achieved. In his annotations to Neri's first book Kunckel says: "that which you call a mixture is here termed frit". The same process is termed by Kunckel calcination, that is to desiccate the ingredients (pre-heating).

GALLÉ, ÉMILE, 1864-1904: An outstanding French glass artist of the Art Nouveau period. Generally speaking, most of his glasses are cut-overlay vessels modelled on Far Eastern examples. He favours muted shades in his exotic colour schemes, and mainly plant motifs enhancing the basic shape of the vessel. [Figs. 180, 181]

GILDING: Gold-leaf is applied to the vessel, and sealed with a layer of clear glass. Gilt beads were incorporated into necklaces in Egypt at the time of the eighteenth Dynasty, B.C. The gold mottled glasses produced at the time of the Roman Empire are worthy of note; gold-leaf was applied to the hot glass bubble, and during further blowing would break up and form golden speckles; gold dust was also sprinkled on the glass vessels while they were still hot. [Figs. 5, 36, 68]

GLASS: the etymology of the term. There were various words for glass in the Greek language: *hyalos* = a coloured, but transparent glass, *krystallos* = glass transparent as water, *lithos chyte* = "molten stone" = coloured glass. Latin: *hyalus*, *krystallus*, *murra*, and, from the middle of the first century B.C. (Cicero) *vitrum*. The origin of the word *vitrum* remains unexplained; it may be that there is an analogy with *vitrum* = a blue colouring material, from identification with the blue Egyptian vessels. From this word the French *verre* the Italian *vetro* and the Spanish *vietro* are derived. In the Germanic languages the word for amber, *glesum*, was adopted for the new substance.

GLASS BANGLES: Bangles made of glass were known as objects of personal adornment in the Early Iron Age, the La Tène period, and in the time of the Roman Emperors. They were produced in two ways: 1. by bending a glass rod of varying patterns into a bangle shape, (examples of this type have been found in graves of the Roman period); 2. by piercing a mass of hot glass and whirling it round an iron rod. This latter method is described by Theophilus in Vol. I. Book 2, Ch. 31. Bangles, some with an underlay of coloured glass, have been found in the graves of wealthy Celtic women. The Celts used glass for making articles for personal adornment only.

Reference: Thea Elisabeth Haevernick, *Antike Glasarmringe und ihre Herstellung, in*: Glastechnische Berichte, Frankfurt a. M., 25., 7, July 1952, p. 212-215.

GLASS HARMONICA: The earliest mention of a glass instrument, sounded by stroking the rims of glass vessels with the wetted finger-tips, occurs in the inventory of the Ambraser Collection, 1596. In 1762 the American physicist and statesman, Benjamin Franklin, developed the instrument still further. His instrument he called a "glass harmonica", which had rotating glasses controlled by a foot treadle. Many concerts were warmly applauded throughout Europe. The glass harmonica became the fashionable instrument of the *Wertherzeit*. A present day glass instrument is the "Glass Harp" developed by Bruno Hoffmann in Stuttgart.

GLASS MOSAIC: Brightly coloured glass pieces are pressed into cement or a similar substance so as to form pictures or patterns. Descended from the stone or pottery mosaic, (mosaic with both glass and pottery used together existed from the first century A.D.). Mosaic purely from glass dates from the third century A.D., and became the characteristic decoration for Christian Churches. The art spread from Byzantium to Venice, other parts of Italy, and Russia. The art was at its height at the time of the Early Christian and Byzantine mosaics, such as may be seen at S. Vitale in Ravenna. A revival of the art occurred in Germany at the end of the nineteenth century.

GLASS PAINTING: Painting on the inner surface of a glass panel or bottle (China, eighteenth to nineteenth centuries), also used in the Bohemian *Zwischengoldgläser*. The paint is not translucent and never fired. A special effect is obtained by applying gold- or silver-leaf, which is sometimes also engraved, behind the decorated surface. [Fig. 160]

Reference: Otto Freytag, *Hinterglasmalerei*, Ravensburg, without date; Josef Vydra, *Die Hinterglasmalerei*, Prague 1957.

GLYPTOGRAPHY (GEM CARVING): Gem carving may be divided into two types: 1. deeply incised cutting 2. cameo-relief carving. Precious stones were originally used as seals, the earliest examples dating from the ancient Mesopotamian civilisations. Glyptic work is seen at its best in Mycenaean, Greek, Etruscan and Roman art. One of the most famous ancient cameos is the "Apotheosis of Augustus" in the Kunsthistorisches Museum in Vienna. The gems used were principally amethyst, zircon, agate (q.v.) and carnelian. The cameos are usually cut from semi-precious stones which have several layers of contrasting colours, such as onyx, chalcedony and sardonyx. The stones were cut on the lapidary's wheel. Since the time of the early Roman Emperors, glass had also been subjected to this technique, first of all in the city of Alexandria. The most famous example of this art is the Portland Vase in the British Museum, which is of blue glass cased with white, then cut, resembling the ancient onyx cameos.

Cameo-carved glass was not produced after the first century A.D. It occurs later, but was treated differently in China (snuff-bottles), in Bohemia (*Hochschnitt* goblets) and in the Art Nouveau period, (cut cased glass, especially by Emile Gallé). [Figs. 149, 180, 181]

GONDELACH, FRANZ: A glass-engraver from Hesse, born in 1663 at Almerode near Cassel. He held the post of *Hof-glasschneider* (glass-engraver by appointment to the court of the Landgrave Carl of Hesse-Cassel) in Cassel until the first quarter of the eighteenth century. Some of his work was executed on Potsdam glass and is similar to the engraving done by Spiller (q.v.). A few of his pieces were marked by an eight-rayed star.

Reference: Gustav E. Pazaurek, *F. Gondelach*, Berlin 1927.

GRAALGLAS: Trade name for coloured mosaic-like glasses produced by the Orrefors Glasbruk AB in Sweden, invented by Simon Gate and Edvard Hald.

GRAL-GLAS: Products of the Gralglashütte Dürnau near Göppingen in Germany, established 1930. Chief designers are Ch. Baumann, Konrad Habermeister and Josef Stadler. [Fig. 237]

GRAPE-CLUSTER BOTTLE: A small bottle-like vessel with wide foot and two handles, blown into a mould to form the shape of a grape cluster. In use in the second and third centuries A.D. in Italy, Gaul and the Rhineland. [Fig. 15]

GREENWOOD, FRANS, 1680–1762: A Dutch glass engraver of English descent. Together with David Wolff (q.v.) he was the most outstanding exponent of stipple engraving. A large number of glasses decorated by his hand were signed. The earliest glass which bears his signature was made in the year 1720. So far only one glass line-engraved by him is known; all the others were stippled. His designs comprise genre pictures and mythological scenes and, to a lesser extent, still-lifes and calligraphy. [Fig. 138]

Reference: Francis Buckley, *Frans Greenwood*, London 1930.

HALL-IN-THE-TYROL: Glasshouse founded by the Augsburg glassmaker Vitl under the patronage of the Archduke Ferdinand in 1534. During the first decades of its existence, fine glasses in an adapted Venetian style were produced with the assistance of Italian glassmakers, but not without difficulties, for the necessary soda had to be imported. The glasshouse was still flourishing in the seventeenth century but without any important production. The majority of the surviving glasses are now in the Hofmuseum in Vienna whence they were taken from the Ambras Castle in the Tyrol. Typical Hall-glasses are covered goblets and ewers in the Venetian fashion. They are characteristically diamond-engraved and they are also decorated with cold painting in red and green colours. [Fig. 87, 89]

Reference: Erich Egg, *Die Glashütten in Hall und Innsbruck im 16. Jahr-bundert, Tiroler Wirtschaftsstudien*, 15. Folge, Innsbruck 1962.

HALLORENGLAS: Large cylindrical or slightly conical drinking vessels, usually with Saxon enamel painting, made for the "Halloren", members of the Salters Company in Halle, for the annual Whitsuntide beer-drinking ceremony. *Halloren* glasses dating from the seventeenth to the mid-eighteenth century have come down to us. The painted decoration, executed in vigorous simplicity, shows in four zones a panorama of the town of Halle, the Talamtshaus, the procession of the Halloren, and the arms of the guild supported by two saltworkers. [Fig. 132]

HEAD-SHAPED VESSELS: These are the development of mould-blown glasses taking the form of a Medusa head. They bear strong resemblance to Greek pottery of naturalistic design. It is thought that such glasses were produced in various parts of the Roman Empire, most probably in Sidonian, Alexandrian and Rhenish glasshouses. They reached the height of their popularity in the third century A.D., a favourite type being the portrait caricature. The Emperor Tacitus, who is said to have blown glass himself, owned a collection of glass curiosities. Nero's court fool, a crippled shoemaker, was the inspiration for the design of one of them. [Figs. 17–19]

HEDWIG BEAKER: eleventh century Egyptian glass cut in high relief. The name derives from St Hedwiga, the patron saint of Silesia. Twelve specimens of this glass are known. The relief-cut decoration consists of stylised lions, griffons or formal palm-leaf pattern. [Fig. 57]

HESSE: In the late Middle Ages this *Land* was one of the most important glass producers. As early as 1406, forty glass-makers in the Spessart Mountains and surrounding forest districts had formed themselves into a strict guild. The Spessart guild controlled working hours and level of production. After 1525 the centre of this guild was transferred to the forest region of Kaufungen, to the village of Almerode. In the seventeenth century enamel-painting was being executed throughout Hesse. Typical of the style in this area are the yellowish-green metal and the gold leaf borders with engraved scale pattern and white enamel dots. In the eighteenth century a goblet peculiar to Hesse was evolved with a high, bell-shaped foot and an air-bubble at the bottom of the bowl. The most important glass engravers were Franz Gondelach and Franz Trumper.

References: Margarete Killing, *Die Glasmacherkunst in Hessen, ein Beitrag zur Gewerbe- und Kunstgeschichte der deutschen Renaissance*, Marburg 1927.

HOCHSCHNITT: A manner of cutting glass, so that the design of the decoration remains in relief, while the remaining parts are ground away with the wheel (cf. Glyptography). The Alexandrian and Roman glass reliefs (such as on the Portland Vase), the Hedwig-glasses, the Silesian goblets of about 1700, the Chinese snuff-bottles of the eighteenth century and the Gallé vases were ornamented in this way. Modern glass manufacture, particularly Bohemian, has fruitfully exploited this technique again. [Figs. 57, 149, 176–178, 180, 181]

HOFFMAN, JOSEF, 1870–1955: Viennese architect and handicraft expert, one of the most prominent initiators of the Vienna Secession 1897, the Vienna Crafts Centre (*Wiener Werkstätte*) 1903, and the Austrian Werkbund (Arts and Crafts Society) 1912. Well-known for his glass designs, especially the so-termed broncit-glass (q.v.). [Fig. 187]

HOFKELLEREIGLÄSER: Drinking glasses of the royal residences in Saxony, with armorial bearings and usually the initials and titles of the ruler in enamel pigment, from the royal cellars of Dresden, Moritzburg, Königstein, Lössnitz, Torgau, Pretzsch, Magdeburg, Halle, Merseburg, Weissenfels, Naumburg, Querfurth, Christiansburg, Altenburg, Gotha. Mostly decorated in Saxony. Considerable numbers of these glasses have come down to us.

References: Karl Berling, *Die sächsischen Hofkellereigläser*, in: *Festschrift zum fünfundsiebzigjährigen Jubiläum des Königlich Sächsischen Altertumsvereins*, Dresden 1900, Beiheft zum *Neuen Archiv für sächsische Geschichte und Altertumskunde*, Vol. XXI.

HUMPEN: Cylindrical drinking vessels of the sixteenth, seventeenth and eighteenth centuries, usually decorated with enamel and less often with cut or engraved decoration. Their frequently enormous size can be traced to the custom of passing a drinking glass round a group of people. [Figs. 117, 125–131]

HUNGARIAN GLASS: Glasshouses founded in the fourteenth century; strongly influenced in the sixteenth century by Venetian, and in the seventeenth and eighteenth centuries by German and Bohemian glass. Worthy of note is the peasant-like art of the more ancient Hungarian glass productions. Jugs and bottles are the most common vessels. In the eighteenth century the faïence made in Habane no doubt had its influence on the style of decoration executed on Hungarian glass.

Reference: Béla Borsos, *Die Glaskunst im alten Ungarn*, Budapest 1963.

HYALITH GLASS: A black, more rarely red opaque glass, invented in Bohemia in the first quarter of the nineteenth century. In 1820 an eight-year monopoly for its production was granted to the glasshouse of Count Buquoy. The purpose behind this glass was to imitate the extraordinarily popular Wedgwood ware. Patterns in the spirit of Wedgwood designs were painted in gold and silver on the glass.

ICE-GLASS: An invention of the sixteenth century, the hot glass is dipped for a moment in water and then re-heated. The crackles caused by the sudden change of temperature are thus fused together again. Ice-glass with a rough surface is also made by rolling a gathered lump of soft hot glass over tiny glass splinters. The surface of ice-glass can also be treated with hydrofluoric acid; if covered with a resinous substance, which crackles when dried, the acid affects only the crevices, and the covered areas retain their smooth surface.

IRIDESCENCE: A shimmer on the surface of the glass which may have its origins a) from prolonged burial in the soil or weathering; in this case the surface is scaly and the light broken up prismatically, producing an attractive rainbow effect in some ancient glass, b) from the application of a metallic lustre, c) and most recently from the use of chemical substances.

IRISH GLASS: Glass was produced for the first time in Ireland in 1585. Irish glass was at its best from the end of the eighteenth to the middle of the nineteenth century. The most important manufacturers are Waterford, founded in 1783, Cork, also founded in 1783, and Belfast, founded 1776. These glasshouses fashioned excellent lead-crystal into heavy, solid shapes with restrained cut decoration. Typical motifs are the fine diamond-patterned arches or half-moon shapes, and the shallow or deep cut stars. Waterford Glass Ltd, Waterford, still produces glass in the traditional style. [Fig. 169]

References: E. M. Elville, *The Collector' Dictionary of Glass*, London 1961; W. A. Thorpe, *A history of English and Irish Glass*, London 1929.

JADE: The name given to three semi-precious stones: Nephrite, Jadeite, and Chloromelanite; the first two are usually green, sometimes grey or brownish, often mottled, and have a waxy appearance, the last is dark green to black in colour. The word jade is derived from the Spanish *piedra de ijada*, (*piedra = stone, ijada = side* – pain in the side), and this stone was said to relieve kidney trouble. Jade is a material much favoured by artists, particularly in China, where it was also imitated in glass.

KANTHAROS: Shallow drinking vessels with foot and two handles, used in Ancient Greece from the sixth century B.C. Often shown in pictorial representations of Bacchus. [Fig. 30]

KEULENGLAS: Club-shaped glass of a rather impure light-green or yellowish-green metal with several indented horizontal trails, about 1500 A.D. [Fig. 94]

KÖPPING-GLASSES: Lamp-blown glasses executed after designs by the Berlin painter and etcher Karl Köpping, 1848–1914. [Fig. 185]

KOTHGASSER, ANTON, 1769–1851: Viennese porcelain and glass decorator. He was introduced to glass painting by Gottlob Mohn. Most glasses by Kothgasser have a heavy-cut foot, and a concave wall. Views of towns and landscapes within an area of yellow-stained glass surrounded by a goldleaf border are painted in translucent enamels. [Fig. 164]

References: Gustav E. Pazaurek, *Gläser der Empire- und Biedermeierzeit*, Leipzig 1923; Hermann Trenkwald, *Gläser der Spätzeit (um 1790–1850)*, Vienna 1923.

KRATER: Ancient vase with wide mouth and small handles, of various types, e.g. Corinthian, Bell, Calyx.

KRAUTSTRUNK (CABBAGE-STEM) GLASSES: Cup-like glasses of the fifteenth and sixteenth centuries with large flat-based tapering applied prunts. They are referred to in contemporary literature. Mathesius has in mind the glasses with large upward-drawn blobs when he uses this term. [Fig. 103]

Reference: Franz Rademacher, *Die deutschen Gläser des Mittelalters*, Berlin 1963.

KRONGLAS: Trade term for the best quality grade of Bohemian crystal glass.

KUNCKEL, GEORG ERNST: Thuringian glass engraver, born in Ostheim on the Rhön and employed from 1721 at the court of Gotha. Died in 1750 in Eisenach. His signature is found on three of his works, of which two are in the Coburg collection. A further thirteen of his products are dated. Annegrete Janda-Bux has ascribed approximately seventy glasses, dating from the years 1721 to 1748, to this artist. These examples have found their way to various parts of the world. Kunckel probably studied the art of engraving in Nuremberg, learning from the work of Friedrich Killinger and H. W. Schmidt. Later he worked for a time on Nuremberg glasses. Characteristic of his work are leafy festoons strewn with tiny polished-cut berries, pearl garlands, flower-head chains and trellised lambrequins with pearl tassels.

Reference: Annegrete Janda-Bux, *Der Thüringer Glasschnitt im 17. und 18. Jahrhundert*, Leipzig, thesis 1962.

KUNCKEL, JOHANN: Chemist and glass technologist, stems from an old family of glass-makers in Hesse. The family name is already known in connection with the Spessart Ligue in 1406. Johann Kunckel was born in about 1630 at Rendsburg where his father worked as a mastercraftsman. From 1679 till 1693 he was in charge of the Potsdam glasshouse, and there he produced among other things the famous ruby glass with gold chloride, the so called Kunckel-glass. In 1679 he published his book *Ars Vitraria Experimentalis or Vollkommene Glasmacherkunst* (*Complete art of glass-making*). It appeared in five successive editions, and is regarded as the first fundamental work on the subject of glass technology in modern times. In 1693 Kunckel went to Sweden, where a knighthood was conferred on him. As Johann Kunckel von Löwenstein he died on his estate in the Electorate of Brandenburg in 1703. [Figs. 142]

Reference: Robert Schmidt, *Brandenburgische Gläser*, Berlin 1914.

KUTTROLF OR ANGSTER: The German term *Kuttrolf* is derived from the latin *gutta* = drop, and *Angster* from the Latin *angustus* = narrow. A description of the vessels will show why such names were chosen. The common characteristic of these vessels of varying shapes is the pinching of the neck to form a number of narrow tubes through which liquid will pour slowly or emerge in drops. In the Middle Ages the terms embraced vessels of many shapes, but later three types were distinguished: the many-tubed Kuttrolf

with a wide mouth, which has East Gallo-Roman origins, the many-tubed version with a bottle mouth, first made in Syria, and, also Syrian, the type with one tube which was still in use in Persia during the seventeenth and eighteenth centuries. These peculiar forms, particularly those with bent necks consisting of several entwined tubes, were very popular in the Middle Ages, and are often depicted in the art of the period. [Figs. 112–115]

References: Franz Rademacher, *Der Kuttrolf, eine antike Glasform und ihre Fortbildung im Mittelalter und in der Renaissance*, in: *Zeitschrift für Bildende Kunst*, 62, 1928–1929, Leipzig 1929, p. 37–43.

KYLIX: Ancient drinking vessel consisting of two-handled, shallow bowl on tall foot.

LACE GLASS, *Vetro a reticelli* was produced in Venice at the end of the sixteenth century. White threads in a crisscross pattern, each "square" enclosing a tiny air-bubble, are sealed within the double wall of the vessel. This glass was made by arranging white glass rods, equidistant one from the other, on the hot glass-bubble; the rods are then pinched together at top and bottom and the glass-bubble twisted so that they form a spiral round it. By sucking air out of the bubble, the craftsman collapses one half of it into the other, thus producing a double-walled vessel with the rods or threads lying criss-cross. Another method was to fuse together two bubbles which have spiral threads in opposite directions. [Figs. 77, 78]

LAGONA: a Roman water-jug with a single handle.

LAMP-BLOWN GLASS: articles which were not made in the factory at the furnace, but by a cottage industry using glass tubes softened into shape in a flame; at one time oil-lamps and bellows were used. This technique was probably discovered soon after glass-blowing itself, and was used at first for the manufacture of glass-beads. In Venice, small figures and other objects were also made in the seventeenth century. The technique spread to France (Nevers) and Holland (Amsterdam). At the end of the eighteenth century it was taken up in Bohemia and Thuringia. Lauscha is still the centre of an extensive cottage industry in the Thuringian Forest, especially for the production of beads, toys and Christmas-tree decorations. Since the turn of the century efforts have been made to adapt this technique to the manufacture of glass vessels; the delicacy of the methods was ideally suited for the purposes of the Art Nouveau movement. After 1920 W. v. Wersin succeeded in making small vases of coloured glass rods. Arround 1930 fresh efforts were made by Wilhelm Wagenfeld to extend the Thuringian glass industry. At the present time, besides the glass makers Albin Schaedel, Volkmar Precht and Edmund Müller, the designers Ilse Decho, Ilse Scharge-Nebel and Professor Horst Michel are engaged in the production of lamp-blown glass. [Figs. 238, 240, 241]

References: Johann Kunckel, *Ars vitraria experimentalis*, 3. d. Nuremberg 1744, p. 398: *Vom kleinen Glass-Blasen, so mit der Lampen geschieht*; Gustav

E. Pazaurek, *Kunstgläser der Gegenwart*, Leipzig 1925, p. 232–240: *Vor der Lampe geblasene Glasarbeiten*; Albin Schaedel, *Lampengeblasene Gläser*, Museum des Kunsthandwerks Leipzig, Ausstellungskatalog, Leipzig 1962.

LATTIMO, LATTICINO, LATTICINIO: the Italian term for white glass, sometimes referred to as milk glass or *Milchglas*. Used since the fifteenth century in the manufacture of Venetian glass of various patterns, such as the *vetro di trina* or *vetro a reticelli*, and the terms are sometimes loosely applied to refer to vessels which have such insertions of white glass. Canes covered with a layer of colourless glass and canes of completely colourless glass are arranged according to the desired effect against the sides or in the middle of a cylindrical mould, and the remaining space is filled with molten colourless glass. After being taken to the fire to ensure complete fusion, the lump of glass is drawn out and twisted into a long thin rod, containing fine threads of coloured glass. It is then cut into canes of the desired length, which in their turn are used, in a similar process, to produce the final vessel. They are arranged around a stoneware mould, colourless glass is blown into it, then removed, the canes adhering to it; the outer surface of the bubble is then also covered with clear molten glass. The whole is heated and thus fused, and the resulting patterned glass is used to make a vessel.

In the seventeenth and eighteenth centuries, pure white glass was used as a substitute for Chinese porcelain, and decorated with Chinoiserie enamel painting. In the nineteenth century Bohemia produced many *Milchglas* vessels with red or blue overlay.

The opacity of white glass is obtained by the use of tin oxide, arsenic or calcined bones. [Figs. 69, 76-78]

LAUENSTEIN: glasshouse at Osterwald near Hamelin in Westphalia, founded in 1701. An English glassmaker introduced at an early date coal for firing the furnaces. The glass produced at Lauenstein is considered to possess the material quality of English lead-glass, and its features resemble English contemporary glass. Typical products are goblets with bell-shaped, folded feet, drawn stems, facet-cut knops, and the bowls are frequently facetted at the base; there is almost always an air-bubble in the bottom of the bowl. Engraved decorations are not elaborate.

References: Christian Scherer, *Zur Frage der sogenannten Lauensteiner Gläser*, in: *Cicerone*, Leipzig, V. 1913, p. 403 ff.; Christel Mosel, *Die Glassammlung*, Katalog des Kestner-Museums, Hannover 1957.

LAUSCHA: village near Neuhaus in Thuringia (Germany), a well-known centre of glass-blowing in the Thuringian Mountains. A glass-house is known to have existed there in 1595. [Fig. 144]

References: Rudi Hoffmann, *Das Museum für Glaskunst Lauscha*, Steinach 1954; Barbara Pischel, *Die thüringische Glasbläserei*, Weimar 1936.

LEAD GLASS: English invention, second half of the seventeenth century; see RAVENSCROFT.

LEBENSALTERGLAS: Drinking glasses produced mainly in the first half of the nineteenth century in Germany. The decoration depicts the ages of man. Whole figures representing each age group are posed on a flight of steps. [Fig. 165]

LEHMANN, CASPAR: German gem-cutter, employed at the Court of Prague under the Emperor Rudolf II. In 1609 he obtained an Imperial privilege for engraving glass. He is regarded as the first master of the art of glass-engraving in modern history. [Fig. 146]

LEKYTHOS: ancient Greek vase or jug with a cylindrical or round, squat body, and narrow neck, originally used for oil. Used mainly as a funeral offering since the fifth century B.C.

LITHYALIN: reddish-brown marbled glass (with the appearance of sealing wax), invented in 1829 by Egermann (q.v) of Blottendorf in Southern Bohemia.

LOBMEYR: well-known Viennese glass-manufacturer, established in 1823. The successive managers of the firm, Josef Lobmeyr (1823–1855), Josef Lobmeyr Jun. (1855 to 1864) and Ludwig Lobmeyr (1864–1902) are important in having perpetuated the tradition of glass-engraving of northern Bohemia in their glasshouses at Steinschönau and Haida. After 1902 came a re-orientation towards the modern Viennese style under the artistic direction of Stefan Rath. After 1910, Josef Hoffmann (q.v.) was one of the co-directors. The firm of Lobmeyr is still one of the leading manufacturers in the field of glass-making. [Fig. 226]

References: Robert Schmidt, *100 Jahre österreichischer Glaskunst*, Vienna 1925; *Stefan Rath Lobmeyr*, Vienna 1962.

LYCURGUS BEAKER GLASS: dark-green glass with five figures in high-relief cut out of the solid wall of the vessel representing the punishment of Lycurgus by Bacchus. Probably Alexandrian workmanship of the fourth century In the British Museum, Rothschild Collection.

References: Eberhard Schenk zu Schweinsberg, *Der Becher des Lykurg, Bemerkungen zu der Arbeit von E. Coche de la Ferté* in: *Glastechnische Berichte*, Frankfurt a. M. 31. 1958, p. 470–472; *Journal of Glass Studies*, The Corning museum of glass, vol. 2. 1960, Corning, New York, Ill. 9, p. 138.

MAIGELEIN: German drinking glass of the fifteenth and sixteenth centuries usually in the form of a beaker or tallish bowl, mould-blown, ribbed or fluted, and with a high-kicked base, although this term has been extended to include bowls of somewhat different shape. [Figs. 98, 99]

References: Franz Rademacher, *Die deutschen Gläser des Mittelalters*, Berlin 1963.

MATHESIUS, JOHANNES, 1504–1565: parson of Joachimsthal, (now in Czechoslovakia), published the *Sarepta oder Berg-Postill, darin von allerlei Bergwerk und Metallen ... Bericht gegeben wird*. The fifteen sermons deal with glass-making and are the source of much important information about medieval glass.

MAUDER, BRUNO: Glass artist born in Munich in 1877, died in Zwiesel, 1948; studied at the Kunstgewerbeschule,

Munich, and was from 1910 director of the Staatliche Fach-schule für Glasindustrie in Zwiesel. Mauder was one of the first post-1900 artists to revert to the natural shapes of the material, the ball and the pear-shape, as a basis for his creations. This principle led away from the Art Nouveau designs, for although that movement had recognised the unique qualities of glass, it had nevertheless subjected it to preconceived ideas on design. Bruno Mauder gave the German glass industry an impetus which still has its effect to-day.

References: Bruno Mauder, *Glas*, Berlin 1944; Wolfgang von Wersin, *Bruno Mauder, Glaserzeugung und Glasveredelung, Werkstattbericht 11*, hrsg. vom Kunst-Dienst, Berlin 1941.

MERCURY BOTTLES: A group of ancient bottles, blown, four-sided and with a long tube-like neck and flat rim, showing a relief of the god Mercury (hence their name – they were not made for containing mercury!) under the base. Occasionally they are stamped with the name of the maker.

MERRET, CHRISTOPHER: 1616–1695, English naturalist, chemist and physician. He translated into English Antonio Neri's *Arte Vetraria*. The translation with his annotations, which were commented on by Johannes Kunckel in his *Ars Vitraria*, appeared in 1662. Merret must be regarded as one of the first scientists whose aim was to disseminate scientific knowledge.

METAL: Glass-makers' term for the material after it has been fused in the furnace.

MILDNER GLASSES: Glasses by Johann Josef Mildner, 1764 to 1807, of the Gutenbrunn Glasshouse in Lower Austria. Signed works exist from the period 1787 to 1808. The glasses are cylindrical and their decoration consists of *Zwischengold* medallions; in the double-walled base there is often a picture, gold-etched over red. These glasses are among the best work produced in the Empire period. [Fig. 162]

References: Gustav E. Pazaurek, *Gläser der Empire- und Biedermeierzeit*, Leipzig 1923.

MILK GLASS: see *Lattimo*

MILLEFIORI GLASS: literally "thousand flower glass", manufactured from the second century B.C. in Alexandria, and later in Rome. The flower or more rarely figure-pattern is spread through the entire vessel. Bundles of small glass rods, with a pattern in cross-section, were fused together, producing a multiplication of this pattern in one piece of glass, which was then cut into the desired thickness. The resulting pieces were then in their turn fused side by side to give a sheet of glass large enough for the object required. [Figs. 7, 85]

MIRROR-GLASS: In ancient times and the early Middle Ages mirrors were made of polished metal, but a mirror of silver-ed glass was already known in Egypt in the first century B.C. In the thirteenth century, mirrors produced by a layer of lead behind a glass-frame were in use in France, Germany, and Italy. In the sixteenth century Venice took the lead in mirror-making, after the technique of silvering by means of mercury had been invented there. France took over in the seventeenth century, her most important centre for mirror-glass being St Gobain. The magnificent Venetian mirrors of the eighteenth century are widely known.

MIXTURE: term for the ingredients before they are fired in the furnace.

MOHN GLASSES: Drinking and souvenir glasses with trans-lucent enamel-painting by Samuel Mohn, born 1762 in Weissenfels, died 1815 in Dresden, and by his son, Gottlob Samuel Mohn, born 1789 in Weissenfels, died 1825 in Vienna. The glasses are often in the shape of the so-called *Ranftbecher* form, which is typical of the beginning of the nineteenth century. The painting consists of a coloured flower garland below the rim, and an area of illustration embracing many motifs, but mainly of town views and landscapes. [Fig. 163]

References: Gustav E. Pazaurek, *Gläser der Empire- und Biedermeierzeit*, Leipzig 1923.

MOSQUE LAMPS: Syrian vessels of the thirteenth and four-teenth century, richly painted with gold and enamel. Suspended from the ceiling by chains attached to six loops on the vessel, and containing oil-lamps. Approximately 230 pieces are known, almost all of them from Cairo mos-ques. The inscriptions in Kufic script always consist of a text from the Koran and praise the reigning Sultan, so that an accurate dating can be made. [Fig. 65]

References: Carl Johan Lamm, *Mittelalterliche Gläser und Steinschnittarbeiten aus dem Nahen Osten*, Berlin 1929/30.

MURRHINE BOWLS: ancient vessels, usually bowls in mosaic-glass. Highly prized during the time of the Roman Emperors, they are often mentioned in Roman literature, and it was Anton Kisa who first discovered that these allusions referred to glass vessels. The earliest Murrhine bowls, made in Alexandria in the second century B.C., are cut out of a solid block of many coloured glasses fused together. Later the following technique was applied: coloured glass rods were arranged in bundles and fused together; the resulting mass was horizontally sliced, and the slices, each showing a flower-like pattern, were sub-sequently fused into a larger slice, or applied to a hot bubble of glass, cased with clear glass and then worked as desired. It is probable that the majority of such vessels were then polished by grinding. They were produced by Alexandrian glassmakers during the last century B.C. and the first century A.D. The technique was adopted by the Venetians, and glasses of this type were named by them "Millefiori glasses". [Fig. 7]

NERI, ANTONIO: died 1614, a Florentine priest and chemist. who published in 1612 his *Arte Vetraria*, seven books on glass-making. Neri himself worked in glass-houses in Florence, Pisa and in Flanders, so we see that his knowledge is based on experiment and experience. Ch. Merret (q.v.) and J. Kunckel (q.v.) wrote commentaries on the "Arte Vetraria".

NUPPENGLAS: German glasses decorated with applied drops or prunts, in their turn subdivided into *Näpfe*, *Stangengläser* or *Krautstrunk*. The *Nuppen* are produced by dabbing the vessel with a molten glass rod. The point of the resulting blob may be drawn upwards or downwards as required. Glasses may be dated according to the size and type of drops, the general shape of the glass being taken into consideration also. The drops developed from the sharp little snail-like *Steinchen* of the mid 1400's to sharp thorny appendages at the end of the fifteenth century, then became larger and flatter during the sixteenth. Forms related to the *Nuppenbecher* are to be seen in the *Rüsselbechern* or Claw beakers of the fifth and sixth century with their hollow trunk-like attachments, and in the *Daumenhumpen* (Thumb glasses) of the sixteenth and seventeenth century, where they are inverted. These techniques are again being used by modern glass-artists. [Figs. 99, 102–105, 107]

NUREMBERG GLASS ENGRAVING its main period dates from 1622, the year when Georg Schwanhardt (q.v.) returned to Nuremberg from Prague, to the end of the seventeenth century. Nuremberg engraving is shallow, as a result of the thin-walled glass; unpolished and polished areas and diamond-engraving (q.v.) are at times effectively combined. The Nuremberg goblets have a flat foot, a shaft with hollow ball-knops, or hollow balusters and discs, and an oviform bowl. The most talented engravers were Georg Schwanhardt the Elder, Heinrich Schwanhardt (q.v.), Hermann Schwinger (q.v.), Hans Wolfgang Schnidt (q.v.), Paulus Eder, Georg Friedrich Killinger and Christoph Dorsch. Around the year 1700, Nuremberg glass-engraving was largely ousted by that of Bohemia and Silesia, which gained through the discovery of a better quality vehicle for it, Bohemian potash-lime glass.

References: Erich Meyer-Heisig, *Der Nürnberger Glasschnitt des 17. Jahrhunderts*, Nürnberg 1963.

OBSIDIAN: apart from rock crystal the only natural glass, normally shiny black or green, of volcanic origin, used by man for weapons, bowls and ornaments since the early Stone Age. Hence man-made black glass is often termed obsidian glass.

OENOCHOE: ancient one-handled ewer, often with trefoil mouths, certainly used for wine.

OMOM: Syrian vessel for the sprinkling of rose water and other sweet-smelling essences. The form developed from the pilgrim-bottle. [Fig. 64]

ONYX GLASS: dark glass with a multicoloured, predominantly white streaking, produced by mixing various molten glasses together.

OPAL GLASS: this term is sometimes used to embrace various kinds of whitish metals. Opaque white glass has for a long time been produced, either for making the entire vessel (at one point in imitation of porcelain) or as a decorative insertion, as in the Venetian *latticino* glass. Semiopaque or opalescent white glass has also been produced by using the ashes of calcined bones. Tinges of other colours were introduced (Antonio Neri mentions opal glass as a peach-coloured glass) and the glass may glow blue, green or pink. The nineteenth century referred to this as "opaline". White glass is known as *Milchglas* in German for obvious reasons: *Milch* = milk (cf. the Italian *latticino*). [Fig. 83]

OPAQUE GLASS: glass of any colour which is not transparent, although it usually has a translucent effect.

PASSGLAS (German), PASGLAS (Dutch): tall cylindrical drinking glasses in use in the seventeenth and eighteenth centuries in Germany and the Netherlands. They are decorated at even distances with thin pincered horizontal trails. At gatherings the glass was passed from mouth to mouth, and each man had to drink from one ring to the next in one draught. [Fig. 120]

PELLATT, APSLEY: born 1791, died 1863. His father had founded the Falcon Glasshouse in Southwark. Apsley Pellatt, Jun., is best known for his perfection of the crystallo-ceramic (q.v.) technique, the inclusion of medallions in glass. This demanded a flawless glass which was supplied by his firm. Imitations by rivals are of poorer quality.

PERSIAN GLASS: important during several epochs in the history of glass-making; a) in the Sassanian period, 226 to 642; b) in the Islamic period, especially in the thirteenth and fourteenth centuries, when it shows to a certain extent Chinese influence in the style of enamel-painting; c) from the seventeenth to the nineteenth century, mass-production of decorative bottles and jugs with Shiraz as its centre. [Figs. 58, 64, 172, 173]

References: Carl Johan Lamm, *Mittelalterliche Gläser und Steinschnittarbeiten aus dem Nahen Osten*, Berlin 1929/30.

POKAL: German word for goblet (from the Italian *boccale* = ewer). The early Venetian glass goblets of the fifteenth century indicate that they were modelled on gilt vessels. The goblet is a typical vessel of the European baroque period. [Figs. 69, 147–151, 154]

POLISHING OF ENGRAVED GLASS SURFACES: (*Blankschnitt*) Joachim van Sandrart in his *Academie der Bau-, Bild- und Mablereykünste* ascribes the invention of BLANKSCHNITT to the Nuremberg glass-engraver Georg Schwanhardt (q.v.). The matt surfaces of the ground part of the *intaglio* engraving are polished by wheels, edged with cork, leather, lead, pewter or brushes. All the deeper parts of the cutting, which are usually of an even, greyish tinge and are not transparent, are heightened by this process and form a sculptural effect. The play of light, caught and softly reflected by the rounded, polished contours of the engraved surface, deepens its relief considerably. The Nuremberg school of glass-engravers applied this method of polishing to the thin potash glasses at their disposal, and achieved a finesse which has never been surpassed. The human body, in particular, is depicted with richness and luminosity.

Thus before the advent of the heavier and more brilliant Bohemian glass the aim of the Baroque to express movement, light and space was realised in glass engraving. [Fig. 147]

PONTIL OR PUNTY: the iron rod to which the glass vessels are transferred before their removal from the blowing-iron for further working, such as the smoothing of the mouth, the forming of the neck in the case of bottles etc. A scar known as a "pontil (or punty) mark" in the base of the vessel often shows where it has been attached to the rod. It is seen in nearly all glasses made before the nineteenth century, when glass-makers began to erase it, sometimes by grinding the base to make it slightly concave, or by cutting a star-shape.

PORRÓN: Spanish drinking vessel, seventeenth to nineteenth century; a conical ewer with a long tapering spout which is inserted near the base. People drink from it without brushing it with their mouths. The *porrón* is derived from skin bottles. [Fig. 90]

PORTLAND VASE: This very famous glass vessel was at one time in the Palazzo Barberini in Rome, was bought by Sir William Hamilton in the 18th century, was then owned by the Duchess of Portland, and is now housed in the British Museum. In 1845 the vase was wilfully broken by a visitor to the Museum, but has been carefully pieced together once more. It is made of blue glass cased with white, the latter then being cut away to form a decorative mythological scene. The vase was probably made in the first century B.C. in Rome.

References: Erika Simon, *Die Portlandvase*, Mainz 1957.

POTASH: an alkaline substance obtained originally by burning vegetation such as bracken, beechwood etc. and used as a flux. After soda, the most important alkali used for glass manufacture. Ancient glass, Roman, Gallic, and Rhenish has a soda, not a potash content. The break with Rome occasioned by the invasions of the tribes compelled glass-makers in the north to turn to potash, and its use was retained in those regions until the beginning of the nineteenth century and the Industrial Revolution in Europe. A certain amount of lime was inevitably also included in the glass because of the use of potash, giving the metal resistance to glass disease.

Today potash obtained from molasses charcoal (found in the residues from the process of producing sugar from beet, and also produced synthetically) is used in the manufacture of good quality glass.

Since the chemical composition of beechwood is liable to changes according to the locality (trace elements), a chemical analysis of old glass vessels can assist research into their place of origin. The results are, however, not always conclusive, since cullet (broken or refuse glass) is often used for the production of glass.

References: Wilhelm Geilmann, *Beiträge zur Kenntnis alter Gläser III, Die chemische Zusammensetzung einiger alter Gläser, insbesondere deutscher Gläser des 10. bis 18. Jahrhunderts*, in: *Glastechnische Berichte*, Frankfurt/M., 28., 1955, 146–156.

POTSDAM: Foundation of the first glasshouse near Drewitz in 1674 but transferred to Potsdam 1679. Because it was found unprofitable it was leased into private hands by the Elector Friedrich Wilhelm. From 1679 to 1693 it was run by Johann Kunckel (q.v.). In 1763 the glasshouse was moved to Zechlin, where it flourished till 1890. The most important engravers of this glasshouse were Friedrich Winter (q.v.), Gottfried Spiller (q.v.), and Elias Rossbach (q.v.). The glasses were richly ornamented by both cutting and engraving. Characteristic of them are decorative borders of formal flower motifs, polished in the early period of the eighteenth century and otherwise unpolished. Later, borders of lozenge-shaped cutting became fashionable After 1730, lavish gilt decorations were favoured. For the same period heavy feet and variously cut baluster stems, often with a large air-bubble inside, are typical. Mythological and military scenes in unpolished engraving grace the entire surface of the vessel. [Fig. 154]

References: Robert Schmidt, *Brandenburgische Gläser*, Berlin 1914.

PRESSED GLASS: Molten glass is poured into a mould, and a plunger presses the glass mass into the mould giving it the desired shape and pattern. The technique was developed in England and in America at the beginning of the nineteenth century, although it did exist in the ancient world, as shown by Roman ribbed bowls or the Murrhine bowls. In the nineteenth century pressed glass was first produced as a cheap substitute for cut crystal glass, but modern glass-makers use this technique to produce vessels which are not intended as imitations of finer products, but which exhibit certain qualities of their own.

PROCHUS: Ancient cone-shaped ewer, certainly used for wine. [Fig. 28]

PYXIS: Ancient cylindrical vase with or without cover.

RAVENSCROFT, GEORGE: 1618–1681, English glass-maker, founded a glasshouse in Savoy in 1673. A year later he obtained a patent running for seven years for the production of glass-of-lead. Many of his glasses bear the raven's head seal.

References: W. B. Honey, *English Glass*, London 1946; W. A. Thorpe, *English Glass*, London 1949.

REICHSADLERHUMPEN: cylindrical glasses with a representation of the Imperial Eagle in enamel paint, and the coats of arms (usually forty-eight) of the *Heiligen Römischen Reiches samt seinen Gliedern* (The Holy Roman Empire together with its Member States) arranged on the wings in the so-called Quaternion System. This heraldic scheme is derived from Peter von Andlaus's *Imperio Romano* of 1460, and from the related illustration in Hartmann Schedel's *Weltchronik*, Nuremberg 1493. *Reichsadlerhumpen* were made in the last quarter of the sixteenth century and throughout the seventeenth, mainly in Bohemia. Until about 1590, a crucifix is to be seen in the centre of the eagle, later the imperial orb. [Fig. 130]

Reference: Walter Stengel, *Reichsadlergläser, Gruppierungsversuche*, in: *Kunst-und Kunsthandwerk*, Vienna, 19, 1916, p. 322–338.

ROCK CRYSTAL: clear, translucent natural product, pure quartz (SiO_2). In ancient times it was cut by artists into splendid vessels and was favoured from the time of the Renaissance for cutting in intaglio and, after 1600, in high relief. In the history of glass-making and glass refinement rock crystal had great influence. The main epochs of glass-cutting, the Roman period, the Fatimid era, the beginning of glass engraving in Europe in the seventeenth century, and Bohemian engraving in the eighteenth century, were strongly influenced by rock crystal cutting.

RÖMER: Drinking glasses consisting of a core-wound foot; they have hollow stem with prunts and a spherical bowl. They are almost always green in colour. The *Römer* was produced when the lip of earlier vessels was transformed into the liquid-containing part at the beginning of the sixteenth century in the Rhineland, achieving enormous size in Holland during the seventeenth and eighteenth centuries, and often engraved in diamond-point technique. It has remained the typical German form of wine glass up to the present day. Rademacher states that the name results from the admiration for Roman glass still felt in Cologne in the late Middle Ages. [Fig. 106]

Reference: Franz Rademacher, *Die Deutschen Gläser des Mittelalters*, Berlin 1963.

ROSSBACH, ELIAS: glass-engraver who worked in Berlin from 1727 to 1741, then in Zechlin until his death in 1765. Eight of his pieces are known, signed "Rossbach Fecit Berlin". Rossbach is one of the best glass-engravers of the eighteenth century. His delicate work is the equivalent on glass in spirit and technique of the Watteau painting executed on porcelain. [Fig. 154]

Reference: Ekhart Berckenhagen, *Berliner und Märkische Gläser*, Darmstadt 1956.

RUBY GLASS: Produced by adding gold chloride. The question of whether Johann Kunckel (q.v.) was actually the inventor of ruby glass is much debated amongst experts. A physician, Andreas Cassius of Hamburg, in 1676 reported to Kunckel his discovery of the red-colouring properties of gold chloride. In 1679 Kunckel mentioned ruby glass in his *Ars Vitraria*, but kept the recipe secret. At the same time, however, ruby glass was produced in southern Germany. The peculiarity of the process for making ruby glass lies in the fact that the glass attains its deep red colour only after reheating; at first it appears grey. [Figs. 141, 142]

RÜSSELBECHER: Variously known as trunk beakers or claw beakers, are Rhenish and Frankish vessels of the fifth to seventh century, in green, or more rarely blue glass, with hollow trunk-like appendages drawn downwards in two to three rows of five to seven trunks. [Fig. 47]

Reference: Fritz Fremersdorf, *Zur Geschichte des Fränkischen Rüsselbechers*, *Wallraf-Richartz-Jahrbuch*, N. F., Cologne, 1933/34, p. 7ff.

RUSSIAN AND SOVIET GLASS: The centre of Russian glass-making in the eighteenth century was St Petersburg, which surpassed Moscow, where glass-houses had been in existence since the seventeenth century. The St Petersburg engraved glasses, like those produced in Hamburg in the second decade of the eighteenth century (both were produced exclusively for the Tzar's court and the aristocracy) differ very little in style from the usual European glass of the time. In the second half of the eighteenth century a certain resemblance to St Petersburg porcelain is noticeable, particularly in the milk glasses of the late eighteenth and early nineteenth centuries. A Russian speciality is a fondness for mosaic-work, which has been evident in all periods, in the eighteenth and nineteenth centuries as well as the present day. The Soviet Union now possesses a modern and versatile glass-industry which can supply the country's enormous need for plate-glass, technical and industrial glass. The main manufacturer is Gusj.

Reference: B. A. Shelkownikow, *Glaskunst in Rußland*, in: *Kunstglas und seine Verwendung in der Architektur*, Leningrad-Moskau 1953 (Russ.); B. A. Shelkownikow, *Russian Glass of the Eighteenth Century*, in: *Journal of Glass Studies*, The Corning Museum of Glass, Corning Glass Centre, Corning, New York, Vol. 2, 1960.

SANDBLASTING: a stream of sand is directed under high pressure onto the surface of the glass, attacking it and rendering it matt. Skilful use of the technique can produce effects of different quality and depth, from slight grazing to deep cutting of the glass. Sandblasting was invented in the U.S.A. in 1871. [Figs. 229–231]

SANG, ANDREAS FRIEDRICH: Thuringian glass-engraver of considerable importance. Court engraver to Duke Ernest Augustus of Saxe-Weimar. The records show that he was in Erfurt during the year 1719, in Weimar from 1723 to 1732, and then in Ilmenau until 1747. He later worked in Holland, and fundamentally influenced Dutch engraving in the second half of the eighteenth century. Four signed pieces by Sang are known (Cologne, Kunstgewerbe-museum; Dessau, the Castle), showing his style. He was probably first influenced by Gottfried Spiller (q.v.) and the Berlin school of engravers. Later his large scale designs were abandoned for more finely detailed representations or landscapes, enhanced by delicate *Laub- und Bandelwerk* patterns. The engraved areas are enhanced by surrounding cutting.

References: Walther Scheidig, *Andreas Friedrich Sang*, in: *Glastechnische Berichte*, Frankfurt a. M. 10, 1932, p. 382–386; Annegrete Janda-Bux, *Der Thüringer Glasschnitt im 17. und 18. Jahrhundert*, Leipzig, Theses 1962.

SAXON GLASS: There have been numerous glasshouses in Saxony since the Middle Ages in the forest regions of that area, in the Vogtland and the Erzgebirge. Enamel painting on glass was carried out in Saxony from the sixteenth century onwards, influenced by that of its neighbours, Bohemia and Franconia. It is characterized by rim borders in white enamel dots on a gold ground, the remaining ornament being in various colours. The metal is mainly colourless. From 1610 till the beginning of the eighteenth century glasses unique to Saxony, the *Hofkellereigläser*, were made and used in Saxon castles. Saxon engraving and cutting was influenced both by the east and the west. A typical feature of the Saxon covered goblets – probably manufactured at the Dresden glasshouse – is the horizontal oval facetting on the lower part of the bowl. The relief portraits on the bowl are also usually indicative of Saxon origins. The court glass-engraver in Dresden was Johann Christoph Kiessling, who died in 1744, and whose goblets were mainly decorated with hunting scenes. Also belonging to the Saxon group of artists are the Weissenfels glass-engravers Johann Naumann from Zittau, from 1680 to 1697 court glass-engraver to Duke Johann Adolf I of Saxe-Weissenfels, and Johann Georg Müller from Lauscha, who died in 1783 as glass-engraver to the court of Saxony in Weissenfels. [Fig. 132]

References: Sabine Baumann, *Studien zum Sächsischen Glas des 18. Jahrhunderts*, Leipzig, Theses 1954; Sabine Baumann, *Sächsische geschnittene Gläser des 18. Jahrhunderts*, Leipzig, Theses 1958; Paul Frenzel, *Weissenfelser Glasschneider und ihre Pokale*, in: *25 Jahre Städtisches Museum Weissenfels 1910–1935*, Weissenfels 1935, p. 35–40.

SCHAPER, JOHANN: A Nuremberg glass-painter working from 1640 to 1670. The Schaper glasses show fine translucent enamel painting on the typical Nuremberg ball-footed beakers. Usually in coloured enamel, more rarely in *Schwarzlot*. [Figs. 133, 134]

SCHMELZGLAS (ACHATGLAS, CALCEDONIO): Mottled glass, produced by allowing glass of different colours to mingle when still liquid. The terminology is confused in older literature. It was first made in Egypt, but it played a most important role in the Venetian art of glass-making. Antonio Neri describes several methods of making a *Calcedonier*. A similar product is *Karneolglas*, which has reddish veins and was produced in Venice from the seventeenth century onwards. It must not, however, be mistaken for Egermann's lithyalin glass which was made in Bohemia in the first half of the nineteenth century. [Fig. 82]

SCHMIDT, HANS WOLFGANG: A Nuremberg glass-engraver working from 1676 to 1710. In contrast to Hermann Schwinger, who was fond of idyllic scenes showing shepherds, fisherman and hunters, Schmidt preferred stirring representations of a battle or a hunt taking place in a towering forest or on a wide plain encircled by tress.

Reference: Erich Meyer-Heising, *Der Nürnberger Glasschnitt des 17. Jahrhunderts*, Nuremberg 1963.

SCHWANHARDT, GEORG, THE ELDER: 1601 to 1667, a Nuremberg glass-engraver. He inherited the privilege of glass-cutting accorded to his master, Caspar Lehmann, and after his return from Prague in 1622 spread his knowledge of glass-engraving in Nuremberg. He is recognised as the artist who first employed the technique of polishing certain parts within the matt engraving in order to achieve an appearance of greater depth. Erich Meyer-Heisig has identified approximately fifty of his pieces.

Reference: Erich Meyer-Heisig, *Der Nürnberger Glasschnitt des 17. Jahrhunderts*, Nuremberg 1963.

SCHWANHARDT, HEINRICH: 1624 to 1693, Nuremberg glass-engraver, son of the above.

Reference: As above.

SCHWARTZ, SAMUEL: Born in about 1681, died in 1737 at Arnstadt in Thuringia (Germany). A glass-cutter and engraver, he was employed at several Thuringian courts but worked mainly at Arnstadt. He received his training most probably in Brandenburg in the first decade of the eighteenth century. The frequently recurring decoration with pointed leaves at the base of the bowl is typical of Brandenburg glasses. Schwartz's glasses were mainly produced at the time when festoon and ribbon decorations were in fashion; many of them have cut stems.

Reference: Annegrete Janda-Bux, *Der Thüringer Glasschnitt im 17. und 18. Jahrhundert*, Thesis, University of Leipzig.

SCHWARZLOT: Method of decoration. For explanation see (pl. 133/134).

SCHWINGER, HERMANN: 1640 to 1683, a Nuremberg glass-engraver. He signed some of his pieces "Herman Schwinger" e.g. a hollow baluster-stemmed glass with forest scenes, architectural representations and military illustrations as seen in the Narodní Galerie, Prague. Characteristic of his work is the idyllic landscape of the early Baroque type with small figures and atmospheric effects such as the heat of a fire, achieved by a slight grazing of the surface, which is partly polished or emphasized by diamond-point engraving.

Reference: Erich Meyer-Heisig, *Der Nürnberger Glasschnitt des 17. Jahrhunderts*, Nuremberg 1963.

SCYPHUS: Ancient Greek drinking vessel, squat, round or bell-shaped, with handles on the sides.

SHEET GLASS: Trade term, as opposed to glass vessels. It comprises window glass, mirrors or any glass which is used in flat panes. In the beginning it was simply produced by pouring the glass-mixture onto a suitable surface. Later a large blown bubble was given the form of a cylinder, and, after both ends had been removed, it was cut lengthwise with shears and flattened into a rectangular sheet. In another process, the bubble was opened at one end and then rapidly rotated on the rod after reheating in the furnace. Thus by making use of centrifugal force it was turned into a circular pane, which was later cut into pieces as desired. Since 1688 a rolling process has been in use; it was invented by Lucas de Nehou. By this method the liquid metal is poured onto a flat iron surface and then rolled in a semi-liquid state. In this century sheet glass is produced mainly by the "broad glass" process; the molten glass is directly drawn from a tank. This technique is possible on account of the tenacity and ductility of the material.

SIDONIAN MOULD BLOWN VESSEL: These were made in the first century A.D. in the Eastern Mediterranean, with Sidon as the main centre of manufacture. They are in blue, green or clear glass. They were blown into clay moulds with a decorative impression on the inside. The decoration thus obtained bore a strong resemblance to that of Greek pottery of the Hellenistic period. The Sidonian mould-blown glasses are sometimes furnished with the name of the maker in raised letters on the handle or body of the vessel. The most frequent names are Ennion, Artas, Ariston, Meges, Eryneios, Sometimes Sidon is mentioned as the place of manufacture, e.g. Ariston Sidoni. In view of the trade with Rome, the names are sometimes given in two languages, Greek and Latin (Sidon became Roman in 63 B.C.; today it is known as Saida, in the Lebanon). Some Sidonian glasses bear the inscription in Greek "Buyer, think of the giver". The vessels take the form of bottles, beakers, and amphorae, often six-sided or cylindrical; the decoration consits of Greek motifs. [Fig. 13]

SILVER STAIN: Silver chloride in an acid solution used to produce a yellow coloured surface in glass. Silver nitrate is used to obtain a metal which is yellow throughout.

SITULA: Egyptian bucket-shaped bowl.

SNAKE-TRAILED VESSELS: Glass vessels produced mainly in Cologne glasshouses in the second, third and beginning of the fourth century A.D., with applied thread-decoration usually in irregular winding patterns, although sometimes in spirals, ivy motifs and other motifs related to Germanic symbolism. They constitute a small group among those vessels showing trailed decoration. The best piece of this type is the pilgrim's bottle, known as the *Meisterstück*, in the Römisch-Germanisches Museum in Cologne. [Figs. 32–35]
Reference: Fritz Fremersdorf, *Römische Gläser mit Fadenauflage in Köln, Die Denkmäler des römischen Köln*, Vol. V, Cologne 1959.

SODA: An alkaline substance, sodium carbonate (Na_2CO_3). Used as flux in glass making. Egyptian glass of the second milennium B.C. contained about 15% soda obtained from the alkaline lakes or indirectly by burning certain marine plants. Inscribed tablets of the Assur-Bani-Pal revealed recipes for glass, mentioning the use of ash of *Salicornia herbacea* or Glasswort. Venetian glass was made with soda which was mainly imported from Egypt and Syria. In modern times soda is prepared from water, salt (NaCl), ammonia and carbon dioxide (Solvay process).

SPANISH GLASS: In its earliest period Spanish glass was a mixture of Moorish-Islamic and Venetian influences, developing in the seventeenth century indigenous forms such as the *porrón*, *cántaro* and the *almorrata*. [Fig. 90–93]
Reference: Alice Wilson Frothingham, *Hispanic Glass*, New York 1941.

SPECHTER: A tall cylindrical glass, or *Stangenglas*, with an applied foot. The name is derived from the area which first produced it, the Spessart Forest Region.

SPILLER, GOTTFRIED: Glass-engraver, born c. 1663 in the Hirschberg Valley in Silesia, a pupil of Martin Winter (q.v.) from 1675 in Potsdam, worked as a glass engraver from 1683 in Berlin, and was from 1702 until his death in 1728 *Königlicher Glasschneider* in Berlin. His work belongs to the High Baroque period. The figures in his designs are deeply cut (up to 7 mm) into very thick glass (up to 10 mm), resulting in a three dimensional effect. Spiller signed one rock-crystal jug "G. Spiller" (Cicerone 1916, p. 89). All his pieces are identifiable by their unique style.
Reference: Robert Schmidt, *Brandenburgische Gläser*, Berlin 1914.

STANGENGLAS: Cylindrical drinking vessel dating from the fifteenth to the seventeenth century, usually showing decoration in the form of prunts, diamond-point engraving or enamel-painting. [Fig. 104]

STEUBEN GLASS: Art pieces from the Steuben Glassworks in Corning, New York. Since the reorganisation which took place in 1933, the Steuben Glassworks have been among the leading manufacturers in the U.S.A. They produce highly individual pieces, employing the best craftsmanship and high quality material. Attractive glass-engraving is a characteristic of their work. The main designers are Sidney Waugh and John Monteith Gates. [Fig. 200]
Reference: E. M. Elville, *The Collector's Dictionary of Glass*, London 1961.

SULPHIDES: See Crystallo-Ceramie.

SURFACE STAINING: This is achieved by the application of metal-oxides to the glass surface and reheating. For example yellow tones are obtained by using silver oxides; ruby colours by copper oxide, etc. [Figs. 163, 164]

THURINGIAN GLASS: *Waldglas* was made in the Thuringian Forest from the fifteenth century, possibly earlier. Numerous glasshouses were founded in the sixteenth and seventeenth centuries. From 1633 to 1639 under Duke Bernhard of Saxe-Weimar a glasshouse employing Venetian craftsmen existed in Tambach, producing the *Tambacher Flaschen*, bottles with six or eight pass rings. From the end of the seventeenth century glass-engraving of a good standard was carried on at some of the neighbouring courts, only to be eclipsed by the growing porcelain industry in the mid-eighteenth century. The most important glass-engravers of this period are Caspar Creutzburg, Gotha, from 1690; the artist J. H., Sondershausen and Arnstadt; Samuel Schwartz (q.v.), Gotha and Arnstadt; Andreas Friedrich Sang (q.v.), Weimar, Ilmenau, Arnstadt; Georg Ernst Kunckel (q.v.), Gotha. A Thuringian characteristic is pseudo-facetting, i.e. moulded stems of covered goblets. No glass-cutting of particular interest developed in Thuringia. During the nineteenth century Ilmenau became important as the centre of technical pharmaceutical glassmaking, whereas Lauscha, founded in 1595, turned to the production of simpler bottle-glass and to pieces made at the lamp. [Figs. 144, 151, 241]

References: Walter Scheidig, *Thüringer Glasschneider und Glasmaler im Dienste des Herzogs Ernst August von Sachsen-Weimar (1708-1748)*, in: *Zeitschrift des Vereins für Thüringische Geschichte und Altertumskunde*, N.F., Jena, Vol. 29 1931, p. 476-482; Walther Scheidig, *Andreas Friedrich Sang*, in: *Glastechnische Berichte*, Frankfurt a. M. 1932, 10, p. 382-386; Annegrete Janda-Bux, *Der Thüringer Glasschnitt im 17. und 18. Jahrhundert*, Leipzig, Thesis 1962; Wilhelm Stieda, *Thüringische Glashütten in der Vergangenheit*, Leipzig 1910; Barbara Pischel, *Die Thüringische Glasbläserei*, Weimar 1936.

TIFFANY; LOUIS COMFORT, 1848-1933: New York glass-artist and painter, son of a silver-ware manufacturer, founder of the Tiffany Glass and Decorating Company, New York. His "Favrile" glass, with its metallic, lustred surface had a great influence on the glass of his European contemporaries, and is a typical product of the Art Nouveau period. His pieces bear a finely etched signature under the foot. [Figs. 183, 184]

Reference: Hans-Ulrich Haedeke, *Glas*, in: *Jugendstil, Der Weg ins 20. Jahrhundert*, Helmut Seling, Heidelberg/Munich 1959, p. 325-340, figs. 183, 184.

TRAILING: A decoration known since Roman times. A lump of softened glass is drawn out into a thread and attached to the surface of a heated vessel. This technique has been applied throughout the ages, but was especially favoured in medieval glass-decoration and for popular glass of the following centuries. Handles of ancient glass-vessels are often made of twisted glass-threads; the feet of fifteenth and sixteenth century *Römers* were produced by winding soft glass-threads concentrically round a wooden mould. Theophilus in his *Schedula diverarum artium* (2nd book, chapter X) gives the following instructions for trailing: "Take also a lump of glass out of the furnace in such a manner that it produces a thread, which you then attach to the desired point on the vessel, turning the latter near to the flame so that it clings to it." See also *latticino*.[Figs.76-78]

TRICK GLASSES: Constructed so as to render the process of drinking difficult for the would-be imbiber, or to produce some amusing effect. They were most popular during the late Renaissance, although all periods have produced this kind of trick vessel, including the Roman and all post-medieval periods.

The *Kutterolf* might be considered to belong to this group of glasses, as might all other vessels designed to show the virtuosity of the glass-blower, such as human and animal figures, musical instruments and vessels in the shape of all kinds of objects, if they were intended as drinking vessels. Some trick glasses were of religious origin; for example the glasses made in the shape of a head, and particularly the Phallus glasses, which can be traced to the fertility rites practised by many ancient civilisations, but whose function degenerated into the realm of vulgar joking during the Middle Ages. [Figs. 121, 122]

TRULLA: A shallow ladle for serving wine.

TRUMPER, JOHANN FRANZ: Hessian glass-engraver of the first half of the eighteenth century. The only signed work we possess, an engraved cylindrical vessel in the collection of the Museum für Kunsthandwerk in Leipzig (about 1730), shows a certain resemblance to the Silesian style of decoration (foliage borders).

References: Walther Scheidig, *Thüringer Glasschneider und Glasmaler im Dienst des Herzogs Ernst August von Sachsen-Weimar (1708-1748)*, in: *Zeitschrift des Vereins für Thüringische Geschichte und Altertumskunde*, N.F., Jena, Vol. 29 1931, p. 476; *Kunsthandwerk und Plastik aus Deutschland im Museum des Kunsthandwerks Leipzig*, Annelise Hanisch, Leipzig 1961, fig. 43.

UNFIRED PAINTING: The ornamentation of glass with enamels which are not subsequently fired. Unfired painting is easier to execute, but less durable than fired enamel decoration. [Figs. 87-89]

VENETIAN GLASS: Glass produced in Venice, i.e. in the Murano glasshouses. The term is often applied to articles in the *façon de Venise*, but produced elsewhere, and tends to refer to any thin-walled soda glass as opposed to the medieval *Waldglas* or the Bohemian cut potash-lime glass. Because of her world-wide trading connections, Venice was in the happy position of having an assured supply of raw materials and a ready market for her glass products. These advantages, combined with the skill of her craftsmen, made Venice the capital of glass-making during the sixteenth and seventeenth centuries. The finest products of the industry are the enamelled glasses of about 1500, the crystal glasses of the sixteenth century, the *latticino* glasses of c. 1600 and the winged glasses of the seventeenth century. Changes in artistic taste towards the end of the seventeenth century transferred the supremacy Venice had enjoyed to Bohemia. [Figs. 66-86]

References: Gudmund Boesen, *Venetianske glas på Rosenborg*, Copenhagen 1960; Karel Hetteš, *Venezianisches Glas*, Prague 1960; Giovanni Mariachen *Edle Gläser von der Antike bis Murano*, Munich 1962; Ignaz Schlosser, *Venezianer Gläser*, Vienna 1951; *The Corning Museum of Glass, Three Great Centuries of Venetian Glass*, Exhibition catalogue, Corning, New York 1958.

VERZELINI, G.: Italian glass-maker who founded the first London glass-house for vessels in the *façon de Venise* in 1575. He died in London in 1606.

References: Robert Schmidt, *Europäisches Glas, Die Sammlung Wilfried Buckley*, Berlin 1927; Francis Buckley, *A History of old English Glass*, London 1925; W. B. Honey, *English Glass*, London 1946.

WALDGLAS: A glass of primitive quality, not deliberately coloured and therefore usually green, or sometimes brown, produced in Central European glass-houses from the fifteenth to the eighteenth centuries. These glass-houses were mainly found in the wooded regions of the Mittelgebirge mountain-range, where an abundance of fuel was at hand. Hence the name *Waldglas*, for *Wald* = wood. The glass consisted of sand containing iron and therefore green, and potash obtained from beechwood ash. German *Waldglas* provides the strongest possible contrast to the thin, colourless Venetian metal, which as a flux contained soda imported from the Orient. [Figs. 100–118]

WILLKOMM: A type of *Humpen* of remarkable size, made from the sixteenth to the eighteenth century, usually enamel painted. The name of these glasses, sometimes capable of holding more than five litres, derives from the custom of using the *Willkomm* to drink to the health of a visitor, thus welcoming him. Mathesius (q.v.) mentions the "*unflätig grossen Willkomm*" as "foolish vessels which one can hardly lift", (*unflätig* = coarse, ugly).

WINDOW-PANES: Already known in Rome in Caligula's time. Pieces measuring 30 × 60 cm. (1′ × 2′) are extant. They are about 4 cm. (1³/₄″) thick in the centre and taper towards the edges; they were produced by rotation on the iron (see sheet glass) and bull's eyes.

WINGED GLASS: Originally Venetian wine-glasses with wing-like appendages, made from pinched glass threads, sometimes adopting the form of a double-headed eagle, sometimes that of two horses. They came into the fashion about 1600. They were popular throughout Europe and were imitated in glasshouses in other parts of the continent. Sometimes the appendages take over the role of the stem, and become heart-shaped, or are ingeniously curved into a figure eight. [Figs. 79–81]

WINTER, FRIEDRICH: Silesian glass-engraver. In 1690 and 1691, he set up a water power mill for glass-engraving in Petersdorf in the Hirschberg Valley. The heavy Silesian cameo-relief glasses, which may be grouped together with the goblets showing the coat of arms of Count Schaffgotsch, which date from the end of the seventeenth to the beginning of the eighteenth century, are probably his work.

WINTER, MARTIN: Glass-engraver in the service of the Elector of Brandenburg in Potsdam, brother of the engraver Friedrich Winter of Petersdorf in Silesia. His work shows the Silesian style of engraving. In 1684 he received a privilege for *Hochschnitt* or cameo-relief engraving from the Elector. In 1687 he set up a water-power mill in Berlin for cutting and engraving, and had as his pupil his nephew Gottfried Spiller.

Reference: Robert Schmidt, *Brandenburgische Gläser*, Berlin 1914; Ekhart Berckenhagen, *Berliner und Märkische Gläser*, Darmstadt 1956.

WOLFF, DAVID: Died at the Hague in 1808, foremost Dutch stipple-engraver on glass. Glasses bearing his signature date from between 1784 and 1796. [Fig. 139]

Reference: Fancis Buckley, *D. Wolff*, London 1935.

ZWISCHENGOLDGLÄSER (see also Double-Glass): Bohemian two-layer glasses from the period of about 1730–1740. An outer glass, which was usually without a bottom, was made to fit exactly round an inner one. The outer surface of the inner glass was covered with engraved or painted gold-leaf. The joint is usually beneath the rim or sometimes further down. [Figs. 160, 161]